# TEACHING ENGLISH 3–11

Other titles in the series:
*Mark O'Hara*: Teaching 3–11 (2nd Edition)
*David Owen and Alison Ryan*: Teaching Geography 3–11
*Mark O'Hara*: Teaching History 3–11
*Christine Farmery*: Teaching Science 3–11

Reaching the Standard
Series Editor Mark O'Hara

# Teaching English 3–11

## THE ESSENTIAL GUIDE

Cathy Burnett and Julia Myers

continuum
LONDON • NEW YORK

**Continuum**

The Tower Building    15 East 26th Street
11 York Road    New York, NY 10010
London
SE1 7NX

**British Library Cataloguing-in-Publication Data**
A catalogue record for this book is available from the British Library.

ISBN: 0 8264 7006 8 (hardback) 0 8264 7007 6 (paperback)

Designed and typeset by Ben Cracknell Studios
Printed and bound in Great Britain by Antony Rowe Ltd, Chippenham, Wiltshire

# Contents

# Preface

This book covers the teaching and learning of English and as such makes use of a subject heading that is found in the National Curriculum but not in the Early Learning Goals. Learning in the Foundation Stage is not structured along subject boundaries as it is in the National Curriculum. This difference is based on current understandings of how younger pupils in particular learn, and how they do not necessarily make the same subject distinctions with which adults seek to organize teaching and learning. The under-5s' curriculum is organized into areas of learning that correspond to, but do not replicate, the subjects in the National Curriculum. The area that corresponds to English is 'Communication, Language and Literacy' but in nursery and reception classes activities can offer starting points for learning across a number of areas of learning. In the interests of readability, we use the terms 'English' or 'language and literacy' to refer to the use of reading, writing, speaking and listening.

Clarification is also necessary in relation to two other areas. Firstly, as many early years settings are outside the mainstream education system, the contents of the Early Learning Goals are not compulsory in the same way that National Curriculum Programmes of Study are in schools. However, the Early Learning Goals set out the desired learning outcomes for children upon completion of their reception year, and those nurseries that are part of mainstream education, as well as reception classes, are expected to be using the Early Learning Goals to structure their work with pupils aged 3–5 years. Therefore, although the Early Learning Goals have a slightly different status, the term *curriculum* will be used throughout the book to describe the educational provision for all pupils aged between 3 and 11 years of age. Secondly, the book seeks to address teaching and learning across the Foundation Stage and Key Stages 1 and 2. Once again, there is a danger that, in our efforts to be inclusive, the text will become unmanageable. As a result, we have chosen to use terms like *primary* and *school* as shorthand for those settings where the whole 3–11 age range is represented. In those instances where 3–5 settings are being discussed separately the terms *Foundation Stage*, *nursery* or *reception* are used.

In discussing issues related to children with English as an Additional Language (EAL), we have used the term 'home language' to refer to the language that could also be described as 'first', 'dominant' or 'preferred'. All of these terms are problematic but, for clarity, a single term has been adopted.

# Acknowledgements

We would like to thank all the colleagues, students and children who contributed to this book, by providing examples, support and insights into their experiences as teachers, teacher trainers and learners. In particular we would like to thank the following teachers and their children:

Nina Burton at Grenoside Primary School;
Mary Machin at Hunters Bar Junior School;
Hilary Malden at Meersbrook Bank School;
Jane Price at Chellaston Infant School;
Leni Solinger/Vanessa Langley at Pipworth Infant School;
Staff at Thistly Meadow Primary School;
Fiona Lingard at Derby City Council.

We would also like to thank all the students whose experiences in learning to teach English, grappling with the demands of the curriculum, the changing nature of literacy and the theory underpinning the development of language and literacy provided the incentive for us to write this book. In particular we would like to thank the following students for their helpful comments on early drafts:

Caroline Brake;
Sarah Feeke;
Sue Holling;
Iain McConnachie;
Cath Marks;
Ann Pagin;
Joan Price;
Sue Tewson.

We would also like to thank colleagues at Sheffield Hallam University for their advice and support, in particular Fufy Demissie, Mark O'Hara and John Stirton and members of the English Centre – Paul Dickinson, Jim McDonagh, Guy Merchant and Jeff Wilkinson – for providing inspiration and sharing the benefits of their knowledge and experience with patience and humour.

Final thanks go to friends and family, in particular Mark Whitaker, Joe Ellingham, Ken Brown and, last but not least, Phoebe, for her contributions.

# Standards information

This book is aimed at newly qualified and teacher training students working in the three-to-eleven age range. The knowledge and ability to teach English is required by all teachers, as specified in DfES/TTA (2003) *Qualifying to Teach*. London: HMSO. Although the structure of the book does not track the order of these requirements, it does address the Standards contained in this document. The grid below provides the reader with a quick guide to where particular information can be located.

| Standards (or relevant parts of Standards) | Chapters |
|---|---|
| S1.1 High expectations for all pupils | 3, 4, 5, 6, 11, 12 |
| S1.3 Demonstrate and promote positive values, attitudes and behaviour | 10, 12 |
| S1.4 Communicate sensitively with parents and carers | 10 |
| S1.5 Contribute to corporate life of schools | 13 |
| S1.7 Improve [one's] own practice through evaluation | 9 |
| S2.1 Secure knowledge of subjects trained to teach | 3, 4, 5, 6, 7 |
| S2.1a/b Understand curriculum guidance for the Foundation Stage, National Curriculum and National Literacy Strategy | 2, 7, 8 |
| S2.4 Understand how pupils' learning can be affected by physical, intellectual, linguistic, social, cultural and emotional development | 2, 3, 11, 12 |
| S2.5 Know how to use ICT effectively to teach their subject | 8 |
| S2.6 Understand responsibilities under SEN code of practice | 11 |
| S3.1.1 Set challenging teaching and learning objectives based on knowledge of pupils . . . and expect standards for pupils of relevant age range | 7, 8, 9 |
| S3.1.2 Plan lessons, sequences of lessons showing how they will assess pupils' learning; take account of and support pupils' varying needs | 8, 9, 11 |
| S3.1.3 Select and prepare resources and plan for effective organization | 10 |
| S3.2.1 Make appropriate use of a range of monitoring and assessment strategies | 9 |

| Standards (or relevant parts of Standards) | Chapters |
|---|---|
| S3.2.2 Monitor and assess [while teaching], giving immediate and constructive feedback and involve pupils in reflecting on, evaluating and improving their own performance | 3, 4, 5, 6, 7, 8, 9 |
| S3.2.3 Able to assess pupils' progress using relevant National Curriculum and Foundation Stage assessment frameworks | 9 |
| S3.2.4 Identify and support more able pupils, those falling behind age-related expectations or not achieving their potential and those experiencing social, emotional or behavioural difficulties | 11 |
| S3.2.5 Identify the levels of attainment of pupils learning English as an Additional Language | 9, 12 |
| S3.2.6 Record pupils' progress and achievements systematically | 9 |
| S3.2.7 Use records as a basis for reporting on pupils' attainment | 13 |
| S3.3.1 Establish a purposeful learning environment where diversity is valued and where pupils feel secure and confident | 1, 2, 3, 10, 11, 12 |
| S3.3.2a/b Teach required or expected knowledge, understanding and skills relevant to the age group for which [one is] trained | 2, 3, 4, 5, 6, 7, 8, 9, 10, 11, 12 |
| S3.3.3 Teach clearly structured lessons to sequence of work which interest and motivate pupils | 2, 3, 4, 5, 6, 7, 8 |
| S3.3.4 Differentiate their teaching to meet the needs of pupils | 11 |
| S3.3.5 [Ability] to support those who are learning English as an Additional Language | 12 |
| S3.3.6 Take account of varying interests, experiences and achievements of boys and girls, and pupils from different cultural and ethnic groups | 12 |
| S3.3.7 Organize and manage teaching and learning time effectively | 7 |
| S3.3.8 Organize and manage the physical teaching space | 10 |
| S3.3.10 Use ICT effectively in their own teaching | 8 |
| S3.3.12 Provide homework and other out-of-class work | 8 |
| S3.3.14 Recognize and respond effectively to equal opportunities issues | 12 |

# Introduction

This book is intended as an introduction to English for newly qualified teachers and teacher training students on 3–11 courses. It seeks to provide the reader with insights into the nature of the subject, and effective ways of planning, teaching and assessing English in primary and foundation settings. It recognizes the important role of English within the whole curriculum and considers cross-curricular issues that affect teaching and learning in all subjects, such as equality of opportunity and special educational needs (SEN). The book concludes with an evaluation of the role of an English specialist in co-ordinating English across a whole school. At the end of each chapter the reader will find a set of reflective questions or tasks intended to reinforce the points made and involve the reader more actively in the subject matter.

In Chapter 1, we explore the range and scope of language and literacy and the varied ways in which they are used in everyday life. This highlights a number of concepts significant to the teaching of English. Within this chapter, English as a language is shown to be diverse, flexible and constantly changing; this perspective informs the rest of the book. Chapter 2 examines children's development as language and literacy users and demonstrates the wealth of experience about language and literacy that children bring to the classroom. Key principles for teaching of English are established and an overview of current expectations of curriculum guidelines is provided. In Chapter 3, we focus on the ways in which children acquire spoken language and suggest practical ways of supporting their continued development. Chapter 4 focuses on the development of reading and describes appropriate teaching strategies for encouraging children's enthusiasm, understanding and confidence. In Chapter 5, we consider the teaching of various aspects of writing. Chapters 4 and 5 both highlight the importance of providing a range of texts, but focus on the value of narrative. The reading and writing of non-narrative texts are explored in Chapter 6, which discusses the crucial role of English within the wider curriculum. In Chapter 7, we consider some generic aspects of English teaching and outline the knowledge needed to teach this subject. Chapters 8 and 9 cover planning and assessment of English. In Chapter 10, we explore the role of the learning environment in supporting authentic use of language and enabling children to become motivated, autonomous learners. Chapters 11 and 12 demonstrate how support can be provided to enable all children to enjoy success in language and literacy. Finally, Chapter 13 offers practical guidance on fulfilling the roles and responsibilities of the English co-ordinator.

# The Nature of English

Language and literacy are key to the way people live their lives. You will have used reading, writing, speaking and listening in many different contexts during the last 24 hours. Perhaps you read a chapter of a novel before going to sleep or searched the Internet for details of a cheap holiday. Maybe you sent a text message to a friend or had a chat with a member of your family. In life, we read, write, speak and listen for a range of purposes and indeed it is very difficult to imagine doing anything without using language. Language and literacy enable us to communicate our needs and desires, interact with others and develop relationships. Through language and literacy we can gain information from a variety of sources and can be entertained, challenged and enlightened by what we read. Moreover, we articulate our thoughts in speech and in writing and through these processes arrive at greater understandings of the world around us. Given the centrality of language to our lives, English as a subject has a particularly important role within the curriculum.

In this book we provide support for planning, teaching and assessing English in early years and primary settings. However, in order to contextualize this practical guidance, it is important to have an understanding of the nature of English and its use. In the first part of this chapter, therefore, we begin by exploring the range and scope of language and literacy and the varied ways in which they are used. This is followed by a focus on the English language and texts, investigating the way that these have evolved and are continuing to do so. In the second chapter we consider the implications of these areas for teaching English and provide an overview of English as a subject in early years and primary settings. Subsequent chapters offer practical guidance on implementing effective practice in the classroom.

# The range and scope of language and literacy use

## Language and literacy as social practice

Over the past 20 years there has been considerable interest in the way in which literacy and language are integral to the activities of everyday life (Brice-Heath, 1982; Street, 1984; Gee, 1990; Barton *et al.*, 2000). The following passage illustrates this relationship. Note how the two friends plan their holiday:

> On her way home from work, Jo noticed cards advertising special offers for holidays in a travel agents' window. She went in and talked to an assistant and collected brochures. At home she glanced through them and rang a friend, Emma. During the conversation she jotted down possible places and dates. She then skimmed the brochures to find particular pages which she read carefully, noting dates and prices. When the two friends met, they looked at these notes and the pages in the brochures and discussed possibilities. Searches on the Internet were made to make comparisons of the information available. After much discussion they made a note of their preferences and a few questions and returned to the travel agent. After a conversation with the assistant they completed and signed a form and left discussing plans for the holiday.

These two friends use language and literacy in many different ways. It is evident that reading, writing, speaking and listening are closely linked: throughout they use discussion to drive the process forwards and reading and writing (searching for information and making notes) go hand in hand. The friends' approach to the task is influenced by previous experience of booking holidays. They know that holiday companies can be misleading and this prompts them to use the Internet to supplement brochure descriptions of resorts and hotels. However, they like the security of booking with a travel agent and appreciate the support provided with filling in forms and answering queries. The way they use language and literacy is typical of the way we use language and literacy in life. Uses are driven by a real purpose and influenced by prior experiences and expectations. Barton *et al.* (2000) have noted the way in which uses are not only underpinned by people's attitudes and interests but also their concerns and values. Literacy and language use can therefore be seen as 'social practice' that is 'embedded in other human activity' (Barton, 1994).

Inevitably the types of language and literacy used in life vary considerably. In their extensive work on literacy as social practice, Barton and Hamilton note how different types of literacy are used in different 'domains' of life (Barton *et al.*, 1998). At work, a teacher's writing activities may include marking work, planning and writing reports while reading may involve accessing information from books and Web sites to provide the subject knowledge needed to teach across the curriculum. The same teacher may read and write very differently for pleasure, perhaps curling up with a book or browsing through a magazine. Her hobbies will prompt other types of reading, writing, speaking and listening; for example, if she is keen on the cinema she may regularly read film reviews or watch television programmes about new releases and

2

discuss films with friends. If she is familiar with more than one language she may use different languages in different situations.

As adults we become very skilled at adapting language within these different domains, becoming 'expert' at reading and writing different types of texts within the context of our relationships, hobbies and occupations. Consider what you might say or write if you emailed a friend to arrange a night out, or telephoned a parent for a chat, or wrote to an employer to explain that you were moving to a new job. How would you greet each person? What kind of words and phrases would you use and are there any you would consciously avoid using? All the time, language is adapted according to purpose and audience. Just as we put on different clothes for different occasions, we adapt our use of language according to the person/people *with whom* we are communicating (our audience), *why* we are speaking to them (our purpose) and *how* we are communicating with them (the form).

This language use is affected by social and cultural convention. This can be illustrated by considering a typical conversation between a customer and shop assistant. The precise language used may vary between different shop assistants and customers; for example, the shop assistant would probably address an elderly customer differently from a young child. Interestingly the overall structure of the conversation would be similar in different contexts. It would probably run along the following lines:

Stage 1: sales assistant – greeting and question.

Stage 2: customer – request or question.

Stage 3: responses, perhaps with a request for clarification.

Stage 4: responses – information provided.

Stage 5: goods provided.

Stage 6: customer thanks sales assistant.

Stage 7: sales assistant gives price.

Stage 8: customer pays.

Stage 9: sales assistant thanks customer.

Stage 10: customer thanks sales assistant and says goodbye.

Stage 11: sales assistant says goodbye.

This kind of interaction, which can be described as a 'service encounter' (Halliday *et al.*, 1985: 54), would be similar whether the customer was buying a loaf of bread, a pair of shoes, an expensive piece of jewellery or a washing machine. If a more expensive item was being purchased, the middle stages may take considerably longer but the overall structure would remain the same.

Whilst later chapters of this book use the word 'text' to refer predominantly to written texts, linguists refer to any meaningful examples of written or spoken language as 'texts'. These therefore include service encounters along with other conversations, speeches and films as well as novels, poems, Web sites, emails and diaries. Spoken and written texts with a similar purpose often have a similar form (Halliday *et al.*, 1985). A further illustration of this can be provided by considering the purpose and structure of oral narrative (or storytelling). Over the last few days you will have heard and told many stories: maybe you gave an excuse for a missed meeting, recounted an embarrassing or hilarious incident or told a joke to a friend. Interestingly, it is likely that the stories you have told follow the same basic structure, which is similar to many written narratives. They begin with an opening that establishes the setting and characters ('The other day I was walking down the road and . . .'). Next, something happens to cause a problem or disrupt the status quo ('I couldn't believe my eyes when I saw . . .'). The story eventually arrives at a resolution ('So thanks to him I managed to get home without any problem') and often ends with a comment on the story or its significance ('. . . so I'm never going to do that again' or 'It was the funniest thing that ever happened to me') (Labov *et al.*, 1967).

This form (the structure) of the text is influenced by accepted ways of behaving that we consciously or subconsciously draw upon when we write or speak. These conventions are influenced by our social and cultural background. This can be illustrated by considering how the service interaction described above might differ in different social and cultural contexts: in societies where bartering is accepted as the norm, a significant section of the interaction would be spent in discussion over the price, whereas in others it would be inappropriate to challenge the price when buying an item. Such social and cultural conventions shape the many different ways in which we use both spoken and written language. Texts used for a similar purpose therefore often share a similar form and these may be described as belonging to particular genres. As Martin *et al.* (1987: 59) write, genres are:

> . . . social processes because members of a culture interact with each other to achieve them; goal oriented because they have to get things done; and staged because it usually takes more than one step for the participants to achieve their goals.

The language we use, then, is influenced by cultural conventions and refined within specific personal and social contexts. Many aspects of our use of language reflect age group, social network and occupation, echoing the language used by the groups to which we belong or to which we aspire. This becomes particularly apparent in considering the use of slang, jargon and invented words.

## Slang and jargon

'Slang' refers to colloquial words and phrases that often reflect identity. Any comparison between slang used by parents and their children demonstrates how it quickly becomes outdated. This is because using slang is an important part of bonding to a particular group and so new groups adopt and develop new forms that frequently relate to the popular culture of their times. Over the past 50 years, words meaning 'good' or 'great' have included 'fab', 'wicked', 'cool' and 'bad'. Indeed, words are often invented and used in ways that have particular meanings to a family, group of close friends, colleagues or even pupils.

Just as people use different slang at different times of their lives, they also become familiar with various forms of technical vocabulary (or jargon) to help them articulate experiences, events and concepts in specialized contexts. Teachers, for example, use an extensive range of jargon, such as 'Key Stages', 'levels', 'Early Learning Goals' and 'core and foundation subjects'. Notably language is also often used in unconventional ways in the classroom; comments such as 'Josie's a level four', 'unfortunately it's wet play today . . .' and 'are you a packed lunch or a hot dinner?' may be bewildering to anyone unfamiliar with the education system in England.

As well as jargon related to school, you will know and use other technical vocabulary associated with hobbies, jobs and relationships. Interestingly, although an understanding of educational jargon may develop and indeed change throughout a career, other uses of jargon may be very short lived; for example, when buying a computer, it is necessary to become temporarily expert in associated terminology such as 'megabytes' and 'bandwidth' but much of this specialist vocabulary is forgotten once a purchase has been made. It seems that different types of slang and jargon are learned and developed through involvement in different contexts; language use helps us 'fit in' and survive in differing environments.

Of course, language can be used to exclude as well as include. If using slang or jargon signals those that belong to a particular group, then failing to use it can mark those that do not. This can be illustrated by considering what it feels like to start a new job. New colleagues may use words, phrases and acronyms that are not understood and an inability to recognize appropriate terminology can cause feelings of inadequacy and insecurity. Similarly, overly complex and formal written language is often associated with legality, authority and power. It can seem to be used to inflate the status of individuals, organizations and institutions or deliberately to confuse and overwhelm readers.

The language we use then not only reflects who we are, what we do and what we are interested in but may affect the way we are perceived by others. This leads us to consider the prejudice that still exists in relation to accent and dialect.

## Accent, dialect and languages other than English

English may be spoken using a variety of regional accents and dialects. 'Dialect' relates to the actual language used (vocabulary and grammar), whereas 'accent' refers to the way that language is spoken. For many years, some regarded speaking using received pronunciation (the accent commonly known as 'Queen's English' or 'BBC English') as a prerequisite for success and indeed radio and television presenters were all expected to speak using received pronunciation. Whilst this is no longer the case, accents can still be the subject of negative stereotyping: as recently as 2002, a survey revealed that many business people associated accents from Birmingham, Liverpool and the East End with laziness and unreliability (Hill, 2002).

Dialects are varieties of the same language that differ in their grammar and use of vocabulary. Standard English is a dialect that developed in the south-east of England. As it was used within the Church and academia, it has long been associated with power and status. Consequently, local dialects that differ from standard English may be viewed by some as inferior. Importantly the grammar used in dialect is just as consistent as that in standard English. Trudgill (1994: 6) highlights this effectively in the following text, which is written firstly in non-standard dialect and then in standard English:

> The normal social convention what we operates with in the English-speaking world be that writing, particularly writing intended for publication, should be done in Standard English. This here book ain't no exception – it be writ in Standard English. This, however, be a matter of social convention. There ain't nothing what you can say nor write in Standard English what can't be said nor writ in other dialects.

> The normal social convention that we operate with in the English-speaking world is that writing, particularly writing intended for publication, should be done in Standard English. This book is no exception – it is written in Standard English. This, however, is a matter of social convention. There is not anything that you can say or write in Standard English that cannot be said or written in other dialects.

Note how the forms taken by the verbs ('operates', 'be' and 'writ') in the dialect passage are just as consistent as those in the passage written in standard English. The non-standard dialect passage also uses double verb negatives: 'ain't no exception' and 'ain't nothing . . .' rather than 'is no exception' and 'is nothing'. Demonstrative pronouns are different too, such as 'this here' rather than 'this', as are conjunctions: 'what' is used rather than 'that'. As the passage suggests, however, whilst the grammatical conventions are different in standard and non-standard English, they are just as rule-bound and each version of the text is able to convey the same meaning. As Trudgill (1994: 20) writes, 'All varieties of a language are structured, complex, rule-governed systems which are entirely adequate for the needs of their speakers.'

Such regional differences, however, are not static. Interestingly, there is an increasing tendency for dialects to become less distinct and accents to spread from their region of origin and become less marked, largely because of greater mobility in the population and the influence of the media. Estuary English, therefore, may be heard not just in the south-east of England but in many parts of the country (Crystal, 1995). Standard English is most commonly used in writing and in formal speech. It is important to mention here that there are currently more than 200 different languages used within the UK (QCA, 2000). Users of other languages may not only use other sound and grammatical systems but also varied scripts for recording language in writing. Many people are not only bilingual but multilingual and will often use different languages within specific social, religious or cultural contexts.

The way in which we use language then reflects who we are, the people with whom we communicate, what we do and what we are interested in; it reflects our identity and may in turn affect the way we are perceived by others. Just as our identity evolves as we grow older, meet new people and have new experiences, so the language that we use and the way that we use it changes too. This is affected by both changes

6

in personal interests, occupations and relationships, but also in response to social, cultural and technological developments. In the next section, we explore the effect of these changes on *language itself* and the texts we use.

# The changing nature of language and texts

## Changing language

Languages constantly evolve, reflecting social, cultural and technological change. English developed over many years influenced by the languages brought to England by various settlers. Words are borrowed from other languages to reflect new concepts or experiences. For example, French became the official language of England under the Normans. Words such as 'castle', 'authority' and 'justice' all originate from French words absorbed into English to describe aspects of society that just did not exist in the same way before the Norman invasion. Similarly, as the English travelled to other parts of the world they brought back words for the items they had seen there. Explorers of South America, for example, introduced the words 'tobacco', 'canoe', 'hurricane', 'hammock', 'potato', 'chocolate' and 'jaguar'. This adding of new words to represent new concepts and experiences continues today: for example, relatively recently, 'fatwa' and 'jihad' from Arabic have been introduced along with 'karaoke' and 'sushi' from Japan.

Changes in the English language do not just involve borrowing from other languages. There are many other ways in which new words evolve and old ones adopt new meanings. Whilst many of the words used today would have been recognized 500 years ago, the meanings ascribed to them may have been different. Some words have narrowed in meaning: 'girl' used to refer to a young person of either sex, whilst 'liquor' was any liquid. Other words have broadened: 'manufacture' used to mean 'made by hand' whilst 'holiday' referred specifically to a 'holy day'. As society changes, words fall in and out of use. Just as today we might be unable to define words such as 'mammet', 'wot' or 'fain' (sixteenth-century words meaning 'puppet', 'know' and 'gladly') so a sixteenth-century person would have just as much difficulty in defining many of the words used today, such as:

- those that began as brand names but are now used to refer to all similar products, whether or not they are made by the original company, such as 'hoover' or 'thermos';
- those created by blending two words together, such as 'motel' (from 'motor' and 'hotel') or chunnel (from 'channel' and 'tunnel');
- 'phone', 'fridge', 'mobile', 'lab', 'bus' and 'bike' which are all 'clipped' versions of longer words;
- compound words, such as 'hatchback' and 'laptop';
- metaphors, such as 'mouse' or 'cut and paste'.

Interestingly the way words are written has also changed over time. Spelling was not standardized until the introduction of printing in the fifteenth century and continues to evolve. Particularly interesting examples of innovation in spelling are occurring within the context of text messaging and online chat where phonetic spelling and abbreviations are frequently used as alternatives to conventional spellings. Indeed words such as 'gr8' were included in the 2003 version of the Collins English Dictionary (Collins, 2003).

Analysis of language and the meanings ascribed to words can tell us a great deal about the values held by society. Over the last 20 years, for example, there has been an emphasis on using gender-free terms to describe occupations reflecting a drive towards sexual equality: 'fireman', 'chairman', 'policeman' and 'air hostess' have been replaced by 'firefighter', 'chairperson', 'police officer' and 'flight attendant'. However, despite attempts to address discrimination, lingering prejudices can affect the way words are interpreted. Indeed people may still find it difficult to solve the following riddle:

'A man and his son are in a car crash. The man dies and his son is taken to hospital. The doctor says, "I can't operate – that's my son!" Who is the doctor?'

Despite the fact that there are many female doctors, many people still make an assumption that a doctor is male and this clouds their ability to find the solution. Similar assumptions about gender are often made about dentists, secretaries, lawyers, judges, nurses, caretakers and early years teachers.

English as a language, then, reflects our past and our present, what we do, what we believe and how we experience the world. It is a vibrant and changing language that evolves in response to changes in social, cultural and technological influences. Interestingly the nature of written or recorded texts has also undergone radical changes in recent years. These changes are explored in the next section.

## Changing texts

Advances in technology have provided us with an increasing variety of written and recorded texts that provide ever-widening opportunities for communication and sources of information and entertainment. These include the Internet, CD-ROMs, computer games, email, online chat, digital video and television. It is evident that images and moving images are increasingly important. Whilst in the past images were mainly used to support (or illustrate) words, they now play an increasingly significant role in written texts, such as magazines, adverts, posters and reference books (Kress, 1997). Kress draws attention to the way in which visual images make meaning. Images have the potential to present large amounts of information succinctly, for example a picture can convey a range of information about colour, spatial relationships and size simultaneously and may be far more effective than written words in certain contexts (Kress, 1997, 1998). Importantly, even the use of written

8

words has a visual impact: the layout of texts and font size, shape and colour all affect the way that a reader interprets the tone and intentions of what is written.

These new texts prompt us to read and write in new ways. Reading of traditional print texts often simply involves making meaning from words on a printed page, which are read in a linear way (from start to finish). New texts, however, demand new methods of engagement. For example, many computer games involve non-linear narratives; players make choices as they move between a series of levels and this determines the way in which they experience the story that underpins the game. Similarly in accessing a Web site, a reader not only needs to be able to combine information gained through different modes (verbal, visual and auditory) in order to make meaning but also use hyperlinks to connect with other parts of the same text or even with new texts. Writing too involves new challenges. Traditional notions of writing assume composition relies upon words. However, composing can also involve selecting from different modes of communication such as video, image, sounds and animation. Writers therefore need to understand the possibilities of each mode and find productive and effective ways to combine them.

Forms of electronic communication, such as online chat, email and texting are interesting in this context as, like speech, they enable rapid communication but lack some of the features of face-to-face interaction, such as facial expression, body language and tone of voice. Various studies (Werry, 1996; Merchant, 2001; Crystal, 2001) have therefore explored the way in which participants in these new contexts have used written language in innovative ways to overcome the limitations of these forms and capitalize on their potential. Alternative conventions enable fast communication and create an informal tone. These include:

- the imaginative use of capitalization and punctuation;
- the use of emoticons (symbols such as smileys) to help participants signal their feelings;
- abbreviations (such as 'RU' for 'are you');
- unconventional spellings.

As technology provides new opportunities for communication, it seems that people develop new ways of communicating through these forms.

# Summary

This chapter has highlighted a number of key concepts in relation to language and literacy use:

- Language is used in varied and flexible ways to respond to different situations, audiences and purposes.
- Language is influenced by the social and cultural context within which it occurs.
- Language and texts evolve as does their use in response to societal, technological and cultural changes.

- The range of language and literacy in which people engage is linked to their occupation, interests, concerns, values and background.
- Different types of language are valued differently in society.

# Reflective questions

1. How does your own use of language reflect your identity? How does it differ from that of a friend or colleague? How is your own use of language affected by social and cultural influences? (Consider accent, dialect, use of slang and jargon, literacy practices, and so forth.)

2. Think about the different kinds of language and literacy you use. Which types do you think are valued most highly by society, in your personal life and in your professional life?

3. How are your uses of language and literacy today different from those you used 10 or even 20 years ago? What is the reason for any differences?

## FURTHER READING

Barton, D. and Hamilton, M. (1998) *Local Literacies: A Study of Reading and Writing in One Community*. London: Routledge.
  Provides a detailed overview of the concept of literacy as social practice with reference to a longitudinal study of the literacy used within the life of a community in Lancaster.

Montgomery, M. (1995) *An Introduction to Language and Society*. London: Routledge.
  A comprehensive introduction to aspects of language change.

Trask, R. L. (1995) *Language: The Basics*. London: Routledge.
  An accessible introduction to aspects of language.

Trudgill, P. (1986) *Varieties of English*. London: Macmillan.
  Explores origins and development of standard English and other regional dialects of English. Examines ways in which dialects differ.

## REFERENCES

Barton, D. (1994) *Literacy: An Ecology of Written Language*. London: Blackwell.

Barton, D. and Hamilton, M. (1998) *Local Literacies: A Study of Reading and Writing in One Community*. London: Routledge.

Barton, D., Hamilton, M. and Ivanic, R. (eds) (2000) *Situated Literacies*. London: Routledge.

Brice-Heath, S. (1982) 'What no bedtime story means: narrative skills at home and at school', *Language in Society*, 11, 49–76.

Collins (2003) *Collins English Dictionary*. London: Collins.

Crystal, D. (1995) *Cambridge Encyclopaedia of the English Language*. Cambridge: Cambridge University Press.

Crystal, D. (2001) *Language and the Internet*. Cambridge: Cambridge University Press.

Gee, J. (1990) *Social Linguistics and Literacies: Ideologies in Discourses*. London: Falmer Press.

Halliday, M. A. K. and Hasan, R. (1985) *Language, Context, and Text: Aspects of Language in a Social-Semiotic Perspective*. Oxford: Oxford University Press.

Hill, A. (2002) 'Accent Blocks Business Success Say Bosses' *Guardian*, 21 July 2002.

Kress, G. (1997) *Before Writing: Rethinking the Paths to Literacy*. London: Routledge.

Kress, G. (1998) 'Visual and verbal modes of representation in electronically mediated communication: the potentials of new forms of text', in Snyder, I. (ed.) *Page to Screen*. London: Routledge, pp. 53–79.

Labov, W. and Waletzky, J. (1967) 'Narrative analysis: oral versions of personal experience', in Helm, J. (ed.) *Essays on the Verbal and Visual Arts*. Seattle and London: University of Washington Press, pp. 12–44.

Martin, J. R., Christie, F. and Rothery, J. (1987) 'Social processes in education: A reply to Sawyer and Watson (and others)', in Reid, I. (ed.) *The Place of Genre in Learning*. Victoria and Sydney: Deakin University.

Merchant, G. (2001) 'Teenagers in Cyberspace: an investigation of language use and language change in Internet chatrooms', *Journal of Research in Reading*, 24, 293–306.

Qualifications and Curriculum Authority (QCA) (2000) *A Language in Common: Assessing English as an Additional Language*. London: QCA.

Street, B. (1984) *Literacy in Theory and Practice*. Cambridge MA: Cambridge University Press.

Trudgill, P. (1994) *Dialects*. London: Routledge.

Werry, C. (1996) 'Linguistic and Interactional Features of Internet Relay Chat', in Herring, S. C. (ed.) *Computer Mediated Communication: Linguistic, Social and Cross-Cultural Perspectives*. Amsterdam: John Benjamins Publishing Company.

# The English Curriculum

The preceding overview of language and literacy in life can be used to contextualize our understanding of English as a subject. Firstly, it signals the importance of introducing children to a wide range of uses of language and literacy that will help them speak, listen, read and write for entertainment, information and communication within diverse contexts. Secondly, given that developments in technology have made it possible to access an ever-widening range of texts, it is increasingly important that children are encouraged to read critically. As language is used to mediate thoughts and experiences, studying language and texts can help children understand others' perspectives and evaluate the values and beliefs that underpin society. The study of a variety of texts, including literature, can help children gain insights into their own feelings and experiences and those of others. Finally, English is the area of learning through which the rest of the curriculum is accessed; it enables children to explore ideas and communicate their findings in all subjects.

English as a subject therefore offers opportunities to:

- help children become increasingly effective language users who can use language for varied purposes and respond to the changing nature of language and literacy;
- enable children to learn about language, how it is used, how it has changed and continues to change;
- develop appreciation of literature to enable them to become independent enthusiastic critical readers;
- develop understanding and skills of critical analysis to empower them to question what they see, hear and read;
- develop the skills necessary to access the rest of the curriculum.

In this chapter we begin by exploring some aspects of the way that children develop as language and literacy users, discuss implications for schools and arrive at some key principles for teaching English in the classroom. This is followed by an overview of current curriculum expectations within early years and primary settings.

# Children as language and literacy users

The notion of literacy as 'social practice' discussed at the beginning of the previous chapter can help us understand how children develop as language and literacy users. Given their experience of language and literacy in use around them, it follows that most children enter education being able to communicate in spoken language and already knowing a great deal about how language is used by their family, friends and local community (Wells, 1985; Tizard *et al.*, 1984). Children will also have been surrounded by print in their everyday lives and will have seen people around them reading and writing. It is from this 'situated' literacy (Barton *et al.*, 2000) that children begin to absorb and make meaning from texts. They understand that reading and writing are meaningful activities and bring this knowledge with them to classrooms. This can be illustrated by the following transcript which demonstrates a child's clear understanding of the purpose of specific written and spoken texts.

*D enters the nursery creative area carrying a mobile phone from the role play area. She places it next to her on the table while she begins to paint. After a few minutes she picks up the phone and begins to press the buttons.*
*Adult*: 'What are you doing D?'
*D*: 'I'm texting Julie.'
*Adult*: 'Oh, what's your message?'
*D*: 'To see if she can pick me up from nursery.'
*D places the phone back on the table and starts painting again. A few minutes later she stops again, places the phone to her ear and starts talking.*
*D*: 'Hello Julie, are you picking me up from nursery or is my mum?' (*Pauses for the imaginary reply*) 'Oh, okay.' *D then returns to her painting.*

(O'Hara, 2004)

Naturally, as they grow older, children continue to develop language and literacy in many contexts outside school. Indeed various studies have highlighted the considerable skill demonstrated by children in accessing and using popular texts, such as computer games, television, games, online chat and email (Marsh *et al.*, 2000; Merchant, 2001; Sefton-Green *et al.*, 2003; Willet, 2003). Children at a very young age confidently move between different uses of language and literacy and between two or more languages in different situations (Gregory, 1997; Burnett and Myers, 2002).

Importantly children do not simply reproduce the practices of those around them. Analyses of playground culture (Blatchford, 1996; Grugeon, 1999) have demonstrated the way in which children play with language and use it for their own purposes. Similarly, Dyson (1997, 2001, 2003) has documented the way that children rework the characters and themes of popular culture through their play, their songs, stories and conversations. Her work shows young people drawing from, adapting and reinterpreting the practices of the wider community. In their lives outside school, children demonstrate that they are autonomous active language and literacy users who are able to use and innovate with language for their own purposes.

Given that our social and cultural background influences the reading, writing, speaking and listening that we do, it follows that the kinds of understandings about language and literacy developed by different children will vary. For some children, the types of language and literacy experienced at home are very similar to those they encounter at school and the transition from home to school is straightforward. In contrast, other children find that ways of reading and writing, which are in common use at home, are overlooked in school and that the way that language is used in school is unfamiliar to them (Brice-Heath, 1982; Tizard *et al.*, 1984; Wells, 1985). Acknowledging this diversity in language use beyond the classroom, many have therefore urged schools to recognize and value children's different language and cultural experiences (DES, 1975; Siraj-Blatchford *et al.*, 2000).

# Implications for schools

Teachers need to achieve a balance between equipping children to use language in ways that enable them to access education and recognizing and valuing the language that children bring with them to school. Importantly, schools can provide a supportive environment in which the values placed on different aspects of language can be discussed and prejudices examined. English teaching can therefore be used to help children begin to challenge inequity and prejudice and explore the social systems that support these. If language captures values and ideas, then analysis of language and texts can help children understand the way that society works.

Unfortunately, studies of children's perceptions of language and literacy in school have repeatedly revealed that children often fail to see the relevance of, or be motivated by, school-based tasks (APU, 1988; Grainger *et al.*, 2003). This is particularly problematic given that, as has been explored, audience, purpose and situation impact on language use. If children are not provided with purposeful contexts for language use then they will be unlikely to explore the reasons why language varies. Over the last 30 years a number of influential projects and reports have stressed the importance of providing meaningful contexts for children's language use in the classroom. These have included:

- In 1975, the Bullock Report (DES, 1975), which emphasised the importance of the process of children's language learning.
- The National Writing Project (1985–9), which explored meaningful and motivating approaches to writing.
- The National Oracy Project (1987–91), which explored the value of speaking and listening throughout the curriculum.
- The Language in the National Curriculum (LINC) project, which emphasised the knowledge about language needed by children across the curriculum.

- The Effective Teachers of Literacy Project (Wray *et al.*, 2002), which suggested that the most effective teachers of literacy linked their literacy teaching to purposeful reading and writing.
- A number of studies that have explored the role of popular culture in children's language use within and outside school and have suggested ways in which this can be used as the starting point for children to demonstrate and develop the way they use language and literacy (Marsh *et al.*, 2000; Dyson, 2003).

As well as acknowledging and building upon children's own uses of language, it is important to broaden the range and scope of their language use and competence. In order to harness the kind of motivation and enthusiasm that children exhibit in relation to their language use at home, it is necessary to provide meaningful, motivating contexts within which they can use and encounter language within school.

Producing and responding to texts plays a key part in this. Through encounters with authentic spoken and written texts, children can gain awareness of the ways in which language is used and moreover reflect on the effect it has on them as readers and listeners. As writers and speakers they can create their own texts experimenting with using language in different ways for real purposes. Children's literature has traditionally played a central role here. Picture books, novels and poetry can entertain and amuse, give insights into experiences and emotions, widen knowledge of others' lives, challenge assumptions or prejudices and help find new ways of looking at the world (Benton *et al.*, 1985). By engaging with fiction and poetry children can become enthusiastic critical readers and have the opportunity to discover and learn from what literature has to offer.

A text-based approach, however, is not confined to children's literature but includes information and reference books along with the vast range of texts found in everyday life, such as leaflets, advertisements, newspaper articles and instructions. These provide children with models of language use for a variety of different purposes and can be used to help develop the different skills and strategies involved in reading for information from an early age. Teachers can also build on children's own uses of language and literacy by integrating popular culture into classroom activities. Television, comics and toys can all provide meaningful, relevant and motivating contexts for the development of language and literacy. Debates exist around the appropriateness of such texts in the classroom and it could be argued that these texts have no place in the curriculum due to the gender and racial stereotyping within many popular texts. However, others have explored ways in which these stereotypes can be explored and challenged through discussion in the classroom (Marsh *et al.*, 2000). The use of colloquialism and slang also provokes concern amongst those who believe that such popular texts do not provide an appropriate model for children's language. On the other hand, they can provide a motivating context for children to explore linguistic diversity. Focusing on everyday and popular texts can not only equip children to read the texts they will encounter in the real world but also prepare them to read them critically.

Earlier we explored how texts and the processes involved in reading and writing are changing and will continue to change. Teachers need to recognize these new texts and equip children to use the potential offered by technology. New technologies can, of course, be used to support children in their production of print texts, for example by using word-processing programs to revise, edit and present pieces of writing. However, as Heppell (2000: xii) asks, 'Do we simply use them to do the old tasks faster or use them to engage children in the new digital creativity, and literacy, that we see all around us?' Children need to approach the use of technology critically; they need to be able to evaluate the potential it offers and be flexible in the way they produce and respond to texts. This means that, more than ever, it is important to talk with children about the different kinds of reading that are appropriate for different types of texts.

Interestingly, in their lives outside school, children who have access to technology experience these new texts through multimedia games, text messaging and email, yet opportunities to use technology in the classroom are often limited by the availability of resources or restricted in scope and range (Holloway *et al.*, 2003). It is important to enable children to use the same kind of autonomy and independence in their use of technology in school as they exhibit in their lives outside school. It is impossible to predict the changes that the future will bring but schools can equip children to be flexible and critical in their response.

This brief overview of the relationship between home and school literacies can be considered alongside the overview of language and texts explored in the previous chapter. It highlights the following key points:

- Our society is linguistically diverse.
- Children use language(s) and literacy in a variety of ways beyond the classroom.
- Children are active and autonomous language users.
- Language and literacy in life are used for a variety of purposes and vary widely within different contexts.
- In real life, language and literacy are motivated and affected by specific purposes.
- The nature of language and texts is constantly evolving.
- Texts reflect the purposes, values and experiences of the people who create them.
- Speaking, listening, reading and writing are often interlinked.
- Written texts vary in nature and provide us with a breadth of opportunities for pleasure, gaining information and broadening understanding.
- Confidence and competence in language and literacy underpin effective learning.

From these observations, we can identify 10 principles for language and literacy provision.

It is important to:
- provide opportunities for children to increase their understanding of linguistic diversity;
- recognize and value the language that children bring with them to school;
- treat children as independent, active and autonomous language users whilst at school;
- provide opportunities for children to read, write, speak and listen for a variety of purposes so that children develop their ability to use language appropriately in different contexts;
- provide meaningful contexts for language and literacy use;
- provide opportunities for children to read and write in new ways and encourage them to be flexible enough to respond to future change;
- develop children's awareness that people's values, perspectives and prejudices influence the way they use language in speaking and writing;
- provide activities in which reading, writing, speaking and listening are integrated;
- provide opportunities for children to engage with a variety of texts, including children's literature, everyday texts, popular culture and a range of digital and print-based sources of information;
- recognize and prepare children to meet the demands on literacy and language made by different subjects.

Practitioners in the primary or early years are required to follow various curriculum guidelines. In the following section, we provide a brief overview of these and in later chapters describe practical ways of interpreting them through planning, teaching and assessment. Throughout, however, the principles outlined above are used to underpin recommended approaches. Examples provided demonstrate how teachers may follow national requirements whilst putting these principles into practice.

# Current curriculum guidelines

## 'Communication, Language and Literacy' in the early years

Guidance for planning, teaching and assessing 3–5 year olds is contained within the *Curriculum Guidance for the Foundation Stage* (QCA, 2000). This document outlines six areas of learning that children experience in an integrated way. The area of learning that corresponds most closely to English is 'Communication, Language and Literacy', which emphasizes the use of language and other forms of communication for meaningful purposes. The curriculum acknowledges linguistic diversity and stresses that children should be provided with opportunities to develop both home languages and English across the curriculum within meaningful, integrated and mainly play-based contexts. Children work towards *Early Learning Goals*, which specify what most children will know, understand and be able to do by the end of Reception. Learning in 'Communication, Language and Literacy' relates to five aspects:

- language for communication;

17

- language for thinking;
- linking sounds and letters;
- reading;
- writing.

A number of 'stepping stones' help teachers plan to support children at different stages of development make progress in each aspect. Importantly, it is not suggested that early years practitioners use the Early Learning Goals to plan a rigid curriculum. Children entering the Foundation Stage will have had varied experiences and will progress in different ways. It is recognized that there is a need to acknowledge and value the language and knowledge about literacy that children bring with them into the early years setting and use this as the starting point for further learning.

## English in the primary school

*The National Curriculum for English* (DfEE, 2000) contains three attainment targets: speaking and listening; reading; and writing. Drama is included within speaking and listening despite arguments for it to be recognized as a separate subject in its own right (Hornbrook, 1998). Programmes of Study specify the *knowledge, skills and understanding* that children should develop in these three areas and the *breadth of study* (or range of texts and experiences) they should encounter. Influenced by the work of the National Oracy Project and National Writing Project, the Programmes of Study highlight the importance of encouraging children to read, write, speak and listen for a range of purposes and audiences. This involves investigating the way that language varies:

- according to context, audience and purpose;
- according to levels of formality (including use of standard English when appropriate);
- between written and spoken forms.

As children move through the primary phase, they are expected to be able to communicate effectively in a range of increasingly challenging contexts.

The National Curriculum includes a series of level descriptors against which children are assessed. Standard Attainment Tests (SATs) at the end of each Key Stage are used to aid the monitoring of children's progress and enable comparisons to be made between schools' achievements in core subjects.

## National Literacy Project and National Literacy Strategy

Most schools in England currently use the National Literacy Strategy Framework for Teaching (DfEE, 1998) to structure their teaching of reading and writing. The Framework, designed to cover literacy teaching for all years from reception to year 6, provides termly lists of objectives relating to the 'knowledge, skills and understanding' required by the Programmes of Study for reading and writing. These objectives are linked to a suggested range of texts, which reflect the 'breadth of study'. The single set of objectives for the reception year is in line with the Early Learning Goals. From Year 1 objectives are taught through daily literacy hours, which include a large proportion of whole-class and group teaching. Such provision is intended to be more efficient than the cross-curricular and often individualized teaching that had preceded it.

The implementation of the National Literacy Strategy has been accompanied by a rigorous programme of target setting at national, local education authority (LEA) and school level. Children's performance in SATs is seen as a key indicator of school improvement and schools are encouraged to set increasingly challenging targets for pupil attainment and demonstrate improvements in SATs results to external agencies, such as OFSTED and LEAs. This has prompted many schools to spend large amounts of curriculum time in preparation for SATs. In response to concerns about the consequent narrowing of the curriculum, the government introduced a new primary strategy. 'Excellence and Enjoyment' (DfES, 2003) encourages schools to develop a broad-based curriculum and to recognize the role of creativity, problem solving and discovery.

## Conclusion

English is a vibrant and wide-ranging subject. Its scope and range have evolved over time to reflect changing beliefs about the aspects of language and literacy that children need to develop. Indeed, just as language itself evolves to reflect social, cultural and technological developments, so has the curriculum for English. Importantly, whilst current guidelines describe the range and scope of the curriculum, they do not have to be seen as prescriptive and can be interpreted in many different ways. In this chapter we have recognized that children themselves engage in rich and varied experiences of language and literacy outside school and have emphasized that an understanding of this is necessary for teachers to plan for children's development. Every class is different and teachers need to be confident in interpreting current and future curriculum guidelines in ways that are relevant and appropriate for the children they teach.

Later chapters provide more specific guidance on planning, teaching and assessing aspects of English, but they are underpinned by the principles identified earlier in this chapter.

# Reflective questions

1. Consider the list of questions below, which echo the kind of questions that inform curriculum planning.

   • How can we/should we capitalize on the language and literacy that children develop outside school?

   • How important is it for children to communicate in standard English and when might they be expected to do so?

   • If we want children to be able to write for different purposes and audiences, which purposes should we prioritize? Should we teach children to write for formal purposes (for example, essays, letters, reports) and ignore the informal (for example, emails, lists, diaries)?

   • Which particular skills do we want children to concentrate on as they develop their use of language? Is it more important for children to spell and punctuate properly, or for them to be able to express themselves through their writing, or use visual or moving images?

   • Which kinds of texts should we look at with children? (Should we be introducing children to a literary heritage of classic texts or giving them the tools to analyse the popular texts that are most familiar to them?)

   • How far should we encourage critical analysis of texts? Should we simply give children opportunities to enjoy what they read?

   • Would your answers to the questions above be different for children in the nursery, in year 1, year 4 or year 6?

2. What is your opinion of the aspects of language and literacy addressed through the 'Communication, Language and Literacy' area of the Foundation Curriculum and the National Curriculum Programmes of Study for English? Is there anything that you feel should be added/deleted? Do you feel there are any strands that are more important than others?

## FURTHER READING

Bearne, E. (1998) *Making Progress in English*. London: Routledge.
  Written prior to the National Literacy Strategy, this book provides practical guidance on teaching all aspects of English and places children's language learning within its social and cultural context.

Browne, A. (2001) *Developing Language and Literacy 3–8*. London: Paul Chapman Publishing.
  An overview of teaching English in the early years which links theory and practice.

Marsh, J. and Hallet, E. (eds) (1999) *Desirable Literacies: Approaches to Language and Literacy in the Early Years*. London: Paul Chapman Publishing.
  A collection of articles exploring how children develop as users of language and literacy and identifying features of effective practice.

Wyse, D. and Jones, R. (2001) *Teaching English, Language and Literacy*. London: Routledge Falmer.
  A comprehensive overview of the English curriculum that links theory and practice.

# REFERENCES

Assessment and Performance Unit (APU) (1988) *Language Performance in Schools: Review of APU Language Monitoring 1979–1983*. London: HMSO.

Barton, D. and Hamilton, M. (2000) *Situated Literacies*. London: Routledge.

Benton, M. and Fox, G. (1985) *Teaching Literature 9–14*. Oxford: Oxford University Press.

Blatchford, P. (1996) 'Taking pupils seriously: recent research and initiatives on breaktime in schools', *Education 3–13*, 24(3), 60–5.

Brice-Heath, S. (1982) 'What no bedtime story means: narrative skills at home and at school', *Language in Society*, 11, 49–76.

Burnett, C. and Myers, J. (2002) 'Beyond the frame: exploring children's literacy practices', *Reading: Literacy and Language*, 36(2), 56–62.

Department for Education and Employment (DfEE) (1998) *National Literacy Strategy Framework for Teaching*. London: HMSO.

Department for Education and Employment (DfEE) (2000) *The National Curriculum for English*. London: HMSO.

Department for Education and Skills (DfES) (2003) *Excellence and Enjoyment – A Strategy for Primary Schools*. London: HMSO.

Department of Education and Science (DES) (1975) *A Language for Life (The Bullock Report)*. London: HMSO.

Dyson, A. H. (1997) 'Rewriting for, and by, children'. *Written Communication*, 14(3), 275–312.

Dyson, A. H. (2001) 'Where are the childhoods in childhood literacy? An exploration in (outer) space', *Early Childhood Literacy*, 1(1), 9–39.

Dyson, A. H. (2003) *The Brothers and Sisters Learn to Write: Popular Literacies in Childhood and School Culture*. New York: Teachers College Press.

Grainger, T., Gouch, K. and Lambirth, A. (2003) 'Playing the game called writing: children's views and voices', *English in Education*, 37(2), 4–15.

Gregory, E. (1997) *Making Sense of a New World*. Clevedon: Multilingual Matters.

Grugeon, E. (1999) 'The state of play: children's oral culture, literacy and learning', *Reading: Literacy and Language*, 33(1), 13–16.

Heppell, S. (2000) 'Foreword', in Gamble, N. and Easingwood, N. (eds) *ICT and Literacy: Information and Communications Technology, Media, Reading and Writing*. London: Continuum, pp. xi–xv.

Holloway, S. L. and Valentine, G. (2003) *Cyberkids: Children in the Information Age*. London: Taylor & Francis.

Hornbrook, D. (1998) *Education and Dramatic Art*. London: Routledge.

Marsh, J. and Millard, E. (2000) *Literacy and Popular Culture: Using Children's Culture in the Classroom*. London: Paul Chapman Publishing.

Merchant, G. (2001) 'Teenagers in cyberspace: an investigation of language use and language change in Internet Chatrooms', *Journal of Research in Reading*, 24, 293–306.

O'Hara, M. (2004) *ICT and the Early Years*. London: Continuum.

Qualifications and Curriculum Authority (QCA) (2000) *Curriculum Guidance for the Foundation Stage*. London: QCA.

Sefton-Green, J. and Willet, R. (2003) 'Living and learning in chatrooms (or does informal learning have anything to teach us?)', *Education et Societes*, 2: http://www.wac.uk/sharedspaces/research.php. Accessed 24/07/03.

Siraj-Blatchford, I. and Clarke, P. (2000) *Supporting Identity, Diversity and Language in the Early Years*. Buckingham: Open University Press.

Tizard, B. and Hughes, M. (1984) *Young Children Learning*. London: Fontana.

Wells, G. (1985) *The Meaning Makers: Children Learning Through Language and Using Language to Learn*. London: Hodder & Stoughton.

Willet, R. (2003) 'New models for new media: young people learning digital culture', *Medeinpadagogik*, 4: http://www.wac.uk/sharedspaces/research.php. Accessed 24/07/03.

Wray, D., Medwell, J., Poulson, L. and Fox, R. (2002) *Teaching Literacy Effectively in the Primary School*. London: Routledge Falmer.

# 3

# Speaking and Listening

In this chapter, we explore the way that children acquire spoken language and suggest practical ways of supporting their continued development. We investigate the link between language and learning and the value of using drama and storytelling in the classroom. We begin by discussing the use of speaking and listening in everyday contexts.

## Types of talk

The following utterances are taken from a series of conversations. They take place in different contexts and show language being used for different purposes.

'Oi! We're off!'

'Perhaps we should make a move?'

'Yes, but on the other hand . . .'

'You'll never guess what just happened to me . . .'

'I wonder if there could be another reason . . .'

'Please could you tell me which train I need to catch to be in London by 12.30?'

Perhaps the first involves commanding, the second asking, and the others challenging, narrating, speculating and enquiring. Interestingly, the first and second examples might both prompt a similar outcome (a start to a journey) but the first is a little more assertive than the second. This could be due to the relationship between the speaker and listener – maybe the first is spoken by a mother talking to her children and the second by a newly appointed personal assistant speaking to his boss. Or perhaps the context is different: maybe both are spoken by a mother to her children but the first occurs as the children get ready to go to school and the second at the end of a relaxed family picnic.

In Chapter 1, we explored ways in which forms of language alter according to context, audience and purpose. The examples above show speech being used in very different ways for different purposes. As Halliday *et al.* (1985) explored, talk always occurs within a social context; the way it is used is affected by what we are trying to say, why we are saying it and the relationship between speakers. Spoken language may be used in many different ways that include:

| | | | |
|---|---|---|---|
| explaining | suggesting | discussing | reporting |
| instructing | speculating | arguing | narrating |
| summarizing | negotiating | clarifying | directing |
| persuading | planning | informing | presenting |
| questioning | disagreeing | analysing | hypothesizing |
| evaluating | describing | expressing feelings | reasoning |

In our lives, we use talk in different ways for different purposes and audiences. We need to support children to develop their capacity to do the same.

# Children's development of spoken language

When children arrive in early years settings and school environments, they are already experienced in using talk in a variety of ways. They are aware that they need to use language to make their needs known and will be beginning to adapt their use of talk in different situations. By the age of three, children may use about a thousand words. This will increase to 2,000–10,000 by the age of five. They will understand many more (Crystal, 1987). At three they will use many simple three or four word sentences and by five will probably be able to use most of the grammatical structures in their home language. Evidently children have not learned all this within educational settings.

Children learn to speak in an environment in which language is widely used around them. From their first days they will have been spoken to in a meaningful way ('have you got a stomach ache?' 'I think you're hungry') and will have learned that they need to communicate with others to get what they need and want. They will have heard models of effective language use and know that language is used for a purpose. Children learn about language use through interaction with others; through conversation they grasp the conventions of spoken language and absorb the values and beliefs placed on language by those around them. They do not just copy the language they hear, but are active in making meaning. When children refer to 'sheeps' or 'feets' or report that they 'goed to the shops', they are using their existing knowledge of language to make sensible guesses at new words or grammatical constructions.

Children's early language, therefore, develops:

- through meaningful interactions with others;
- through hearing models of effective language use;
- as a result of others' response and encouragement.

As teachers in the nursery or classroom, it is therefore important to develop children's language without undermining their attempts to communicate. The following transcript illustrates this approach. (Mehmet is in the early stages of developing English as an Additional Language.)

*Teacher*: Did you have a picnic?

*Mehmet* (3 years, 9 months): A picnic. Yes. Over there. (*He points to the next photo*.)

*Teacher*: Oh I can see you sitting at the bench having a picnic lunch. Did you bring sandwiches?

*Mehmet*: No sandwiches. I meat. Barbecue.

*Teacher*: Oh a barbecue with meat. Did your dad make that?

*Mehmet*: No Dad, me and Khan.

*Teacher*: Oh not your dad, you and your brother Khan.

(Siraj-Blatchford *et al*., 2000: 54)

Note how the teacher asks Mehmet genuine questions as she is interested in his answers. She listens and responds to what he has to say, encouraging him to use what he knows about English to communicate. Whilst she does not correct his language, she provides models of more conventional language use.

Supporting children's continued language development in school involves providing:

* opportunities for learning language in context;
* opportunities for children to interact with one another and adults;
* effective adult models for talk and ensuring that children are exposed to a wide range of spoken language;
* activities in which children communicate for meaningful purposes;
* plenty of support and affirmation;
* an environment that fosters children's continuing interest in language.

# Creating a supportive context for talk

Most of us have been in some situations where we felt uncomfortable talking. Consider the factors within the following situations that might inhibit talk.

A new teacher is attending a staff meeting on her first day working at a new school. She is the least experienced member of staff. The discussion concerns the school's behaviour policy, which was developed during the previous term.

A teacher is giving a talk to a group of parents about his school's approach to teaching reading. As he makes his first point, two parents in the front row exchange knowing glances. The other parents stare back at him expressionless.

Effective speaking and listening may be inhibited by:

* *topic*: insecure knowledge about the subject under discussion or confusion about expectations;

25

- *audience*: lack of familiarity with those being spoken to or uncertainty about their reactions;
- *type of talk*: lack of confidence in using the kind of talk that is expected (e.g. gauging the right level of formality or using appropriate specialist language);
- *response*: an apparently unresponsive or uninterested audience;
- *the wider context*: other issues or concerns in the speaker's personal or professional life or negative prior experiences of similar situations.

Observing children within different contexts can show how the confidence with which they use language varies. Indeed it is common to observe children who are reticent in the classroom using talk in highly effective ways in the playground. It is also important to recognize that, for some children arriving in the nursery, the classroom environment will provide contexts for talk which are unfamiliar. Much of their previous experience will have been rooted in the home. Now they must find ways of communicating in new contexts with people who may not share knowledge about their experience of the world or culture. Children who feel inhibited by the situation in which they are expected to talk are unlikely to speak or listen as effectively as they would if they felt more comfortable. Teachers, therefore, have a key role in creating a supportive environment for talk. They need to show a genuine interest in what children have to say and provide an environment where their talk is clearly valued.

The range and scope of children's speaking and listening will be expanded through their experiences in early years and primary classrooms. This means creating opportunities for children to speak and listen about varied topics to different audiences in diverse contexts. However, it is important to think carefully about the degree of challenge in any speaking and listening task. If children are to use talk to discuss an unfamiliar topic, then it may be unfair to ask them to do this in front of the whole class. If they are to make a formal presentation, it is important to ensure that they are confident about what they are going to talk about. In the following examples, children have been asked to talk for a variety of audiences and purposes. In each example, the children are meeting new challenges, which may relate to the topic, audience, type of talk or context. The teacher in each case has thought carefully about how to create a supportive context and ensure that the children know their talk is valued.

At the beginning of the day, **nursery** children are encouraged to talk informally about things they have done at home and bring in souvenirs and toys to discuss with the whole group. The nursery nurse often photographs this activity and mounts the photographs on a wall display.

A small group of **year 1** children is working with the teacher to sort materials that are magnetic/non-magnetic. The children are encouraged to make predictions and hypotheses about their findings. The teacher writes each child's suggestions on a sheet of sugar paper in speech bubbles next to their name. Once they have tested the materials, they look back at the sheets and compare their results with their predictions. The sheets are stuck into a group book, which also contains photographs of the experiment and a record of the results.

During circle time, **year 3** children are encouraged to share their thoughts and feelings. The whole class sits in a circle and only one person may speak at a time. A 'magic pebble' is passed around and only the person holding it may speak. Using 'sentence starters' helps the children structure their contributions. Sometimes the circle time is light-hearted: 'My favourite colour is . . . because . . .' or 'What I like about the weekend is . . .' Sometimes it is used to share positive experiences: 'Something I'm proud of is . . .'; and to value members of the class: 'What I like about Craig is . . .' At other times, it is used to discuss problems: 'Something that worries me about school is . . .'; and to find solutions: 'I think playtime would be better if . . .'

The **year 4** class holds regular 'class council' sessions to discuss issues that are important to the children. Children take turns to chair the discussion. Those nominated to speak hold a toy microphone. These discussions have resulted in revisions to the class rules and recommendations to the head teacher on improvements to the playground.

A **year 6** child has recently arrived in the school from Libya. He speaks Arabic but no English. The teacher pairs him with another Arabic-speaking child. This child sits with him in the classroom, plays with him at playtime and makes sure that he knows how to find his way around the school.

# Listening

Speaking and listening are rarely separated in life. However, when children arrive in early years or school contexts they will be expected to listen for sustained periods of time. It is unlikely that they will have much prior experience of this and they need to be encouraged actively to develop their listening skills. One of the most powerful ways that teachers can do this is by being effective listeners themselves. Appreciative and responsive listening can be modelled by using appropriate body language (looking at the listener, nodding, and smiling), being interested in what children have to say, commenting on their ideas and asking them questions. Behaviour associated with active listening can be discussed explicitly with children, who can be encouraged to use similar strategies themselves in group and class discussions.

### *Activities to promote sustained listening:*

- devising charts and guidelines for 'being an effective listener';
- listening to a description of an image (a shape, a picture, a map, a diagram) and trying to draw it;
- following spoken instructions to complete a task (for example, to make a simple toy);
- repeating key points from a presentation or set of instructions and asking questions for clarification;

- note making (for example, listening to and making notes from a talk by a visiting nurse);
- sound stories (making sound effects at appropriate points of a story);
- playing listening games (for instance, 'Simon says', 'Heads, shoulders, knees and toes', 'The keeper of the keys', or 'I went shopping . . .');
- listening to and responding to stories and music on tape.

# Linguistic diversity

Over the years, commentators have remarked that many children, often from working-class homes, come to school with 'limited language' (Board of Education, 1921; Wells, 2003). Such views have been linked to a perception that the spoken language outside school is deficient in some way. However, as explored in Chapter 1, there is little evidence to support this assumption and the majority of children grow up in a rich language environment. Moreover, whereas some homes may offer more support to language development than others, these differences are not linked to social class. This means, of course, that children come to school knowing a lot about language even though this may differ from the ideas about language that are inherent within the school environment. The challenge for teachers is to enable children to demonstrate and use what they already know within the school setting.

As explored in Chapter 1, children will use a range of accents, dialects and languages. The National Curriculum requires teachers to equip children to use spoken standard English. However, this does not mean that children must use spoken standard English exclusively. The way that children use language is closely linked to their identity; if schools do not value the language they bring with them to school, they risk devaluing the child. Schools and early years settings need to:

- accept, encourage and use the children's own language skills;
- challenge any possible prejudice that may be linked to such differences;
- actively value linguistic diversity;
- provide opportunities for children to develop their use of standard English in appropriate contexts;
- ensure that children are comfortable with using the language(s) of the home in school, particularly when using talk to support learning.

Importantly, classrooms in which linguistic diversity is valued are rich, vibrant places offering many opportunities for learning about language. The following scenarios illustrate the kind of activities that can be used to recognize and explore linguistic diversity:

Children in a **reception** class have been asked to go home and learn a traditional rhyme to share with the other children. Some parents and siblings have written down versions of rhymes for the children to bring into school. As some of the children are bilingual, many of these are in languages other than English. They learn the rhymes and record them on tape.

A **year** 2 class has been exploring speech in stories. The children have collected different greetings (used by their friends, relatives and characters in books and soap operas) and made an interactive display which involves matching the greetings to pictures of the people that said them. They also discuss which greetings would be most appropriate in formal situations.

A group of **year** 3 children has been investigating dictionaries and glossaries. As homework, they spoke to parents and grandparents and listed dialect words their relatives use. They have now compiled these lists and made dialect dictionaries.

A group of **year** 4 children is exploring issues around friendship through drama. They are grouped according to languages used and encouraged to improvise using their home languages. The children are then given some moments to discuss themes explored in their home language before contributing to a class discussion in English.

As part of work on persuasive language, a **year** 5 class has designed a new mobile phone and created a poster advertising it. The children now prepare a presentation, supported by PowerPoint slides, to convince a mobile phone company director to produce the phone. During their preparation, they discuss the kind of language appropriate to this formal presentation.

A **year** 6 class has been investigating different forms of communication during a transition project with the local secondary school. They have exchanged information about themselves and their respective schools using face-to-face conversation, online chat, email, and texting. They are now comparing how language is used differently within each form.

# Planning purposeful tasks for speaking and listening

Encouraging children to talk will not necessarily provide the conditions necessary to develop speaking and listening. If the activity does not actually require children to speak to one another they may simply work in silence or talk about matters unrelated to the task. Successful work on developing children's ability to speak and listen for a variety of audiences and purposes has been built on the premise that motivating contexts for talk must be provided (Norman, 1992). However, as Norman (1990) points out, activities involving children in speaking and listening for a variety of purposes and audiences provide motivating contexts for talk. Children are far more likely to communicate effectively if they feel it is important to do so.

Opportunities for many of the types of talk listed earlier arise across and beyond the curriculum. The following activities all involve using different types of talk in meaningful contexts. (Whilst each activity is linked to one key type of talk, each task will inevitably involve other types too.)

### Negotiating

Two **year 4** children are collecting atmospheric words and phrases that describe the desert from *Muhamad's Desert Night* (Kessler, 1995). They write each one on a separate strip of paper and then decide how to arrange the phrases they like into a new 'found' poem.

### Describing

A group of **nursery** children is playing a guessing game. The children have a number of objects on the table in front of them. They describe one of the objects whilst the other children try and guess what it is.

### Persuading

Some **year 3** children have been studying the local area and are now recording a television advert intended to attract tourists to the area.

### Instructing

In PE, a group of **year 1** children has devised a simple throwing game involving a hoop and a large ball. The children tell another group how to play the game.

### Evaluating

Children in **year 5** have read the books submitted for the shortlist for the Carnegie Prize for children's literature. In groups, they decide which book they think should win.

### Informing

The teacher has heard the **reception** children talking about a cartoon they have been watching. The teacher knows very little about this and asks the children to tell her about it.

### Reporting

The teacher has produced a video of the school's latest football match. The **year 4** children work in groups to prepare a commentary on the video. One group presents their commentary with the video during a school assembly.

### Explaining

A **year 2** child has made a vehicle driven by an elastic band. During the plenary session, she explains how it works to the class.

### Selecting

**Year 6** children have used a digital video camera to film activities throughout the school and are working in groups to produce short videos for an open day. They use digital editing equipment to select the footage they want to use. They discuss and make decisions about transitions between shots, sound, voice-overs and title sequences.

**Hypothesizing**

A class of **year 3** children is looking at a selection of World War II artefacts in groups of 5. The children's task is to find out as much as they can about the artefact and discuss its purpose. Later they will make labels for the artefacts, which will be placed in their class museum.

# Organizing activities to promote talk

When planning for collaborative work, careful thought must be given to group size and composition. Reticent children may be inhibited by a child with a dominant personality and may work more effectively alongside children who enable them to take a more active role.

There are various ways of grouping children, including:

- ability grouping;
- mixed-ability grouping;
- friendship grouping;
- by languages spoken;
- by gender;
- by personality;
- in self-selected groups.

Careful observation of children engaged in collaborative work will help inform these grouping decisions. Note that paired work is very supportive and easy to organize. In many classes, children have *talk partners*, with whom they discuss their thoughts during whole-class and group activities, for instance strategies to tackle a maths investigation or ideas for an opening line of a story.

Expecting children to share what they have discovered with other children can provide a clear focus for collaborative work. However, feeding findings back to the whole class can be repetitive and boring. Various organizational strategies help provide motivating opportunities and purposes for talk.

## 'Jigsawing'

Children are organized into 'home' groups with a shared focus, for example researching the experience of the rich and poor in Tudor Britain. Each group member is responsible for investigating a different aspect, for example Child A: food; Child B: homes; Child C: health; Child D: leisure. The children leave their home groups to form 'expert groups' with others with the same research interest. After researching their particular aspect, the children return to their home groups to report back on their findings. The 'home' group then completes a shared task using all the information it has gathered (for example a leaflet comparing the lives of rich and poor in Tudor times).

### 'Envoying'

After collaborative group work, each group sends out an 'envoy'. The 'envoy' visits each of the other groups and passes on her/his group's findings and/or gathers ideas from the groups he or she visits. He or she then returns to report back any findings to his or her base group.

### 'Snowballing'

Children work in pairs to investigate a subject or discuss an issue (such as ways of overcoming the litter problem in the school playground). Each pair then joins another pair to share its findings. The new groups of four can then work together, using the ideas they have pooled, for example deciding on the most effective solution to the litter problem and creating a poster to recommend it to the rest of the class.

### 'Rainbowing'

Children start off in groups and are given a task to complete. For instance each group carries out a different investigation into the growth of runner beans (one group looks at the effect of light, whilst another explores the effect of water, and another looks at the impact of different growing media, and so on). Individuals within each group are allocated a different colour. Once the task is completed, the children form new groups according to their colours. In these colour groups they share their findings, for example by listing the conditions for healthy plant growth.

## Talk and learning

Interestingly, when faced with a particularly challenging puzzle to solve, it is often helpful to talk it through with someone else. Many of us find that, by explaining an idea to others, we clarify it to ourselves. Moreover, a discussion about concepts or problems can help us deepen understanding or find more appropriate solutions. Talk and learning are often closely linked. Thoughts and ideas are shared through language and knowledge is created as people communicate their discoveries and negotiate meaning from them with others. As Mercer (1995: 67) writes: 'Individually and collectively, we use language to transform experience into knowledge and understanding. It provides us with both an individual and a social mode of thinking.'

In transcript A, three children are talking as they work together to paint some sky for a display.

### Transcript A

1. *S*   Blue . . . This sky is blue.
2. *M*   Like, like . . . the sky in the book.

3. *T*   Is it? I mean . . . just . . .
4. *S*   Course it is . . . the sky in South Africa's always blue, like the sun is always shining.
5. *M*   Doesn't.
6. *S*   Does . . . What do you mean?
7. *M*   Has to rain sometimes . . . that's why, that's how they got the mud . . . and in the winter.
8. *S*   Yeah, I remember it rained.
9. *T*   They got paint pots to get the water.
10. *M*   But it's not in the book.
11. *M goes to find book and brings it back to show the others.*
12. *M*   Look . . . nowhere . . . nowhere blue.

(Browne, 2001: 7–8)

As the children paint, they explore ideas (2), use reasoning to justify their opinions (4, 7, 10, 12), draw on prior experience (8), and challenge or build on one another's suggestions (3, 6, 9). This is typical of what Mercer (1995) calls 'exploratory talk'. It involves collaborators developing each other's ideas and adopting a critical stance to their own and others' contributions. This kind of talk supports learning.

Importantly, learning talk is very different from the well-rehearsed talk often used in formal situations, such as interviews or presentations. Barnes (1992: 126) describes it as: '. . . often hesitant and incomplete; it enables the speaker to try out ideas, to hear how they sound, to see what others make of them, to arrange information and ideas into different patterns'.

Effective learning talk requires a supportive environment in which all are encouraged to talk through emerging thoughts and ideas. Plenty of opportunities for collaboration need to be provided within an environment that encourages children to experiment. The teacher's role in promoting learning talk through class and group discussions is discussed in Chapter 7.

Despite the potential for learning through discussion, it has been noted that much collaborative talk is unproductive (Dunne *et al.*, 1990; Phillips, 1994). Transcript B records a classroom conversation held by two children using Draw, a computer art program. This was recorded as part of an investigation into the way that pairs of children work collaboratively (Lomangino *et al.*, 1999).

## Transcript B

1. Beth:   You're not doing it right, Tyler.
2. Tyler:  Arrr.
3. Beth:   Just a second [ *frustrated tone, she reaches over to the mouse and begins clicking down on the rubber stamp icons causing them to show up on the screen*].
4. Tyler:  Oh, what'd you do?

5. Beth: Just a second, Tyler . . . I know what I'm doing.
6. Tyler: Beth, don't.
7. Beth: [*sound of paint icon in background*]. Hold it a second [*continues clicking on paint bucket*].

(Lomangino *et al.*, 1999: 217)

This conversation occurs against a background of existing relationships and identities. The children are engaged in a constant power struggle. Each child's need to dominate the other sees them rejecting their partner's moves and asserting their own ideas (1, 4, 5, 6). Interestingly, this means that they do not explore their ideas through talk or sound them out with each other. Their talk can be described as 'disputational' (Mercer, 1995). They make individual decisions and direct rather than negotiate (3, 7). Unsurprisingly this pair was far less successful in the task than those that were supportive to one another. Their talk did not support their learning.

The National Oracy Project identified three dimensions of talk that are significant within any discussion (Norman, 1990):

- *communicative*: talk as a means of transferring meaning between people;
- *social*: concerned with people getting along together;
- *cognitive*: a means to learning.

Considering these three aspects of talk can be useful when evaluating classroom discussion. In Transcript B, for example, the social dimension seems to provide an obstacle to exploratory talk. Had the children been supportive towards one another and willing to try out each other's ideas, the cognitive dimension of their talk may have been more effective. The most successful learning talk occurs when communicative, cognitive and social aspects are all addressed effectively.

Studies (Dawes *et al.*, 1992; Mercer, 2000) have suggested that children's interactions become more focused and productive when they have been given opportunities to reflect on their talk. This can be encouraged through agreeing guidelines for group discussion, giving children talk logs (for children to make notes on how they interacted with others) or simply spending time evaluating talk and sharing effective strategies. Children can be asked to discuss ways to:

- make sure that everyone has a chance to contribute;
- encourage others to give reasons for their suggestions;
- respond when someone challenges their ideas;
- be encouraging to someone who is reluctant to take part in discussion;
- summarize ideas and make sure the discussion stays on track;
- arrive at a consensus following a disagreement;
- challenge someone without being rude;
- ask for clarification;
- make sure that all options have been considered;
- actively listen to others' contributions;
- deal with a dominant group member.

Of course, communica...
speaking, facial expressio...
just as much as the wor...
with others, it is necessary...
using turn-taking skills)...
people stand, use eye co...
vary according to social...
issues about these con...

36

to retell the story. She talks the chi...
first? And then? And what did...
Children from a year 1 cla...
available in Punjabi an...
children listen to th...
conveying the m...
A teacher...
children...
then...

# Storytelling

Exploring narrative t...
English curriculum an...
also have a significant co...
demonstrates the confidenc...
orally and experiment with...
classroom can build on these ea...
can be encouraged to share jokes and anecdotes, or listen to ...
stories.

### Benefits of storytelling

- children absorb the patterned, rhythmic language used within storytelling and this can help broaden their repertoire of language use;
- telling stories to children can encourage active listening; they can be encouraged to join in refrains, make sound effects and contribute their own ideas about characters, setting and events;
- when children tell stories they are involved in a highly sustained speech event. This gives them experience of structuring a presentation and finding ways to capture and retain their audience's interest;
- given that it is quicker to generate a story orally than in writing, storytelling can give children a sense of control over their story and help them develop their understanding of story structure;
- it provides children with an opportunity to be creative within a supportive context. If children retell a story, they can use the original narrative but embellish it as much as they wish, for example by adding details about characters, telling the story in a new setting, or using voice tone and gesture to create atmosphere;
- it builds upon the oral tradition of passing on stories between individuals and communities and can help children understand how traditional tales have evolved.

The following scenarios provide examples of storytelling being used in the classroom.

A **nursery** teacher reads *Jasper's Beanstalk* (Butterworth *et al.*, 1993) to a group of children. She then helps the children use props (a fork, some beans, a toy cat, and so on)

dren through it: 'Do you remember what happened
ne do after that?'

ss listen to a story using headphones. The story is also
Bengali versions recorded by a bilingual teacher and parent. The
tape in one or both languages and sequence a series of illustrations
ain events of the story.

lls her **year 2** class one of the traditional Anancy stories (Berry, 1989). The
make a map of the places visited in the story, and use it as a prompt to help
retell their story to a partner. Once all the children have revised the story in this
ay, one child volunteers to sit in the 'storyteller's chair' and begin telling the story to
the rest of the class. As soon as she begins to falter another child takes over and
continues with the story and a third child finishes it off.

The **year 4** children have all 'collected' a story about a family incident from home. The
children work in pairs to record their stories on audiocassette. Next, they listen to their
tellings and find ways of making them even more exciting for their audiences, developing
their use of pace, volume and tone. Following this 'oral re-drafting', they record a final
version of their story. Several children opt to share their versions live with the rest of the
class. These are videoed to be shown at the next parents' evening. Some children record
versions of their story in both their home language and English.

The **year 6** class is investigating life in Britain since 1948. Some of the children's
grandparents offer to come and talk to the children. The children conduct interviews and
record the childhood stories they are told. They then use the stories as the starting point
for their own oral stories, which they rehearse, refine and share with the rest of the class.
This prompts a discussion about the value of oral history as historical evidence.

## Drama

Drama provides children with simulated experiences through which they can develop
a deeper understanding of their own and others' lives. It offers many rich opportunities
for developing speaking and listening for different audiences and purposes (for
example, talking to a character who does not understand or to someone who is upset
or angry) and within different contexts (for example, using standard English within
a formal situation). Many children reluctant to speak in other situations will make
valuable and extensive contributions during drama work. Drama also provides
motivating contexts for collaboration.

# Working in role

During early childhood, children engage in 'socio-dramatic play'. Through behaving 'as if' they were doctors or nurses, shopkeepers or parents, children explore and rehearse the behaviours and experiences they encounter in the world around them. In this way they make sense of the world they experience. Role-play areas therefore provide a key resource within early years classrooms. Practical suggestions for establishing and supporting children's play in these areas are contained in Chapter 10. More extended and even whole-class role-play within and beyond classrooms can build on children's early play to provide opportunities for children to meet new challenges, empathize with others and explore relationships. A visit to a local ruin, for example, can provide the starting point for children to explore aspects of life in the past.

A key strategy is 'teacher in role' (Bolton, 1975). By interacting with children in role, teachers can provide them with challenges, dilemmas to face and problems to solve (for instance, by asking them to help sort out a dispute or solve a mystery). Importantly, being in role does not imply 'acting' but simply adopting the attitudes of the person represented. The choice of role is important. A teacher may choose to take a high-status role that will enable him/her to direct the children (for example, the teacher is the king/the children are the subjects) or a low-status role (for instance, the teacher is someone new to the local area who comes to the children for advice) or a peripheral role (for example, a messenger).

Another useful strategy (often used in conjunction with 'teacher in role') is 'mantle of the expert' (Heathcote *et al.*, 1995) in which children are treated as experts and asked to use and apply their knowledge in a given situation. For example, reception children who have been exploring the story of *Goldilocks and the Three Bears* can be asked to console the teacher in role as one of the three bears. They might be invited to explain what happened at the bears' house and give advice on how to approach Goldilocks to sort things out. In challenging the traditional teacher/pupil relationship, this strategy can be empowering for children; it often prompts them to assume high levels of responsibility for their actions within the drama and gives them confidence to speak out and take responsibility within the situation being explored.

Working in role can also provide a valuable stimulus for writing and deepen children's engagement with and response to texts. Examples of this are provided in Chapters 4 and 5.

# Making, performing and responding to drama

Being involved in making, presenting and responding to performance develops children's confidence and provides them with a powerful means to express themselves. As children move through school, they gain increasing confidence in using a range of dramatic techniques. Importantly, performance does not have to be large scale. Much of the most valuable work involves children in finding their own ways to interpret and present ideas, stories and experiences. These will only occasionally be performed in formal situations in an assembly or for parents; more often they will be shared informally in the class.

Children need plenty of opportunities to evaluate dramatic performance. This may be work presented by their peers or other classes, recorded performances (television, film or radio) or professionally produced performances within or outside school. As children evaluate the work they see, they develop a language with which to discuss dramatic performance. They become aware of dramatic tension and the impact of elements such as gesture, voice, pause, eye contact and use of space. This helps them understand the possibilities of dramatic form and in turn informs their own work. The relationship between making, performing and responding to drama can be seen as cyclical (see Figure 3.1).

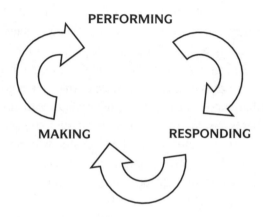

Figure 3.1. Making, performing and responding (a cyclical process)

The following scenarios show children exploring aspects of performance. Note that children start at different points in the cycle.

The **year 1** children have watched a visiting puppet company's version of Hansel and Gretel. They discussed what they liked about the performance, including their thoughts on characterization and use of lighting and sound. They are now making puppets and scenery for their own puppet play.

**Year 2** children have been exploring the conversation poems of Michael Rosen and Allan Ahlberg. Each group is allocated a poem and asked to find a way of dramatizing it. The children decide who is speaking, the relationship between the characters and what each character could be thinking at different moments. Then they find a way of representing this in their performance.

The **year 4** children are creating short scenes based on *Children of Winter* (Doherty, 1995). They are asked to prepare a scene focusing on a key moment from the story, when three children must decide whether or not to give shelter to a man who could threaten their survival. The children work in small groups. They are only allowed to speak four lines of dialogue in their scene so cannot rely on words to communicate feelings and relationships. One child acts as director giving feedback to the rest of the group.

The **year 6** children have been exploring *Macbeth* and have reached the point at which the three witches appear on the heath. The children work in threes to find a way of making the witches 'appear'. Next the class watch the *Animated Tales* cartoon version of the same scene and compare it with their own. They discuss the way that atmosphere and tension were created, the different interpretations of the witches and the impact on the audience. Finally they decide which version they prefer.

## Useful drama techniques

- **Freezeframes**: children make a still image or tableau representing a key moment, a concept or an emotion.
- **Thought-tracking**: ask the children to speak the thoughts of characters in a freezeframe.
- **Hotseating**: question a child or group of children in role as characters from a story.
- **Decision alley**: focus on a moment when a character has to make a decision. Sit the children in two parallel lines to form an 'alley'. One child (as the character) walks down the 'alley' whilst the others tell her/him what they think s/he should do.
- **Forum theatre**: ask a pair/group of children to improvise a scene. Others suggest alternative ways in which the character could have acted and replay the scene to accommodate these suggestions.
- **Role on the wall**: draw a large outline of a character. Record words to describe the character in and around the character. Alternatively scribe a character's thoughts and feelings, actions or speech.

# Summary

In planning for speaking and listening, we need to:

- help children broaden the range and scope of their language while valuing the language they bring with them to school;
- include a range of opportunities, purposes, audiences and groupings to promote a variety of types of talk;
- organize groups appropriately, taking into consideration the children, their personalities and the task;
- model attentive listening and the use of different types of talk, including tentative exploratory talk and the use of genuine questions;
- make explicit the value of collaboration and of speaking and listening skills;
- provide opportunities for talk to support learning across the curriculum;
- develop children's understanding of effective talk through encouraging reflection;
- plan tasks which require collaboration/discussion;
- recognize the place of drama and storytelling in the curriculum.

# Reflective questions

1. It is clearly important to develop children's ability to use standard English. How can we do this without devaluing children's home experience of language? How do we make sure that 'correctness' is not emphasized at the expense of fluency?

2. Find time to observe a child's speaking and listening within different contexts: in whole-class situations; in groups with and without an adult present; during different types of classroom activities; in the playground. Are there times when the child seems more confident than at others? Which kinds of situations seem to encourage/inhibit talk for this child? How do differences in topic, audience, type of talk and wider context seem to affect their confidence?

## FURTHER READING

Grainger, T. (1997) *Traditional Storytelling in the Primary Classroom*. Leamington Spa: Scholastic.
  Explores the importance of narrative and provides practical suggestions for storytelling in the classroom.

Grainger, T. and Cremin, M. (2001) *Resourcing Classroom Drama, 5–8* OR *8–14*. Sheffield: NATE.
  Two highly useful books giving practical suggestions for sequences of drama lessons using a variety of stimuli.

Grugeon, E., Hubbard, L., Smith, C. and Dawes, L. (eds) (2001) *Teaching Speaking and Listening in the Primary School*. London: David Fulton Publishers.
  Practical guidance on developing a range of types of talk along with suggestions for assessment.

Mercer, N. (2000) *Words and Minds*. London: Routledge.
  Provides a detailed overview of the relationship between talk and thinking.

Whitehead, M. (1997) *Language and Literacy in the Early Years*. London: Paul Chapman Publishing.
  Provides a detailed overview of theoretical perspectives on early language development.

## REFERENCES

Barnes, D. (1992) 'The role of talk in learning', in Norman, K. (1990) *Teaching Talking and Learning in Key Stage 1*. London: National Curriculum Council.

Board of Education (1921) *The Teaching of English in England (The Newbolt Report)*. London: HMSO.

Bolton, G. (1975) *Towards a Theory of Drama in Education*. London: Longman.

Browne, A. (2001) *Developing Language and Literacy 3–8*. London: Paul Chapman Publishing.

Crystal, D. (1987) *Child Language Learning and Linguistics*. London: Arnold.

Dawes, L., Mercer, N. and Fisher, E. (1992) 'The quality of talk at the computer', *Language and Learning*, 10, 22–5.

Dunne, E. and Bennett, N. (1990) *Talking and Learning in Groups*. London: Routledge.

Fox, C. (1993) *At the Very Edge of the Forest: the Influence of Literature on Storytelling by Children*. London: Cassell.

TEACHING ENGLISH 3–11

Halliday, M. A. K. and Hasan, R. (1985) *Language, Context and Text: A Social-Semiotic Perspective*. Oxford: Oxford University Press.

Heathcote, D. and Bolton, G. (1995) *Drama for Learning*. London: Heinemann.

Lomangino, A. G., Nicholson, J. and Sulzby, E. (1999) 'The influence of power relations and social goals on children's collaborative interactions while composing on the computer', *Early Childhood Research Quarterly*, 14(2), 197–228.

Mercer, N. (1995) *The Guided Construction of Knowledge: Talk Amongst Teachers and Learners*. Clevedon: Multilingual Matters.

Mercer, N. (2000) *Words and Minds*. London: Routledge.

Norman, K. (1990) *Teaching Talking and Learning in Key Stage 1*. London: National Curriculum Council.

Norman, K. (1992) (ed.) *Thinking Voices: the Work of the National Oracy Project*. London: Hodder & Stoughton.

Phillips, T. (1994) 'The dead spot in our struggle for meaning: learning and understanding through small group talk', in Wray, D. and Medwell, J. (eds) (1994) *Teaching Primary English: the State of the Art*. London: Routledge.

Siraj-Blatchford, I. and Clarke, P. (2000) *Supporting Identity, Diversity and Language in the Early* Years. Buckingham: Open University Press.

Wells, A. (2003) 'Skills chief bemoans the "daily grunt"', in *Guardian*, 8 January 2003.

## CHILDREN'S BOOKS

Berry, J. (1989) *Anancy-Spiderman: 20 Caribbean Folk Stories*. London: Walker.

Butterworth, N. and Inkpen, M. (1993) *Jasper's Beanstalk*. London: Hodder Children's Books.

Doherty, B. (1995) *Children of Winter*. London: Mammoth.

Kessler, C. (1995) *Muhamad's Desert Night*. London: Puffin.

# 4 Reading

Reading
_____

In this chapter, we begin by discussing reading in everyday life, explore the range of purposes, texts and approaches to reading involved and discuss the implications for classroom teaching. We then examine the development of understanding and response and ways in which enthusiasm for literature can be encouraged in children of all ages. This is followed by consideration of the reading process, how children learn to read and the teaching of phonics. The last part of the chapter presents a range of strategies for teaching reading.

## Reading in daily life

There are many different ways to read the same text. As you read this book, you may be flicking through the pages, wondering whether you can find anything useful and relevant to support your current needs; you may be reading intently, ready to make notes, or glancing over someone else's shoulder trying to guess the subject matter.

Clearly, reading does not only involve following a text with deep concentration in order to gain a full appreciation of its meaning. It also includes all the incidental bits of reading that take place in glancing at an advert, headline or label, as well as quick checks for information, such as the time, the date, a street sign or bus destination. Sometimes reading entails scanning a text for a specific piece of information, for example finding a telephone number in a phone book or a price in a catalogue. At other times, it involves skimming contents to gain a gist of the meaning, for example looking through a newspaper. In contrast, closer reading is often needed when detailed understanding is required, for example when absorbed in a novel, following instructions or reading a useful section from a text book. Such different ways of reading are not independent of each other. Often one type of reading leads to another. Skimming the headlines of the paper may lead to close reading of a specific article. Scanning a holiday brochure for a particular place of interest may lead to careful reading of descriptions, small print and figures to check prices and suitability.

In adult life, reading is often motivated by a need or desire for information, required in order to complete an action: a recipe is read to prepare a special meal; a timetable is examined before a journey is made; a brochure is considered before a holiday is booked. In such examples, the text is read, the information is processed and then an action takes place. Reading in daily life can also be important in providing relaxation and enjoyment. Reading a novel, magazine or a text relating to an interest often offers a source of pleasure. It may present an escape from the world around, an insight into the lives of others or opportunities for informal learning and the stimulation of new ideas.

The different purposes for reading and ways of reading a text are not the only aspects of variation. As discussed in Chapter 1, texts also differ widely in their organization, presentation, use of language and levels of formality. Academic texts are written in standard English, whereas an email or note from a friend is likely to be far more informal, using slang, jargon, abbreviations and smileys. Texts also vary in their use of illustrations, figures, moving images and sound. Many texts, for example a note, email, letter or novel, are organized and presented in a way that assumes that the whole text will be read from beginning to end. Others, such as Internet pages and information sheets, are often presented in a far less linear sequence so that readers choose their own paths through them.

Another important aspect of reading is the ability to be critical. At its simplest, this enables a reader to decide which text will be most useful for a specific purpose and to discard those that seem irrelevant or unsuitable. It also involves awareness that texts carry particular messages and bias according to their authorship, readership, funding and purpose. As a result, a reader is able to recognize the ways in which language is used to influence others, for example in advertising and the media. Given the increasing presence of print in daily life in paper and electronic form, the ability to read critically is particularly important.

In order to encourage children to become keen, competent and confident readers in the world beyond the classroom, their experience of reading in school needs to provide:

- meaningful purposes for reading;
- a range of different texts;
- opportunities to read for pleasure;
- encouragement to select and evaluate texts.

If children are to be encouraged to develop enthusiasm for reading, they need to encounter texts that are interesting, appropriate and relevant. In this chapter, we focus on the teaching of reading mainly in relation to fiction, but it is clear that children need to explore a wide range of texts that reflect those found in the world beyond the classroom, such as advertisements, instructions, packaging, Internet sites and leaflets. The value of such texts and the reading of non-fiction will be examined in depth in Chapter 6.

# Children's literature

Before considering the value of children's literature, it is useful to reflect on the role of narrative in your own life. Narrative, the telling of a sequence of events, is an essential part of human experience and a dominant form of entertainment in many people's lives. You may well enjoy watching videos or soap operas and sharing stories of experiences with friends. You may also find pleasure in reading fiction. Such experience may entertain you, provide relaxation or humour or the chance to escape from daily life. It may also offer puzzles to solve and the opportunity to be involved in different lives. It may be that you enjoy the challenge of being provoked to think, to question assumptions or consider issues and viewpoints previously taken for granted.

Picture books, novels, short stories, plays and poetry offer all children opportunities for similar enjoyment and satisfaction. At every age, children can gain pleasure from the humour of texts, the entertaining plots, characters, situations and use of language. They may find reassurance in encountering familiar situations and feelings or enjoy escaping into different worlds and broadening their experience. They can also gain satisfaction from being challenged to consider issues and reflect on preconceptions and prejudices.

Such rich and varied opportunities are available to the youngest children. Texts aimed at this age group often feature a simple, predictable structure, repetitive text and illustrations, which enable children to enjoy the narrative and gain understanding of the characters and setting. However, illustrations do not always simply support the written text but may contribute essential meaning. A well-known example of this is *Handa's Surprise* (Browne, 1995), in which a child takes a basket of fruit as a surprise to her friend in a neighbouring African village. The pictures show that the fruit is taken by animals and replaced, without Handa's knowledge. The written text focuses on her thoughts as she walks, her anticipation of how pleased her friend will be with her surprise. The difference between the meaning conveyed by the words and images heightens the reader's eagerness to find out what will happen when she arrives. Understanding and appreciation of the text therefore rests upon the contribution made by both media.

At other times the contradictions between illustrations and text may raise issues and questions that are left for the reader to answer. An example of this is *Zoo* (Browne, 1992) in which the illustrations are used to provoke thought about the experience of animals in the zoo and the attitudes of visitors. In contrast, the written text offers a child's narrative of his family's day out. In *Lost Thing* (Tan, 2000), the written text tells the story of a boy who finds a 'thing', a strange but fabulous machine that does not fit in his world. Intricately drawn illustrations show that this is a world dominated by order, work and logic. They not only add to the boy's narrative but provide the setting and a social commentary on the story. Making meaning from such a text challenges the most able reader.

Picture books should therefore not be seen simply as support for the early readers. On the contrary, the interaction between text and illustrations can enable picture books to achieve a particularly powerful impact which should ensure their place in the class library throughout and beyond Key Stage 2. Multi-layered texts support and benefit from continued re-readings, during which children may discover elements they previously missed. The same book may also be explored on different levels with different age groups: for example, *Gorilla* (Browne, 1995) may be seen by younger children as a fantasy story, but by older readers as a poignant exploration of loneliness and the building of a relationship.

Given the increasing reliance on the visual image as a means of communication, for example in adverts, signs and so on, discussions around illustrations in picture books can help promote visual literacy. Children can consider what is shown in an image and whose perspective is reflected. They can also examine ways in which colour is used to represent mood or atmosphere. For example, in *Farmer Duck* (Waddell, 1991), a story of a farmyard revolution to overthrow a lazy, cruel farmer, they can discuss the significance of the bleak, misty opening scene and the sunny, flower-filled setting at the end.

# Developing enthusiasm for literature

From the earliest stages, children need to see that reading is an enjoyable experience and that books have much to offer them. They need to have a range of appropriate texts read to them with enthusiasm as well as having the opportunity to select and read books independently and to share them with others. As Chambers (1993) and Millard (1997) point out, reading is not simply a solitary pursuit because sharing responses often enhances the experience.

The following examples illustrate different ways in which children are encouraged to develop interest and enthusiasm for literature and confidence and independence as readers.

In a carpeted corner of the **nursery**, there is an armchair, large floor cushions and a well-stocked bookshelf at the children's height. Books recently read to the children are included on the shelves. A small boy selects the book *Rattletrap Car* (Root, 2001) from the shelf and sits down to look at it. He looks at the pictures of the family car which gradually falls to pieces on a journey to a lake. He is joined by another child and then a teaching assistant, who reads the rhyming text aloud to them.

Following a visit to a local library, the role-play area in a **reception** classroom has been set up in the area around the book corner. A large sign welcomes visitors to the class library. There are some chairs and a low table with magazines and newspapers so that the children can sit and read. There is a librarian's desk with borrowers' cards and a date stamp and relevant leaflets collected from the local library. Initially the teaching assistant acted as the librarian, organizing the books, stamping borrower cards and recommending particular titles. Now the children adopt these roles when playing in this area.

The year 1 children are seated in groups at tables. On each table there is a pile of books, both fiction and non-fiction. The room is quiet but not silent. Some of the children share a book in pairs, taking turns to read the text or make their own version from the pictures. Two children are retelling *Eat Your Peas* (Grey, 2002), which has been read to them previously by the teacher; another pair are following the antics of the monkey in the illustrations in *Monkey Do!* (Ahlberg, 1999); another pair is comparing pictures of snakes in a book on wildlife. Four children are using head-sets to listen to a taped story. This 'reading time' takes place most days and lasts for about 10 minutes. The length of the session has increased since it was introduced at the beginning of the year.

The year 3 children have all been asked to select their 'desert island books'. In groups they are now compiling a list of all-time favourites to swap and compare with a class in another school.

It is the end of the day. The year 5 children are sitting down and the teacher is finishing the class novel, *The Turbulent Term of Tyke Tyler* (Kemp, 1979). As she finishes the last line, the class erupts in surprise at the ending. They spend the last 10 minutes exploring their different responses and the teacher notices that their discussions continue as they leave for home.

These examples demonstrate a variety of ways in which the classroom teacher can promote reading as a positive, enjoyable experience and as an independent and shared pleasure. However, the success of such strategies depends upon the teacher's enthusiasm for and knowledge about children's literature. Without knowledge of a wide range of literature it is impossible to find the appropriate text to read aloud, share with a group or offer a reluctant reader. The development of positive attitudes towards reading also requires the provision of opportunities, physical spaces and resources for reading. These aspects are discussed in Chapter 10.

## Developing understanding and response

In the teaching of reading, the development of understanding of texts is crucial. Traditional approaches to supporting this aspect of reading have often relied upon comprehension exercises. As pointed out by the Bullock Report (DES, 1975) and Lunzer and Gardner (1979), such work typically involved a series of questions about a decontextualized extract of text, such as a section from a novel or a piece written for use in the exercise. Many of these questions could be answered without having any real understanding of what the text was about. In addition, the presentation of such exercises, as a set of questions answered in a given order, tended to guide the reader towards a particular interpretation and way of reading the text. Used exclusively, such exercises could discourage children from seeing reading as a meaningful activity and from finding their own ways to gain understanding of texts. They also fail to provide children with practice and experience in aspects of reading that are essential beyond the classroom.

Children need to be motivated to read a wide range of texts and make meaning for themselves. Directed Activities Related to Texts (DARTs) activities, developed by Lunzer and Gardner (1984), provide children with a variety of purposes for exploring texts. These activities not only promote literal understanding but also encourage inferential comprehension – the ability to read between the lines, beyond what is explicitly stated. They can be used to develop understanding of fiction and non-fiction with children of all ages, depending on the complexity of the text and the level of support provided. Explanations and examples of activities are shown in Table 4.1.

As individuals read, they do not simply understand what is written, they interpret texts in different ways. In making meaning, an individual draws on knowledge of the world and knowledge of other texts. This recognition of the individual and unique nature of response was highlighted by Iser (1978) who argued that reading involves active engagement with texts in order to make meaning. As a reader, you may well be familiar with the feeling of being unable to put down a novel because you are eager to find out what happens, anxious about the fate of a character or want to see if your hunch about the cause of a crime is correct. These are all aspects of reader response. Benton and Fox (1985) analysed this process of engagement and meaning making as it takes place in adults' minds during reading. They identified five key aspects of reader response:

- predicting;
- retrospecting;
- picturing (or imaging);
- interacting;
- evaluating.

Children need to experience these aspects of response from the earliest stages. Long before they are able to read independently, young children can be encouraged to engage actively with texts. Children often comment spontaneously on aspects of texts that interest them and their thoughts on issues raised. However, the development of response can also be encouraged through a range of activities and the use of questions and prompts as shown in Table 4.2.

The examples of classroom practice that follow (Tables 4.1 and 4.2) show children actively engaged in making meaning from texts through a variety of activities. Note how the same activity often involves children in more than one of the aspects identified above.

**Table 4.1. DARTs (Directed Activities Related to Texts)**

| | Activity | Example |
|---|---|---|
| **Predicting** | Anticipating what will happen next | Year 5 children read *The Wind Singer* (Nicholson, 2001), a quest story in an alternate world. They stop at a series of bookmarks inserted by the teacher, which prompt them to discuss what they think will happen next. |
| | | Nursery children look at the cover of a recipe book. They discuss what they expect to find and when it would be used. |
| **Cloze procedure** | Finding words to fill gaps in texts, created by the teacher. The children may compare their suggestions with the original | All the adjectives have been deleted from the poem. Year 2 children work in pairs to fill the gaps and then compare their results with the original. |
| | | Year 6 children have a page from a newspaper editorial. Every tenth word has been deleted. They suggest words to fill the gaps. |
| **Sequencing** | Putting pictures, words, sentences, paragraphs or verses of a text in order | Reception children sequence a series of pictures telling the story of *Little Red Riding Hood* using the 'drag and drop' facility on the computer. |
| **Modelling** | Reading a passage and drawing a picture, diagram, timeline or concept map to represent the ideas it contains | Children in year 4 read an explanation of how volcanoes erupt. They draw a series of drawings to show younger children what happens. |
| **Evaluating** | Deciding which aspects of a text are true or valid | In pairs, year 5 children distinguish fact from opinion in descriptions of resorts in holiday brochures. They delete any words which present an opinion. |
| **Comparing texts** | Comparing content, layout or language | Nursery children compare *Walking Through the Jungle* (Harter, 1997), a colourful narrative text, showing the animals a child meets on her imaginary tour of the world, with an information text about animals. They note differences in layout and content. |
| | | Children in year 6 compare reports of a current event from a tabloid and broad sheet newspaper. They list the points made by each article and identify similarities and differences in content, layout, use of captions and images. |
| **Text marking** | Highlighting or underlining key words or phrases from a text | In shared reading, year 1 children look at an account of a day out at the seaside in the 1950s. They underline all the vocabulary which relates to the past and later make a list of these features with their modern day equivalents. |
| | | Year 4 children look at texts on Viking life. They highlight references to food in green, transport in yellow, homes in blue. |
| **Table completion** | Completing table using information gained from information texts | Year 2 children use books and record facts about the habitat, diet and features of different mammals on a chart. |
| **Labelling** | Using information gained from a text to label a diagram | Children in year 3 are given a diagram of the skeleton and a relevant extract from a science book. They add labels to the diagram. |

**Table 4.2. The development of response**

| Aspect of response | Meaning | Activities | Prompts and questions |
|---|---|---|---|
| **Predicting** | Hypothesizing about what the text will reveal, what will happen next in a story | Predicting the content of the text from the cover, title, etc. Continuing stories orally or through drawing, writing or drama. | What do you think is going to happen next? Why? Look at the front cover – what clues can you find that tell you what the story is going to be about? What do you think the first line of the story will be? This is the title – what do you think the chapter will be about? What do you think will happen to . . . ? |
| **Retrospecting** | Thinking or referring back to earlier events in the text, e.g. considering a series of clues in a mystery story | Creating a timeline of events; TV/newspaper reports retelling events; sequencing pictures or written events; individual or shared retelling of stories through spoken, drawn or written retelling or drama; diary entries. | Didn't something like this happen earlier . . . ? What was it? Why does the character feel this way? Is there a reason for this? Can you remember when . . . ? Why do you think this happened? |
| **Picturing** | Visualizing aspects presented through a text, for example imagining the setting or the appearance of a character | Creating new illustrations/front cover; designing illustrations for a picture book on the basis of the written text – comparing with original; drawing scenes, events or characters; creating wanted poster for character; planning scene set for filming of scene, creating postcard or photo; drawing a map or plan of a setting or journey. | What do you think the character looks like? Close your eyes and tell me/draw what the setting is like. |
| **Interacting** | Imagining what it would be like to be in a situation described, for example empathizing with a character | Hotseating; role play; role on the wall; diary entry; letters; retelling/rewriting story from different perspective (oral or written); adding thought/speech bubbles to a picture of a character. | Why does the character feel this way? Is there a reason for this? How have your ideas about this character changed? How do you think the character feels? What would you do in that situation? How will this character react? Why do you think they did this? If I was her, I'd . . . |
| **Evaluating** | Making judgements of what they like and dislike about the text, find plausible, etc. Benton and Fox (1985: 16) describe this element as the 'mark of discrimination and the rejection of indifference'. | Reviewing the plausibility of events or characters' actions; considering the relevance of text to purpose; comparing similar texts; exploring preferences; advertising a favourite text; sharing responses to same text with a. | Did you like the book? Why? Why not? What was your favourite part/character? Prepare the blurb. Compare with the one on the back of the book. Which bits did you enjoy most/least? Why? What do you think about the ending? Were you relieved/disappointed? Why did the writer not tell us about this earlier? Why does the writer . . . ? |

The **reception** teacher is reading aloud *Peace at Last* (Murphy, 1980), the story of Mr Bear who cannot sleep because Mrs Bear is snoring. He tries to sleep in Baby Bear's room and then the living room, but there is still too much noise. The teacher tells the children that Mr Bear then goes to the kitchen and asks them what will happen. The children discuss their expectations and what they think will be shown in the picture.

*(picturing, predicting, retrospecting)*

The **year 1** teacher has been reading *Amazing Grace* (Hoffman, 1993), a story about a girl with a wild imagination who likes dressing up and is very keen to have a key role in the school play. She encounters prejudice on the grounds of her colour and gender and begins to believe that she will not be able to take the part. The teacher stops reading and the class thought-track Grace, speaking aloud her thoughts as she walks home from school.

*(interacting, retrospecting)*

The **year 3** children are enjoying the story '*The pudding like a night on the sea*', a short story (Cameron, 1994) about Julian and Huey, two young boys who are left alone with a delicious dessert that their father has made as a treat for their mother. They are tempted to taste the pudding and eventually eat it all. In fear of being discovered, they go and hide under their bed. The teacher stops reading at the point when the father discovers they have eaten it. The children use 'hotseating' to explore the boys' feelings about what they have done and what will happen. Later the teacher reads '*The chocolate cake*' by Michael Rosen (in Patten, 1998), a poem about a similar incident involving a boy's visit at night to the kitchen. The children compare the presentation of events and creation of tension in the two texts.

*(interacting, retrospecting, evaluating, predicting)*

The **year 6** teacher has read aloud *The Other Side of Truth* (Naidoo, 2000), which tells the story of two children who arrive as refugees from South Africa and their experiences of England. The main character is interviewed on television news about her experiences. The children look at current newspaper articles on asylum seekers, discuss how similar issues are raised in the novel and the media and then produce a short documentary on the case.

*(interacting, retrospecting, evaluating)*

## Critical reading

As discussed earlier, the development of children's ability to reflect critically on what they read is also important. This involves considering the success and relevance of texts and becoming aware of the position and intentions of the author. Critical reading is encouraged when children have opportunities to discuss and evaluate what they have read. It can also be developed through questions and activities enabling them to consider how a text has been written, the choices made in relation to content and presentation and how these reflect the author's purpose in writing. The development of such skills is appropriate for children of all ages, as illustrated by the following examples.

The **nursery** teacher has read aloud *I Want My Potty* (Ross, 2000a), a humorous tale about a princess. The group discusses the illustrations and points to examples they particularly like. The teacher reminds the children they have seen other books by Tony Ross and they remember several, including *Don't Do That* (1998) and *I Don't Want to Go to Hospital* (2000b) which they retrieve from the bookshelf. The children discuss similarities in the illustrations.

The **year 1** teacher reads *Susan Laughs* (Willis, 2001), which describes a young girl's likes and how she spends her day. Before reading the last page, the children discuss what they know about Susan. The teacher then reveals the last page, which shows that Susan is disabled. The children discuss the reasons why the author/illustrator chose to withhold this information until the end.

The **year 2** children look at the first chapter of *The Sheep-Pig* (King-Smith, 1983) and compare it with the opening scenes of the film version: *Babe*.

A group of **year 4** children are looking at *Zoo* (Browne, 1992), a picture book which presents a family's day out at the zoo. The images present a contrast between the experience of the animals and the people who visit them. The children have been asked to discuss what they know about the author's attitude to zoos and to find evidence in the text for their views. (For an interesting extension of this activity with a Year 1 class, see Riley *et al.*, 2000.)

This section has explored how response, understanding and critical reading can be encouraged through a range of focused activities and the use of carefully selected questions for discussion. The provision of regular opportunities for children to hear and discuss texts read aloud, to read together and to share recommendations is also essential to promote interest in literature and critical response. The final section of this chapter shows how a variety of teaching methods can be used to provide such experience. The next section of the chapter examines young children's knowledge about reading and then explores the reading process and its development.

# Children's reading development

Learning to read is challenging. In order to succeed, children must learn to make sense of abstract symbols, learning to distinguish between them and remember their correspondence with the sounds of spoken language. Children need to be aware that spoken language is made up of words and that such words are found in texts, organized into units as sentences. They must also learn the conventions of punctuation and layout. Additional challenges are presented by the need to distinguish between different kinds of texts and the different ways in which they are read.

However, from a very young age, children also have considerable knowledge about reading. As discussed in Chapter 1, most young children are familiar with reading as a meaningful and varied activity. They may be used to sharing texts with an adult or siblings on a regular basis. They will also have considerable experience of seeing print in the world around them. Hall (1987), Weinberger (1996) and Hallet (1999), amongst others, have highlighted children's awareness of such text, for example on packaging, logos on clothing, advertisements and road signs.

Young children's familiarity with the appearance of print is important in their development as readers. Marie Clay used the term 'concepts about print' (1975, 1985) to identify specific aspects of early reading development. Children gain understanding that:

- print carries meaning and can be distinguished from pictures;
- a text contains separate specific words;
- spaces between groups of symbols are significant in indicating words;
- print follows a regular direction (in English, the text is written from left to right and a page is read from top to bottom).

Some children will already be aware that English script differs in presentation and organization from written versions of other languages with which they are familiar.

At an early age, children are often able to recognize a familiar sign; identifying McDonald's golden arches or a supermarket logo is therefore one of the first steps in learning to read. Such recognition does not rely on awareness or understanding of the significance of individual letters, but the ability to identify the shape or pattern of the letters. This has been termed the 'logographic phase' (Frith, 1985). It is a valuable step in children's development of reading in providing access to meaning from print.

By the time they enter the Foundation Stage, some children will therefore have an awareness of the nature of text and a fairly sophisticated understanding of reading as an activity. The challenge for the education system is to move children from this stage to equip them with the skills and understanding of a competent and fluent reader. The next section in this chapter therefore looks at the reading process to identify the range of strategies used by competent readers, before exploring how their use in early reading can be developed.

# The reading process

As fluent readers, we tend to take for granted the strategies we use in order to access texts. However, it is useful to examine more closely what happens when we read. The following version of a well-known fairy tale has therefore been constructed to make reading more problematic and provide an opportunity to reflect on the process involved. In reading this text, notice the strategies you use in order to make sense of it. It may help to read it aloud.

*Wnsupn atym, derwz alidl grl hoo livd wid hr mudu. Wn day hr mudu sed two hr lidl grl, 'Pliz tek thiz bass cit ov cayks two ur granknee hoo livs indu forust. Unid two pooton ured cowt, du redwn wiva hu two kipu wom.' 'Okay,' sed derlidl grl an doff shi wnt.\** (See end of chapter for translation.)

In making sense of this text, it is likely that you used one of more of the following strategies:

- sounding out – saying the sounds of the letters;
- recognizing whole words (for example, 'two');
- knowledge of the genre – fairy tale – to predict the content;
- knowledge of the story to predict what could be included;
- knowledge of English grammar to help you to predict appropriate words, for example expecting that:
  - 'shi' will be followed by a verb
  - verbs will be in the past, following the tense of the other verbs in the passage
  - 'hr' will be followed by a noun – mother;
- knowledge of punctuation to help you to predict appropriate words (for example, speech marks indicate spoken words).

These strategies reflect the following cueing systems used by successful readers: *semantic, syntactic* and *graphophonic*. These cueing systems are explained in Table 4.3.

**Table 4.3. Cueing systems for reading**

| Cueing system | Explanation | Examples |
|---|---|---|
| **Semantic** | Using knowledge of the whole text to predict what words might be. | • Drawing on knowledge of earlier part of text.<br>• Using information from pictures.<br>• Reading ahead to see if understanding is coherent with what follows.<br>• Using knowledge of the genre and content, for example recognition of the type of story or the specific tale in the above example helps in predicting the content. |
| **Syntactic** | Using knowledge of grammar – the sense of the surrounding sentence to check if a word seems to 'fit' with previous experience of spoken or written language and knowledge of word endings to indicate the type of word. | • Using knowledge of word order to suggest that an adjective is likely to be followed by a noun, for example 'hr' in the above passage will be followed by a noun or 'shi' as a personal pronoun is likely to be followed by a verb.<br>• Using endings such as 'ful' to indicate that a word is an adjective. |
| **Graphophonic** | Using knowledge of links between letters or groups of letters and the sounds they represent. Instant recognition of some words. | • Sounding words out by identifying the phonemes represented by each grapheme or combination of graphemes.<br>• Instantly recognizing high-frequency words, for example 'two' in the passage above. |

In order to look more closely at the way in which the cueing systems shown in Table 4.3 are used, it is useful to take a text which is more familiar in presentation than the text used above, but may still present challenges.

> *Drag can be divided into two components, known as induced drag and profile drag. The first is the inevitable price of lift, the second is the term for drag caused by all parts of the aircraft's structure, including the undercarriage and all other excrescences. Induced drag varies inversely as the square of the airspeed, while profile drag increases approximately as the square of the airspeed. This means in fact that induced drag lessens with greater airspeed, but profile drag increases . . .*

(Taylor *et al.*, 1987: 15)

If you are familiar with flying and have considerable knowledge about this topic or a background in physics, it is likely that you will have read this text without any difficulty. Reading involves drawing on existing knowledge to make sense of texts. As a result, without knowledge of flying or the relevant aspects of physics, it is difficult to gain meaning from the extract and necessary to read more carefully, employing each of the cueing systems described above. The semantic cueing system alerts the reader that the first word of the passage is problematic. 'Drag' is commonly used as a verb meaning 'to pull' or in slang as a noun (a hindrance or a type of dress). Clearly none of these meanings apply in this context; the style and content of the passage suggest that it is a technical term and that it represents a scientific concept. The syntactic cueing system enables the reader to recognize that 'drag' is being used as a noun as it is followed by the verb 'can'. If the term 'excrescences' is unfamiliar, it is likely that the graphophonic cueing system will be employed to work out how the word sounds, by breaking down the word and sounding out each syllable.

If you were unfamiliar with this area of knowledge, it is interesting to reflect on how much you understood from your initial reading of the passage. It is likely that because you lacked the relevant background knowledge and there were no illustrations to support it, you were forced to rely more heavily on other strategies and consequently your interest and understanding suffered.

The National Literacy Strategy (DfEE, 1998) describes the cueing systems as four searchlights, which help the reader to make meaning from text:

- *Knowledge of context* (the semantic cueing system);
- *Grammatical knowledge* (the syntactic cueing system);
- *Phonics (sounds and spelling)* and *word recognition and graphic knowledge* (the graphophonic cueing system).

The teaching of reading needs to ensure that children are able to use all the cueing systems or searchlights effectively and are aware of their importance. In encouraging children to develop their use of the cueing systems, it is useful to refer to the third column of Table 4.3. This contains strategies that children can be explicitly encouraged to adopt in their reading.

54

The development of the semantic and syntactic cueing systems has b
in the earlier sections of the chapter, which focused on activitie
understanding and response. The following section turns to the teachn.
graphophonic cueing system.

# The role of phonics

The teaching of phonics has been a high-profile aspect of the teaching of reading for some time and the focus for considerable debate. In this section of the chapter, we explain the meaning of the term and refer to relevant research in this area to identify the nature of knowledge and skills involved. On the basis of this theory, we provide a range of practical activities and games to develop children's use of phonics.

The term 'phonics' refers to the development of graphophonic awareness, the ability to recognize that words can be broken up into separate phonemes (sounds) that are represented by graphemes (letters). It includes the ability to identify the phonemes represented by combinations of graphemes and to put these together to create words. At its simplest, in reading this involves the recognition that graphemes (letters) represent phonemes (sounds), the recognition that the grapheme 'b' or 'B' represents the sound 'b'. If this simple one-to-one correspondence applied in every case, the ability to decode would be relatively straightforward; children would simply need to learn to recognize the letters and their corresponding phonemes. However, the relationship between graphemes and phonemes is far more complex, as the following examples illustrate:

- The same letter 'a' is used in each of the following words: 'hat', 'fall', 'bake', 'arm'. Notice the different phoneme it represents. Similarly consider the different phonemes represented by the letter 'c' in these words: 'circle'; 'cat'.
- The following words all contain the same phoneme – 'o'– as in the letter name or used in the word 'No!'. Notice the different graphemes used to represent this phoneme in the following words: '*toe*', '*flow*', '*go*', '*hope*', 'th*ough*'. Similarly notice the different representation of the phoneme 'f' in 'eno*ugh*', '*f*ish', 'hu*ff*' or 'sh' in '*sh*ip', 'sta*ti*on', 'lu*sci*ous'.

These examples illustrate the following principles identified by the NLS (DfEE, 1998):

- a phoneme can be represented by one or more letters;
- the same phoneme can be represented/spelled in more than one way;
- the same spelling may represent more than one phoneme.

Traditionally, the teaching of phonics tended to focus initially on the development of letter recognition and followed a systematic progression, supplemented by carefully structured reading schemes that incorporate vocabulary based on children's level of phonic understanding, for example *The Big Pig* (Flowerdew, 1968) was aimed at children working on consonant-vowel-consonant (CVC) words. This assumed that progression in reading relied solely upon the development of graphophonic knowledge.

However, as illustrated earlier, successful reading involves the use of all three cueing systems. Focusing on the use of the graphophonic cueing system alone can present reading as a 'code-cracking activity' (Wray *et al.*, 1991: 98) and neglect the development of the other strategies. In addition, dependence on graphophonic cues in the early stages will not equip children to deal with the many common words which do not follow a simple phoneme-grapheme correspondence, for example: 'me', 'want', 'give'.

However, research (Bryant *et al.*, 1985; Goswami *et al.*, 1990) has suggested that the ability to hear and distinguish sounds, known as 'phonological awareness', contributes to success in learning to read. Within this, the ability to detect the sounds within words is known as 'phonemic awareness'. This includes the ability to isolate sounds within words, recognize when they are repeated and reproduce them. The significance of this understanding is that it prepares children for reading by enabling them to appreciate the logic behind the representation of the same phoneme by a consistent set of graphic symbols.

### Aspects of phonological awareness:

- identification of syllables (beats in a word);
- identification and re-production of phonemes, in particular in:
  - *rhyme*: repetition of final phoneme(s), e.g. day – play; sing – bring
  - *alliteration*: repetition of initial phoneme, e.g. 'wiggly wet worms'
  - *onset and rime*: most syllables have an 'onset', a consonant or consonants which precede the vowel, and a 'rime' – a part which includes and follows the vowel, e.g. in 'park' – 'p' is the onset, '-ark' is the rime;
- blending – the ability to put the individual phonemes together to form a word;
- segmenting – the ability to distinguish individual phonemes within words. (This is explored in Chapter 6.)

As highlighted by Bryant and Bradley (1985) and Riley (1996), children's ability to label the letters of the alphabet when they begin formal schooling tends to correspond with later success in reading. Such recognition of letters is significant because it reflects a child's understanding that sounds can be represented symbolically, an essential step in understanding the nature of written text as language recorded in the form of words and sentences.

Another important aspect of graphophonic awareness, highlighted by Goswami (1995), is the use of analogy. This involves the ability to read new words by applying knowledge of familiar words; a strategy often adopted by fluent readers. An example of the use of analogy would be that a child who encounters the word 'reach' may use knowledge of the words 'beach' or 'each' to read it. At an earlier stage knowledge of the word 'cat' helps the child to read 'bat'. The value of analogy to early readers is therefore that it enables them to make use of existing knowledge and provides a tool for tackling words independently.

# The teaching of phonics

This section explores practical ways of developing graphophonic awareness. The following section explores how such understanding can be developed through:

- language play;
- picture books and shared texts;
- games and activities to encourage listening and aspects of graphophonic awareness and recognition of high-frequency words.

## Language play

From the early stages, babies play with sounds and increasingly imitate the sounds of spoken language around them. As their understanding increases, young children continue to enjoy playing with language. In any playground, their delight in tongue twisters, rhymes, advertising jingles, slogans and song lyrics and their creativity in adapting and reinventing them provide evidence of this. Such informal learning not only contributes to the development of phonological and phonemic awareness but also highlights a valuable and motivating focus for activities in an educational context. With encouragement and discussion, children can build upon their language play, recalling and adapting familiar rhymes, jingles, jokes and poems and reflecting upon words and sounds involved. Recording children's alternative versions of these is also useful in reinforcing understanding of written text and validating children's contributions as authors.

## Picture books and shared texts

Picture books have a particularly important role to play in this context. Many texts incorporate entertaining wordplay in various forms and many incorporate rhyme, for example: *Each Peach Pear Plum* (Ahlberg *et al.*, 1989); *This is the Bear* (Hayes, 1986); *New Shoes* (Willis, 2003). As the story is read aloud, children can be encouraged to predict a missing rhyme. Alliteration is also common, particularly in poetry and again children can be invited to guess missing words, identify the repeated phoneme and create their own versions. It is interesting to note that shared enjoyment of such texts can involve children in developing different aspects of graphophonic awareness. Some children will benefit from attention drawn to the phonemes, and others will be ready to explore the written representation of language, moving from the discussion of rhyme and alliteration to the identification of graphic representation of the common phonemes. When working with a group of children of different abilities, it is therefore important to plan for both aspects and direct questions and involvement accordingly. For example, in reading *This is the Bear*, some children can be invited to identify or guess rhyming words, and others can be encouraged to notice the common spelling of the rimes. In *Mister Magnolia* (Blake, 1980), some children may collect the words that rhyme with 'boot' ('chute', 'fruit', 'scoot', 'newt', and so on) and others can be expected to identify, sort and add to these words.

The opportunities offered by language play and literature illustrate the development of graphophonic awareness in a meaningful context. However, it is sometimes useful to reinforce aspects of understanding through more focused activities. The following section provides some suggestions.

## Games and activities to encourage listening

Games and activities which encourage children to listen carefully have an important role to play in the development of early reading. The listening activities presented in Chapter 3 are relevant in this respect.

### *Games that focus on recognizing syllables:*

- clapping names of individuals. For example, 'I'm clapping the name of a girl in this group and it's "clap clap clap" . . . Who could it be?' The children guess – their guesses may be correct but not identify the particular child, but this can be used to reinforce understanding. 'Yes, it could be "Amanda" (three claps) but it's someone else! Who could it be? Yes, it's "Tasmina"!';
- say and clap favourite colours/TV programmes/foods. Taking a theme, the children in the circle each say and clap their favourite item;
- pass the name! An adaptation of the game above – A child, for example Joanna, starts with 'I'm Jo-ann-a' (three beats) 'and this is for . . .' (one beat) – eye contact made with Tom. Tom takes up – 'I'm Tom' (one beat) and this is for . . .' (two beats) eye contact with Hamsa;
- pass the rhythm – with hand clap, drum or tambourine. Start a very short rhythm, which the children in the group practise together. The rhythm is then passed around the circle; each child repeats the same pattern. As the children gain confidence, the teacher interrupts with the word 'change!' and the next child introduces a new short rhythm to be copied.

## Games and activities to encourage recognition and production of phonemes

In the list below, the first four examples focus on alliteration and can be played with children seated in a circle. Each child adds an item. Younger children may need to be prompted or supported in their contributions.

*Alliteration games:*

- I went to market and I bought . . . **c**arrots, cake, coffee . . . and so on.
- The minister's cat is a . . . big, brave, bad, bold cat.
- A variation of 'I Spy' can be played as 'I hear with my little ear' something beginning with the phoneme . . . 'ch' (chair).
- Create alliterative sentences for each member of the class – Mustafa likes music and marching! Jessica likes jumping and jelly! (They don't need to be true!) Turn this into a question – 'Who in this class might like hats and hopping?' – 'Harry!'
- Odd one out! Give the children four objects (or pictures). Three start with the same phoneme. They identify the odd one out.
- Children can group themselves according to the first sound of their first name.

## Activities involving rhyme

In discussing rhyming activities, Layton *et al.* (1997: 16) identify three categories representing increasing levels of challenge:

- **Rhyme judgement** – deciding whether or not words rhyme. For example yes rhyme – no rhyme! Show two objects/pictures. The children identify them and decide whether the words rhyme.

- **Rhyme detection** – selecting words that rhyme from alternatives:
  - Group the rhyming objects/pictures.
  - Odd one out! Which one of the objects/pictures (for example cat, pen, hat) is the odd one out, as it does not rhyme with the other two?
  - Group the rhyming objects/pictures.

- **Rhyme production or generation** – supplying rhyming words:
  - Create rhyming lists of words – pass an object round and the children think of as many rhyming words as possible. For example, pen – hen, when, then, and so forth.
  - Guess the name of a hidden object that rhymes with . . .
  - Create silly sentences with the same rhyme – 'My cat is fat. It likes to sit on a mat. It wears a silly hat . . .'
  - Rhyming riddles (Layton *et al.*, 1997: 21) 'I'm thinking of a something that shines in the sky and it rhymes with fun!'

**Onset and rime**
- Change the onset – how many words can we make? For example, hat, cat, sat, rat, bat . . .
- Group objects or match the pictures according to the same onset/rime.

# The development of awareness of Grapheme–Phoneme Correspondence

The examples of activities presented above focus on the recognition and production of sounds without reference to the written form. In any early years group, it is likely that some children will have limited phonological knowledge whereas others will have already acquired considerable phonemic awareness and will be ready to link this to the written representation. It is therefore important that, when working with children in whole-group sessions, all levels should be considered. Many of the above activities that focus on the identification and production of phonemes could be adapted to support children who are ready to develop graphophonic knowledge, by including discussion of relevant graphemes.

Children's interest and pride in their own names provides a valuable and meaningful starting point for the development of awareness of grapheme–phoneme correspondence. As discussed earlier, children's ability to recognize their names is likely to rely initially upon the recall of features such as pattern, shape and length. However, with encouragement they can move on to make discoveries relating to the individual letters. The initial letter is generally the first to be identified. Recognition of this letter can then be supported through discussion, hunts to find the same letter in collections of letters, identifying words that begin with the same letter and encouragement to create the letter shape in a variety of media.

Displayed on individual cards with accompanying photographs, names provide a useful resource for raising awareness of the nature of written text. Children are likely to notice the different lengths of the written representations and this can be discussed in relation to the corresponding length of their spoken forms. Individual letters can be counted and the cards can be grouped according to length, initial letter or common endings.

In the early stages of graphophonic awareness other relevant activities include:

- matching objects to letters according to their initial letter;
- locating letters in texts;
- letter fans – strips of card showing individual letters are given to each child.
  The child holds up the appropriate letter to match an object shown by the teacher.

As children gain confidence in recognizing single letters, they can be encouraged to read familiar CVC (consonant-vowel-consonant) words. This can be reinforced through the following activities:

- Identifying each phoneme in a written word – for example red – 'r' 'e' 'd' and blending the phonemes into the word.
- Three children are given a card with a letter that will form a CVC word (for instance b/e/d). The group helps to put them in an appropriate order. The teacher asks for suggestions to change the onset. A child suggests 'r' and is given the appropriate card and replaces the child holding 'b'. The class reads the word and the teacher asks for further suggestions for changes.

- Letter swap! Each child in the circle has an object. The teacher (or a child) holds up a card showing a letter. Children who have an object with that initial letter swap places. This can also be played using phonemes at the beginning, end or middle of words.
- Find an analogy. The teacher introduces an unfamiliar word to the children and asks them to identify any aspects which remind them of words they already know, such as 'this – recognize th from this, is from his'.

The ability to use analogy has been shown to be a valuable aspect of children's success in reading as it provides a tool to decipher unfamiliar words and can be relevant at any level of reading.

The activities listed above offer a few examples of ways in which graphophonic awareness may be encouraged. Many more can be found in the suggestions for further reading listed at the end of the chapter. A sequence for the development of phonic knowledge is included in *Progression in Phonics* (NLS, 1999).

# The development of sight vocabulary

Focusing children's attention on the shape and pattern of familiar words provides a means to support their recognition. Flashcards and matching games have been used to promote this. However, such recognition of words is very challenging, particularly when words are presented out of context. It is also limited in its value as a means to support reading because it does not equip children to decode unfamiliar words. In addition, the most common words required by children are often a similar size and shape, lacking in distinguishing features (such as 'have' and 'home'). However, instant recognition of commonly used, 'high frequency', words (DfEE, 1998) is useful and assists children in accessing texts. This can be encouraged through drawing attention to the use of particular words in context, for example in familiar texts and environmental print.

# The organization of the teaching of reading

This chapter has presented a wide range of activities for developing children's understanding and skills in reading. This final section suggests how such provision can be made in the classroom through:

- reading to the class;
- shared reading;
- guided reading;
- group reading;
- paired reading;
- individual reading.

# Reading to the class

Many teachers make time to read aloud to their class. Reading aloud can provide:

- experience of hearing enthusiastic and expressive reading;
- communal enjoyment of a text and the opportunity to share responses;
- access to a range of texts (fiction and non-fiction) that would be too difficult to read independently;
- an introduction to new authors, series or genres.

Texts need to be carefully chosen to capture the interest of the children and reading needs to be prepared beforehand. Reading aloud can be enhanced through:

- introducing the story by talking about an object or toy to represent an item or character in the story;
- using different voices for characters and gestures and facial expressions;
- looking up regularly and making eye contact with the children;
- encouraging participation from the children through actions, sound effects and repeated refrains;
- inviting predictions and responses.

# Shared reading

Shared reading was pioneered by Holdaway (1979) who saw the value of parents sharing books with children and wanted to create similar opportunities in the classroom. During shared reading, texts are introduced that most children in the class would find too difficult to read independently. The text is generally enlarged so that all the children can see it or individual copies are provided. Fiction, poetry, information books and everyday texts may all be used. At any level, shared reading is used to model expressive reading and encourage response to text. It is important to engage the interest of all the children and plan opportunities for interaction and paired discussion.

In shared reading, the teacher models the use of the skills and strategies involved in reading, whilst encouraging as much interaction as possible from the children. This approach is applicable to any age range and should have a clear learning objective, which is relevant to the children. In the early years, shared reading is used to model how books and print work. The teacher makes explicit the use of cueing systems and the direction of print. Children's attention is drawn to the importance of the illustrations and specific words and letters. For older children, shared reading often focuses on extracts from texts, to enable children to explore a specific aspect in detail. Such extracts can be selected from texts read aloud or used in independent or guided work. Several extracts can also be taken from the same novel and used over a few weeks, supported by oral telling of what has happened between them. For all ages, learning from shared reading is often applied, reinforced or extended through independent work.

# Guided reading

In guided reading, the teacher works with a group of children who read individually from multiple copies of the same text. Usually these children have similar needs and the learning objective will be selected to provide them with support in a specific aspect of reading. Texts selected for guided reading may include fiction, non-fiction, Information and Communication Technology (ICT) texts and everyday texts and should be challenging but possible for the children to read independently. Guided reading sessions should help children to become more confident and independent in their reading. They provide a meaningful context for the development of a range of reading strategies.

Possible stages for organizing guided reading are shown below.

## Before reading

The introduction of the text gains the interest of the children. The teacher may ask questions, designed to remind children of similar texts, predict the content or to focus attention on reading for meaning. She may also discuss possible reading strategies, for example cueing systems with less confident readers or skimming and scanning for those working with non-fiction.

## During reading

The children read independently. The teacher may listen to individuals reading or monitor the reading of the group, providing prompts for children who are stuck. For children who are more able, reading may be silent.

## After reading

The teacher encourages the children to discuss what they have read and their response to the text. She may also invite them to reflect on the strategies they used. She may lead a discussion on a specific technique or features, encouraging the children to justify their responses with close reference to the text.

## Follow up

Sometimes a follow-up task is provided. Examples include drawing an image or diagram linked to a text, recording responses in a reading journal or discussing an alternative ending or continuation.

# Independent reading

Independent reading requires children to work without the help of the teacher. Here, the reading skills and strategies learned through shared and guided work are brought together. The role of the teacher is therefore to provide appropriate and motivating tasks, which enable children to draw on previous learning. This may involve children in re-reading or continuing to read a text that has been introduced to them in an earlier teacher-led session. Children may also be involved in collaborative or individual activities which develop understanding and response or specific aspects of reading discussed earlier in the chapter. Guidance on differentiation of activities is provided in Chapter 9.

Children also need opportunities to read widely for themselves. Many schools provide opportunities for children to read self-selected texts independently on a regular basis at a particular time of the day. This is sometimes known as USSR (Uninterrupted Sustained Silent Reading) or ERIC (Everyone Reading In Class). Many children, particularly in the early years, prefer sharing books rather than reading on their own.

## Group reading

Group reading provides a supportive context for developing expressive reading and discussion of books. Children may take turns in reading and then discuss questions provided by the teacher or posed by the group.

## Paired reading

Paired reading often involves children from different age groups working together. Younger children have an opportunity to share their books and older children develop their skills in reading with expression. Such schemes help develop relationships between children in different age groups and can be particularly successful in boosting the confidence of less able older readers.

## Individual reading

Prior to the introduction of the NLS, much of the support given to developing readers was carried out through listening to children read. Effective individual reading sessions involved a sequence similar to guided reading, with discussion before, during and after reading. Although opportunities for individual reading can provide focused support for an individual, the time and level of attention to a single child make it difficult to sustain on a regular basis. Guided reading is therefore often used instead, as it provides help for several children with similar needs at the same time and offers valuable opportunities for group discussion.

# Summary

This chapter has drawn attention to the importance of developing children's interests and skills in reading through providing:

• opportunities to read widely and to hear texts read aloud;

- a wide range of activities to develop understanding and response;
- encouragement to share responses and reflect critically on reading;
- explicit modelling of the use of the cueing systems;
- experience of a wide range of texts;
- recognition of the experience of literacy that children bring from home;
- motivating activities for the development of graphophonic awareness.

The main focus for reading in this chapter has been children's literature. Chapter 6 looks in depth at the teaching of reading of non-fiction.

# Reflective questions

1. Children arrive in the nursery with different levels of awareness of print. How can teachers respond to this?

2. Consider a child you have taught who lacked interest in reading and avoided the activity whenever possible. What steps would you take to engage her/his interest?

3. Consider a child you have taught who seemed to read without understanding. What would you do to change this?

## FURTHER READING

Graham, J. and Kelly, A. (2000) *Reading Under Control: Teaching Reading in the Primary School*. Second Edition. London: David Fulton Publishers.
   Comprehensive and accessible, this text provides an overview of developments in the teaching of reading, classroom organization, resources and assessment.

National Literacy Stategy (NLS) (1999) *Progression in Phonics: Materials for Whole-class Teaching*. London: DfEE.
   A practical guide to the teaching of phonics which includes a range of useful activities and photocopiable resources.

Whitehead, M. (2002) *Developing Language and Literacy with Young Children*. London: Paul Chapman Publishing.
   A stimulating book that presents the early development of reading within the broader context of communication, emphasizing the importance of spoken language and the significance of stories, narrative and language play.

## REFERENCES

Benton, M. and Fox, G. (1985) *Teaching Literature Nine to Fourteen*. Oxford: Oxford University Press.

Bryant, P. and Bradley, L. (1985) *Children's Reading Problems*. Oxford: Blackwell.

Chambers, A. (1993) *Children, Reading and Talk*. Stroud: Thimble.

Clay, M. (1975) *What Did I Write?* London: Heinemann.

Clay, M. (1985) *The Early Detection of Reading Difficulties*. Third Edition. London: Heinemann.

Department for Education and Employment (DfEE) (1998) *National Literacy Strategy Framework for Teaching*. London: HMSO.

Department of Education and Science (DES) (1975) *A Language for Life (The Bullock Report)*. London: HMSO.

Frith, U. (1985) 'Beneath the surface of developmental dyslexia', in Patterson, K. E., Coltheart, M. and Marshall, J. (eds) *Surface Dyslexia*. London: LEA.

Goswami, U. (1995) 'Phonological development and reading: What is analogy and what is not?' *Journal of Research in Reading*, 19(20), 139–45.

Goswami, U. and Bryant, P. (1990) *Phonological Skills and Learning to Read*. Hove: Lawrence Erlbaum.

Hall, N. (1987) *The Emergence of Literacy*. London: Hodder & Stoughton.

Hallet, E. (1999) 'Signs and symbols: environmental print', in Marsh, J. and Hallet, E. *Desirable Literacies: Approaches to Language and Literacy in the Early Years*. London: Paul Chapman Publishing.

Holdaway, D. (1979) *The Foundations of Literacy*. London: Ashton Scholastic.

Iser, W. (1978) *The Act of Reading*. Baltimore: Johns Hopkins University Press.

Layton, L., Deeny, K. and Upton, G. (1997) *Sound Practice: Phonological Awareness in the Classroom*. London: David Fulton Publishers.

Lunzer, E. and Gardner, K. (1979) *The Effective Use of Reading*. London: Heinemann.

Lunzer, E. and Gardner, K. (1984) *Learning from the Written Word*. London: Oliver & Boyd.

Millard, E. (1997) *Differently Literate: Boys, Girls and the Schooling of Literacy*. London: Falmer.

National Literacy Strategy (NLS) (1999) *Progression in Phonics: Materials for Whole-class Teaching*. London: DfEE.

Riley, J. (1996) *The Teaching of Reading*. London: Paul Chapman Publishing.

Riley, J. and Reedy, D. (2000) *Developing Writing for Different Purposes: Teaching about Genre in the Early Years*. London: Paul Chapman Publishing.

Taylor, S., Parmar, H. and Underdown, R. (1987) *Private Pilot Studies (Fifth Edition)*. Calton: Poyser.

Weinberger, J. (1996) *Literacy Goes to School*. London: Paul Chapman Publishing.

Wray, D. and Medwell, J. (1991) *Language and Literacy in the Primary Years*. London: Routledge.

## CHILDREN'S LITERATURE

Ahlberg, A. (1999) *Monkey Do!* London: Walker.

Ahlberg, J. and Ahlberg, A. (1989) *Each Peach Pear Plum*. Harmondsworth: Puffin.

Blake, Q. (1980) *Mister Magnolia*. London: Red Fox.

Browne, A. (1992) *Zoo*. London: Julia McRae.

Browne, A. (1995) *Gorilla*. London: Julia McRae.

Browne, E. (1995) *Handa's Surprise*. London: Walker.

Cameron, A. (1994) *Julian Stories*. London: Yearling.

Flowerdew, P. (1968) *The Big Pig*. London: Oliver & Boyd.

Grey, K. (2002) *Eat Your Peas*. London: Random House.

Hayes, S. (1986) *This is the Bear*. London: Walker.

Hoffman, M. (1993) *Amazing Grace*. London: Lincoln.

Kemp, G. (1979) *The Turbulent Term of Tyke Tyler*. London: Penguin.

King-Smith, D. (1983) *The Sheep-Pig*. London: Gollancz.

Murphy, J. (1980) *Peace at Last*. London: Macmillan.

Naidoo, B. (2000) *The Other Side of Truth*. London: Penguin.

Nicholson, W. (2001) *The Wind Singer*. London: Mammoth.

Patten, B. (ed.) (1998) *The Book of Utterly Brilliant Poetry*. London: Penguin.

Root, P. (2001) *Rattletrap Car*. London: Walker.

Ross, T. (1998) *Don't Do That*. London: Red Fox.

Ross, T. (2000a) *I Want My Potty*. London: Andersen.

Ross, T. (2000b) *I Don't Want to Go to Hospital*. London: Andersen.

Tan, S. (2000) *The Lost Thing*. Melbourne, Australia: Lothian Books.

Waddell, M. (1991) *Farmer Duck*. London: Walker.

Willis, J. (2001) *Susan Laughs*. London: Andersen.

Willis, J. (2003) *New Shoes*. London: Andersen.

---

*Translation of text presented to encourage reflection on the reading process.

*Once upon a time, there was a little girl who lived with her mother. One day her mother said to her little girl, 'Please take this basket of cakes to your granny who lives in the forest. You need to put on your coat, the red one with a hood to keep you warm.' 'Okay,' said the little girl and off she went.*

# 5 Writing

We begin this chapter by reflecting on writing in everyday life. We then examine what young children know about writing and consider the development of skills and understanding that can be expected to take place during the early and primary years. We identify principles for classroom practice and explore these in relation to the teaching of composition, narrative writing, grammar, punctuation, spelling and handwriting.

## Writing in daily life

Writing in daily life is often taken for granted. However, through writing we create meaning. Written language has an enduring quality, surviving after it has been produced. It offers the opportunity to explore and express individuality and create an impression on others. It provides the means to provoke, challenge and complain and yet also to entertain, reassure and declare eternal love! At a more mundane level, it is useful for making arrangements, providing reminders and maintaining contact with others. In many cases, we use writing to communicate with others. The motivation for writing notes, text messages, letters and emails derives from a sense of purpose and an audience who will read the text. We may also write for ourselves, to make a note of something to remember, keep a record or express emotions. Writing may also provide us with a tool to make sense of experience and clarify our thoughts (Kress, 1997; Hornsby *et al.*, 2001).

Writing in everyday life includes a wide range of texts, written in many different ways. As discussed in Chapter 1, the form and presentation of texts vary according to their purpose. A text message to a friend is unlikely to be presented in sentences, and may well incorporate slang, abbreviations and smileys. In contrast, a formal letter is generally written in standard English.

Writing in everyday life is:

- motivated by meaningful purposes;
- varied in form according to audience and purpose;
- produced for a specific audience, often others, but also for oneself.

# The writing process

In discussing writing, it is useful to refer to the terms *composition* and *transcription* (Smith, 1982) to distinguish between aspects of writing. *Composition* involves the process of finding ways to communicate through words, deciding what to say and how to say it. This includes decisions about the overall structure of the piece of writing, considering the most effective way to use sentences for effect and choosing vocabulary. *Transcription* involves the transference of these ideas to paper or screen; the use of spelling, punctuation and presentation, sometimes referred to as 'secretarial skills'.

All writing involves both composition and transcription. Whatever the text, a writer must decide what needs to be written and how to write it (composition) and follow some, if not all, of the conventions for written language in terms of print, spelling and punctuation (transcription) in order for it to be read. However, the amount of attention devoted to each aspect varies according to the type of text, its purpose and intended audience. In writing a formal letter, we are likely to take time in planning and organizing, drafting and redrafting the content. We will also devote attention to our use of language, accuracy and presentation. In contrast, we would write an email to a friend far more quickly and easily, using language that may well resemble conversation in its informality, with limited concern for spelling and punctuation. When writing a shopping list for our own use, we are likely to devote even less attention to transcription, as neither accuracy or neatness are required for us to read it.

The process involved in writing a formal letter, for example a job application, is likely to take considerable time. We might begin by highlighting key points to be addressed and making notes on what will be included. We might then write a rough draft, which is later changed, reorganized and improved. It is interesting to note that in these early stages the focus is on composition, the content and its organization. It is likely that attention to transcriptional aspects, accuracy in spelling and punctuation, will come later. This is not to suggest that the process is strictly linear. Transcription skills are necessary from the beginning in order to plan and draft but composition is generally the focus of attention at first. Once we are satisfied with our draft, we then turn our attention to spelling and punctuation to ensure accuracy. However, even at this editing stage we may still make changes to the content and its organization.

A clear sense of purpose provides the motivation to devote time and energy to this lengthy process, which may take place over several sessions. At any stage, discussion with others may be used to provide ideas, clarification and support in reviewing the content, editing and proofreading.

This review has highlighted that:

- writing is a complex process, demanding skills in composition and transcription;
- a focus on composition precedes attention to transcription;
- composition involves planning, drafting and redrafting;
- the level of concern devoted to composition and transcription varies according to the nature of the text, purpose and audience.

# Development in writing

As discussed in Chapter 1, by the time children arrive in the nursery, they will already be familiar with writing used in various ways. Such experience provides them with considerable understanding of its nature, use and value. However, writing also presents significant challenges. At this stage most young children are able to communicate effectively through speech (Wells, 1985) and will have achieved this level of competence without having become conscious of the nature of individual words or sounds from which language is formed (Vygotsky, 1962). In contrast, writing requires an awareness that:

- language involves individual words;
- words are represented by groups of symbols, produced in a specific order and arrangement;
- these symbols represent sounds in a consistent way;
- these symbols need to be reproduced in a recognizable form.

In order to develop as writers, children therefore need to gain understanding of the nature of written text. They need to acquire the necessary secretarial skills, including the dexterity to form letters, so that they are able to communicate with others. They also need to be able to present and manipulate language appropriately and effectively, creating different types of texts and taking into account the needs of their audience.

It is clear that the development of writing involves many diverse aspects that are both discrete and interrelated. A sense of the progression involved is presented in Table 5.1, developed from work by Bearne (1998), Browne (1993) and Wyse *et al*. (2001). The table is divided into stages of development although it is likely that an individual child will demonstrate competence reflected in more than one level.

# Approaches to the teaching of writing

In the past, the teaching of early writing tended to focus on the development of aspects of transcription, for example the ability to form letters and spell. Teaching in the early stages therefore devoted considerable attention to copy writing. Composition tended to relate to the description of events in a child's life and would be scribed by an adult in order to provide an acceptable model for the child to copy. Once children had gained sufficient skills in transcription they were expected to compose without the support of the adult. The initial stages were therefore seen as an apprenticeship, with the children requiring skills in transcription before they could take responsibility for composition and become writers.

It is interesting to consider how such an approach differs from most children's experience in learning to talk. As discussed in Chapter 3, children learn to speak in an environment in which their earliest utterances are treated as meaningful and encouraged. They experiment with sounds and learn from the models of language in use around them. They use language for real purposes, to ensure their needs are met, express their feelings and communicate with others. Those around them expect them to succeed. Such positive expectations, the valuing of attempts to communicate even if they are not accurate and the development of skills within meaningful and purposeful contexts have implications for the teaching of writing.

In teaching writing, children's early attempts to communicate can also be valued, even though they do not conform to conventional representation. Children can be regarded as writers from the earliest stages; their experience and understanding of writing derived from the world beyond the classroom can be seen as relevant and useful. The term 'emergent writing' was introduced by Hall (1987) to emphasize that from the earliest stages of forming marks, children are using and experimenting with this knowledge. Such mark making is therefore to be encouraged as it provides a focus and context for developing awareness of conventional print. Providing encouragement for children to write for meaning is regarded as essential and the development of transcription skills occurs within this context.

This emphasis on the provision of meaningful contexts for children's writing has implications for the planning of activities and purposes for writing in the classroom. In the past, writing activities tended to be planned to enable children to practise or demonstrate expertise in technical skills or to provide a copy of information as evidence of their learning. In all such writing tasks, accuracy and neatness in presentation were required. The emphasis in writing was on the product, presented in an exercise book to be judged by teacher.

Such an approach to the teaching of writing developed children's skills in a very limited way, which failed to acknowledge or prepare them for the ways in which writing was used beyond the classroom. It did not recognize that writing often requires a more extensive process of planning and drafting and assumed that children were able to focus on aspects of composition and transcription simultaneously. Children's experience of writing lacked a sense of purpose and audience and was limited to a narrow range of texts. Such an approach to teaching did not introduce children to the exciting potential writing has to offer in terms of communication, self-expression and learning.

In contrast, a *process approach* to the teaching of writing (Graves, 1983) involves children in producing a variety of types of texts for a range of different purposes and audiences. They are encouraged to move through the stages of planning and drafting to present their product to an audience. Children are encouraged to be aware of the importance of their skills in transcription in facilitating effective communication.

**Table 5.1. Development in writing**

| Composition | Transcription |
|---|---|
| **Stage i Pre-writing**<br>• Aware of and shows interest in texts<br>• Recognizes difference between picture and writing<br>• Interested in mark making, exploring marks for the communication of meaning<br>• Produces oral recount<br>• Limited range of vocabulary | • Produces scribbles and some shapes similar to letters |
| **Stage ii Early writing**<br>• Aware of narrative and non-narrative texts<br>• Makes marks to communicate meaning<br>• Produces oral narrative and account<br>• Limited range of vocabulary | • Increasing formation of shapes which resemble letters in formation and presentation<br>• Grouping of letter shapes appearing |
| **Stage iii Gaining competence**<br>• Writes to communicate meaning<br>• Recognizes narrative text and produces oral storytelling<br>• Produces simple non-narrative forms of text – labels, notices, etc<br>• Widening range of vocabulary | • Produces increasingly recognizable letters.<br>• Groups letters as words with some reproduction of common words and use of phonic knowledge to indicate the initial sounds of some words<br>• Recognizes full stops and includes them in writing without consideration of their purpose |
| **Stage iv Developing competence**<br>• Distinguishes between narrative and non-narrative forms of text<br>• Produces simple narrative with logical structure<br>• Produces non-fiction texts with support<br>• Shows some awareness of audience and purpose in use of language<br>• Increasing range of vocabulary used<br>• With guidance, is able to produce notes and use them for recording and planning<br>• With support, encouragement and a clear expectation of publishing, understands the need for redrafting and is able to identify aspects for improvement | • Recognizes the need for punctuation and writes in sentences<br>• Sometimes uses full stops and capital letters and is aware of other punctuation marks<br>• Spells some familiar words accurately and uses phonic knowledge to tackle unfamiliar words<br>• With support is able to identify some simple errors in spelling and punctuation<br>• Produces legible writing with ease |

**Table 5.1. Development in writing (continued)**

| Composition | Transcription |
| --- | --- |
| **Stage v Increasing competence**<br>• Aware of a range of narrative and non-narrative forms of text and able to produce them with some support<br>• Recognizes need to take into account the purpose and audience, use of language, organization and presentation of text<br>• Able to provide a structure for narrative writing and include characterization, setting and atmosphere.<br>• Increasing range of vocabulary used<br>• With support is able to produce notes and use them for recording and planning<br>• Recognizes when redrafting is appropriate and is able to identify aspects for improvement particularly in relation to vocabulary and organization | • Recognizes the need for punctuation and writes in sentences of varied length<br>• Increasing use of commas, question marks and exclamation marks<br>• Spells familiar words accurately and uses a range of strategies to tackle unfamiliar words.<br>• Able to identify some simple errors in spelling and punctuation<br>• Developing a comfortable, legible style with attention to presentation when needed |
| **Stage vi Competence**<br>• Able to produce a range of narrative and non-narrative forms of text<br>• Responds appropriately to purpose and audience in selection of type of text, use of language, organization and presentation of text<br>• In narrative writing, able to interest and entertain the reader, taking account of ways of using narrative structure, characterization, setting and atmosphere.<br>• Increasing range of vocabulary used for effect<br>• Independently makes notes for use in recording and planning<br>• Able to redraft, look critically at own writing in terms of content, structure, style and vocabulary | • Recognizes the impact of punctuation on meaning and uses a range of punctuation marks, paragraphing and direct speech accurately<br>• Spells accurately and is willing and able to make a logical attempt at unfamiliar words<br>• Able to edit own writing<br>• Able to write in a comfortable, fluent, legible style with attention to presentation as appropriate |

# Encouraging development in writing

In order to encourage children to develop into confident, competent, enthusiastic writers in their lives beyond the classroom, it is essential that their experience of writing in the classroom provides opportunities for this.

### Writing beyond the classroom:

- write for a range of purposes and audiences;
- produce a range of different types of texts;
- write in order to communicate, express feelings and entertain others;
- use their writing to aid learning;
- engage in writing as a process;
- develop confidence and competence in transcription skills.

Audiences and purposes for children's writing exist within and beyond the school as shown below.

### Within the international and national community:

- emails/letters to children in another school at home/abroad, authors and publishers about favourite books;
- requests for information from organizations, bands, stars, museums, tourist information offices and so on;
- contributions to Internet sites for children's writing and discussion boards of charitable organizations;
- letters in response to issues to the Prime Minister/United Nations/charitable organizations.

### Within the local area:

- complaints or requests to the local council, MP or police, for instance about local litter and the need for new bins or a lack of facilities for skateboarding;
- invitations and posters about school events or local campaigns;
- letters, reviews and articles for the local paper;
- responses and contributions to local TV.

### Within the school:

- guides to the school for new children/visitors;
- lists of children wanting dinners for the school office;
- invitations to events for parents and carers;
- books for younger children;
- posters to advertise events;
- letters of thanks, for example to cleaning staff.

*Within the classroom:*

- labels for a display, resources or property;
- information for other children in the class;
- reminders, e.g. about behaviour, events, items to collect, etc.;
- class books of stories, poems, and so on;
- welcome poster;
- messages and adverts for class notice board;
- letters to the teacher.

*Writing for oneself:*

- diaries;
- jotters;
- reminder notes.

Given an appropriate focus and support, children of all ages can be involved in writing for any of the audiences above. A range of suggestions for using the role-play area to provide opportunities for writing is included in Chapter 8. Further audiences and purposes for children's writing can be created through imaginative activities, such as drama and role play as illustrated below.

The **reception** teacher has told the class the first part of the story of Cinderella, stopping at the point at which she is offered three wishes by the Fairy Godmother. At the beginning of the next session the children receive a letter from Cinderella, asking them for help in deciding what wishes to make. They write letters in response. See Figure 5.1.

The **year 1** teacher brings in a letter from the paper that argues that a proposed extension to a playground in the local park should not go ahead as it is too expensive and there is already too much litter and noise in the area. The children discuss their views and together prepare a shared response.

The **year 3** children have been reading *Bill's New Frock* (Fine, 1990). The book opens when Bill wakes up and discovers that he is a girl. Only Bill seems to be shocked by the change. At home and at school he is treated as a girl and the day is full of surprises. The teacher uses 'hotseating' to encourage the children to explore Bill's feelings. Individually they then write an entry for Bill's diary.

A **year 5** class is involved in a role play about the historic flooding of two villages in Derbyshire. In their role as villagers, the children receive a letter from the Water Board, explaining plans to flood the village to form a reservoir. They decide that they need to reply and send letters of complaint to the local newspaper and councillors. They then plan a protest meeting, producing fliers and posters to encourage others to attend.

Some children act as newspaper reporters; they interview the villagers and produce a report on the campaign.

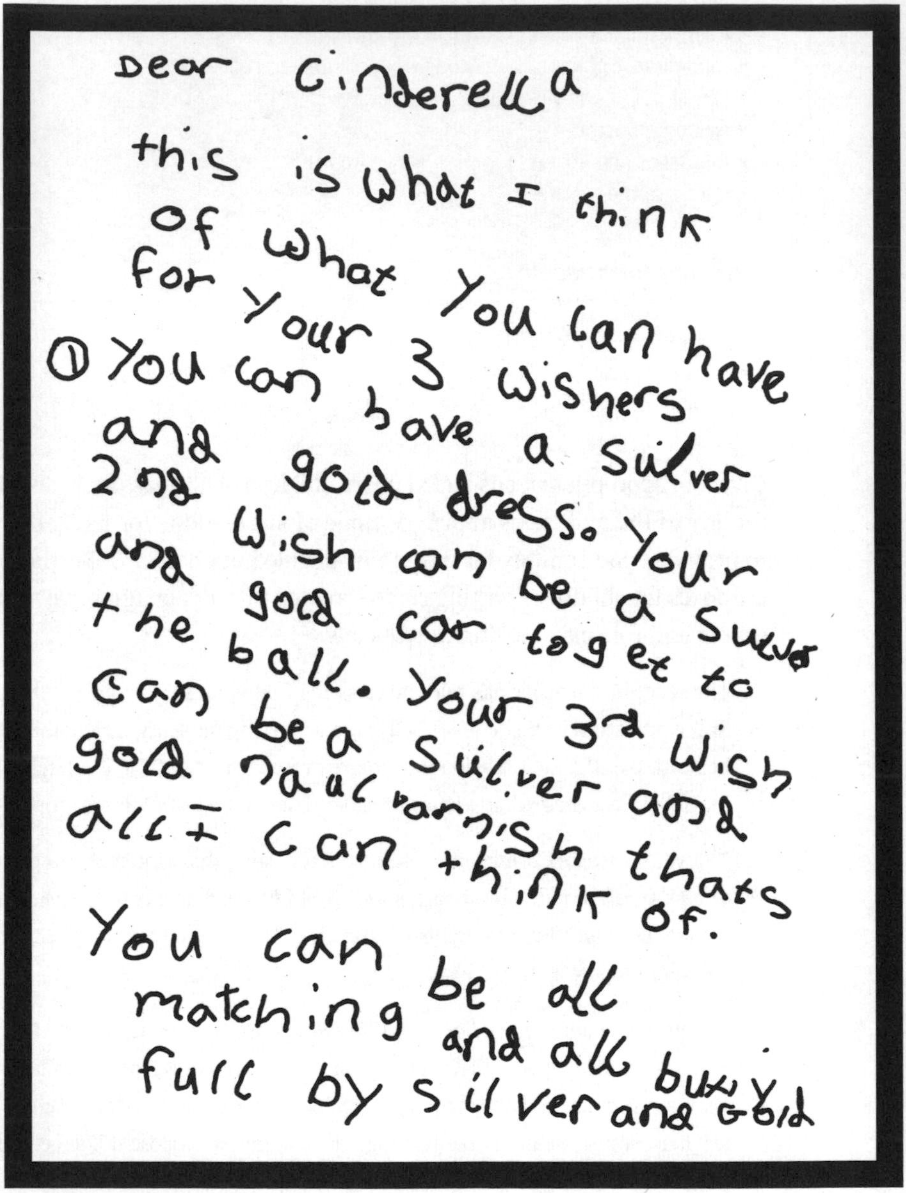

> Dear Cinderella
> this is what I think
> of what You can have
> for Your 3 wishers
> ① You can have a silver
> and gold dress. Your
> 2nd wish can be a silver
> and gold car to get to
> the ball. Your 3d wish
> can be a silver and
> gold nail varnish thats
> all I can think of.
>
> You can be all
> matching and all busy
> full by silver and gold

Figure 5.1. Letter from a child to Cinderella

# Engaging children in the writing process

The writing process can be divided up into different stages. As mentioned earlier, this sequence is not simply linear and children may move between the different stages. These stages include:

- generating ideas;
- planning;
- drafting;
- revising;
- editing;
- presenting.

There is no need for children to work through the whole of the process for every piece of writing they do. As discussed earlier, different aspects will be relevant for different types of writing. Children need to learn that the approach will vary according to the audience and purpose of writing. They need to be able to recognize when drafting, redrafting and careful editing are required and be aware that, at times, such a lengthy process would be inappropriate.

The section below explores what is required at each stage and how this can be encouraged.

## Generating ideas

Providing an appropriate stimulus is essential at this point. This will engage children's interest and give them a sense of the purpose and audience for their writing. It will help them to explore their ideas before they begin to write. At this stage, they may use writing or drawing to record ideas and clarify thoughts.

### Ways of encouraging children to generate ideas:

- drawing, for example sketch a holiday destination and then use it as the basis for a holiday brochure;
- objects, artefacts, a picture or music, for instance collect descriptive words and ideas then produce a poem (see Figure 5.2);
- playground games or science or design technology activities – for example, do the activity and then discuss what instructions other people will need;
- a letter or newspaper article to initiate a discussion or debate about an issue, such as school uniform, environmental issues, children's rights, which will lead into discursive or persuasive writing;
- improvisation to prepare for writing a play script;
- school trips – for example, collect ideas in pictures or words to produce a visitors' guide, or generate words to describe a place, such as a waterfall or busy street, that will later be drafted into a poem;
- create a map in preparation for writing an adventure story – having drawn the map, plan the events that happen there.

At this stage ideas are often recorded; writing and drawing may be useful in clarifying thoughts.

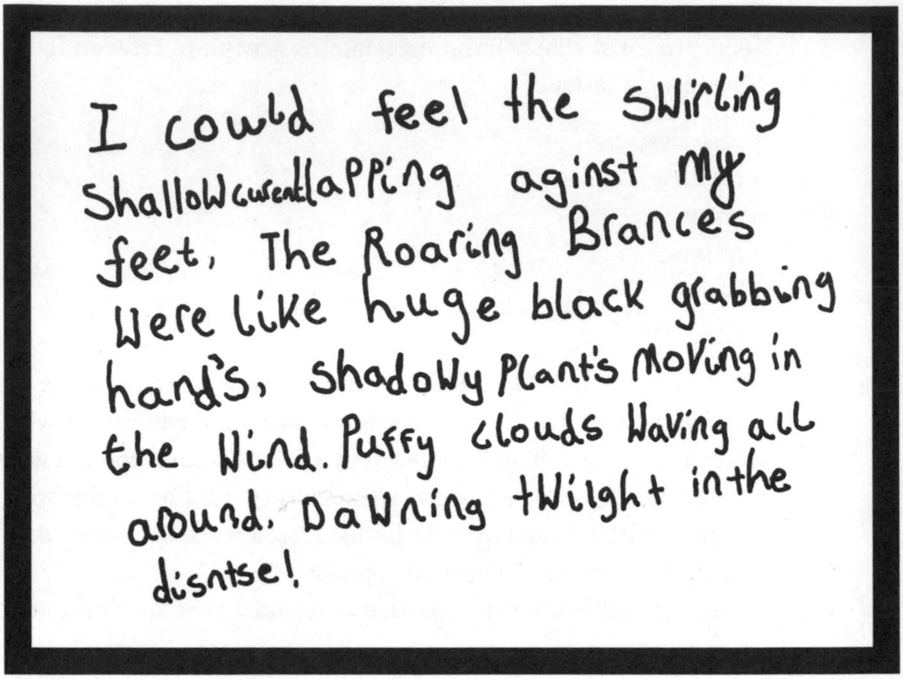

I cowld feel the swirling shallow cwent lapping aginst my feet. The Roaring Branches were Like huge black grabbing hand's, shadowy plant's moving in the wind. Puffy clouds Waving all around. Dawning twilght in the disntse!

Figure 5.2. A child's poem

## Planning

At this stage children need the opportunity to organize their ideas. The form of organization will depend on the type of writing.

*Chronological writing* is organized around a sequence of events and includes stories, recounts of experiences and instructions. These need to be presented in a clear order. When children are planning such writing they therefore need to be encouraged to recognize this sequence and organize their ideas accordingly. Depending on the type of chronological writing, support for such planning could include a storyboard (a page is divided into a series of boxes to be filled with pictures showing key events in order); a flow chart or an annotated map. Depending on the content, children may also benefit from the opportunity to try out their plan through sharing it with others, acting it out using puppets or retelling through drama.

*Non-chronological writing* (writing which is not organized around a series of events), such as a report, advert or explanation of a process, can be particularly challenging as the content itself does not offer a clear system of organization. In planning, children therefore need to make decisions about the sequence of information to be presented and this requires understanding of the structure and features of non-chronological texts. Ways of supporting children in planning and writing such texts are explored in depth in Chapter 6.

# Drafting

At this stage, the children concentrate on composition. They need to be clear about their audience, the purpose and the type of text they are expected to produce. It is helpful for children to rehearse sentences orally before writing and repeatedly reread what they have written. Children need to be encouraged to be adventurous in their choice of vocabulary, rather than worrying about their spelling.

# Revising

In revising, children make improvements to the content and organization of their draft, taking into account the needs of the audience, the purpose and type of text. Children often find it helpful to read the whole text aloud and can be encouraged to consider what is successful or effective and what improvements could be made. Children also benefit from opportunities to discuss their work with a response partner, whose role is to comment on positive aspects of composition and make constructive suggestions. Children need to learn how to take on this role and it is useful for the teacher to model this during shared and guided writing. Reminders about how to provide a useful and supportive response can be displayed in the classroom (see below). These could be supplemented with points relating to the particular learning objective and form of writing, for instance the creation of suspense in narrative writing or the use of diagrams to support an explanation.

---

### How to be a good response partner

Read the whole piece of writing first.

- Tell the writer three things you like about it.
- Talk about anything you don't understand.
- Tell the writer if you would like to know more about anything.
- Suggest up to two things he or she could do to improve it.

---

# Proofreading

When proofreading, children focus on transcriptional aspects, in particular spelling and punctuation. They can be given coloured pens to highlight spellings that need to be checked or missing punctuation. Specific individualized targets relating to proofreading can also be useful, for example:

- Check whether you have used paragraphs/speech marks appropriately.
- Find and change five spellings that you know are incorrect.
- Underline five spellings that you suspect need to be checked.

# Presenting

At this stage, children decide on how to present their work to their specific audience. This may involve making decisions about type and size of font or handwriting and how to use illustrations to help communicate meaning.

The process described is appropriate for occasions when there is a real purpose and audience for the children's work. This will provide the incentive for children to retain their commitment throughout the different stages and activities. A particular advantage of the writing process is that it offers the teacher the opportunity to engage with children's writing and provide support at any stage. Discussion during the process of writing can encourage children to be positive and critical of their own work and to recognize the need for changes to be made.

Word processing is an invaluable asset in supporting children through all the stages of the writing process. It releases children from the physical demands of writing and enables them to reorganize their work easily, experiment with layout and check their spelling.

There is no expectation that children should undertake this process for every piece of written work produced, as this would be laborious, time consuming and demotivating. Depending on the learning objective, it is sometimes appropriate to focus on a single stage of the process, as shown in the following examples:

> The **year 1** children work in pairs to describe the appearance of a character in a photograph. Their descriptions are later read out to the class who guess which photo matches each one. At no stage are the children expected to edit their work or present it neatly as the focus relates to their use of descriptive language.

> The **year 3** children have discussed things they often hear their parents say when it's time to go to bed. These have been scribed by the teacher and printed on individual strips of paper. In groups, they select some sayings and arrange them as a poem.

> The **year 5** children have been planning leaflets and the teacher is pleased with the quality of the content but notices that little thought has been devoted to presentation. She provides an electronic version of a text and asks the children to work in pairs to present it as a leaflet. They later compare the results and discuss the use of layout, font, size of print, and so on, in the presentation of text.

# Narrative writing

As discussed in Chapter 3, by the time children reach the Foundation Stage, most will already have gained a strong sense of narrative from hearing conversations around them, watching cartoons and videos and sharing stories. From this awareness they will need to develop the skills and understanding to produce a written narrative. In order to be successful they will need to gain the ability to:

- structure a written narrative;
- create and develop characters;
- create relevant settings;
- write in a range of narrative genres;
- develop their use of language to engage and maintain the interest of the reader.

In teaching narrative writing it is essential to recognize the complexity of the task involved and to provide support so that children are not being expected to deal with too many demands. For example, in the early years, children are often encouraged to retell a familiar story or relate an experience that happened to them. The reason for this is that the events, their sequence, the setting and characters are known. The children can therefore focus on the telling of the tale.

At every stage, children's literature provides an invaluable resource in the teaching of narrative writing. Children's familiarity with literature has long been assumed to contribute to their development in narrative writing, but it is only relatively recently that attention has focused more closely on enabling children to understand how writers write (Barrs *et al.*, 2001). Literature offers children the experience of language used effectively in a variety of genres and styles. Lewis (1999) demonstrates how understanding of story structure can be developed through work with picture books. She selects different kinds of structures found in children's picture books, for example:

- cumulative stories, in which events or objects are added to preceding items until no more can be added, such as *Mr Gumpy's Outing* (Burningham, 1970), *The Great Big Enormous Turnip* (Tolstoy, 1968);
- journeys from one place to another, such as *Handa's Surprise* (Browne, 1995);
- journeys involving a return, such as *We're Going on a Bear Hunt* (Rosen, 1989).

Lewis (1999: 81) suggests a teaching sequence through which children can be encouraged to gain understanding of the structure and produce their own text. 'The five step approach' involves:

- immersion in the text type – reading several texts of the same type;
- discussion of features of the structure, reinforced by visual recording through mapping or charts;
- independent recording of the structure of a different text from the same genre;
- using a blank version of the same mapping frame to plan their own story;
- drafting the story and sharing the drafts with others in preparation for publication.

Such an approach illustrates the value of texts as models for children's writing and can be used to develop children's understanding of different narrative genres throughout the Foundation Stage and primary years. A series of sessions is needed to familiarize children with features of a genre and to allow them to go through the stages of the writing process in producing their own text. If children are to gain a sense of themselves as writers of fiction, it is essential that they have such opportunities.

They can be involved in producing stories for class collections and often enjoy writing for younger children.

Traditional tales offer a valuable focus for narrative writing. Retelling can involve adaptations and there are many published versions to provide ideas for this. *Snow White in New York* (French, 1987) is an example that can be used as a stimulus for children to create their own interpretation of a familiar story in a new setting. Alternatively, children can be encouraged to re-write a well-known story from a different perspective, as in *The True Story of the Three Little Pigs* (Scieszka, 1991).

Through literature, children can become aware of the ways in which successful texts are constructed and language is used. Through group or class discussions, children can be engaged in identifying particular techniques used by authors. Bearne (2002: 12) argues that, through facilitating such discussions, teachers move children from 'personal and affective responses to texts to more aesthetic and critical responses' that will support them in their own writing.

The following scenarios illustrate how such response can be encouraged through the use of texts as models for writing.

The **reception** children have read *Dear Zoo* (Campbell, 1984), in which requests to the zoo for a pet result in a series of inappropriate animals being supplied. For each episode the text follows a regular pattern: 'I wrote to the zoo to send me a pet. They sent me a . . . He was too . . . so I sent him back.' The children have created a list of the animals sent, with notes of their reasons for being inappropriate. They are now writing a class book: 'Dear Farm'. They list the animals to be sent by the farm and note reasons for their unsuitability. The teacher then scribes as the children tell the story.

The **year 2** class has read *Too Much Talk* (Medearis, 1995), an entertaining West African tale that begins when a farmer comes across a talking yam. He runs off in surprise and encounters a series of people and other talking objects. With the teacher, the children have constructed a map to show the farmer's journey and annotated it to show the people he meets and the objects that talk. The children then plan a similar story set in their own neighbourhood, about a child that discovers a talking object. In pairs they sketch a map of the area, indicating places, people and talking objects. They then tell their story to another pair and later produce a written version for a class book.

The **year 4** class has recently read *Meet Me by the Steelmen* (Tomlinson, 1997) in which a statue in a busy shopping centre captures the attention of a young boy, who is later transported back in time. They have looked closely at how the author makes the settings vivid and believable, noting references to each of the senses. The children are then given the challenge of writing a scene which begins near a local statue of Winston Churchill and involves a trip back in time. They discuss what may happen and the children then sketch pictures of the setting in the present and in the past, including notes of words and phrases to describe sounds, sights and smells. Before the children write their narrative, the teacher returns to *Meet Me by the Steelmen* and they discuss how the writer shows the change in time by gradually introducing features of the historical setting.

The children return to their pictures and number features in the setting in the order in which they will be introduced.

 In teaching narrative it is therefore important to include opportunities for:

- regular reading aloud of a range of children's literature;
- focused discussion of the use of language in extracts from familiar texts;
- drama as a stimulus for narrative writing in role;
- using drawing, talk and storyboards to support planning;
- providing children with support in structuring narratives through using known texts as models;
- work in pairs;
- feedback from others;
- storytelling and oral rehearsal in preparation for writing;
- publication of children's work, e.g. in class books.

# The teaching of grammar

The teaching of grammar has been the subject of controversy over the years. Recently, its position in the teaching of literacy has received considerable recognition in its profile within the NLS Framework (DfEE, 1998). The resulting *Grammar for Writing* (DfEE, 2000) makes explicit its role as a tool to enable children to use written language more effectively. This is important. In the past, grammar has been regarded as prescriptive, setting down rules which needed to be learned and practised through exercises. Such rules relate to standard English which is presented as the correct form of language, as discussed in Chapter 1.

In contrast, descriptive grammar explores how language is *used*. Rather than focusing exclusively on standard English, it examines ways in which dialects differ. Knowledge about grammar therefore provides children with:

- insight into appropriate and effective use of language;
- an ability to recognize differences between standard English and dialect forms;
- tools to facilitate the effective use and understanding of language;
- metalanguage – the means to discuss aspects of writing and reflect on their own language use;
- an interest in language.

Such knowledge about grammar can be promoted through activities which encourage children to:

- explore language use in texts;
- reflect on their own use and knowledge about language;
- apply their learning through using language in meaningful contexts.

The following scenarios illustrate this:

The **year 1** teacher wants to develop the children's ability to form clear questions. She introduces the game 'Who am I?', explaining that the teaching assistant will assume the identity of a member of the class and that the children need to guess who it is. Initially she helps the children to create questions but they soon become confident and are able to take over. Once the solution has been found, a child takes over the role of choosing an identity for others to guess.

At the end of the day, the **year 3** teacher introduces the circle game: 'the minister's cat'. In turn, each child adds a word to describe the fictitious cat . . . 'The minister's cat is an angry, bold, careful . . . cat.' The teacher explains that the words used to describe the cat are all adjectives. The following day the teacher uses an extract from a holiday brochure and the children identify the adjectives used. The children discuss the use of adjectives and their impact on the text. Later they prepare descriptions of holiday places they have visited for a class brochure.

The **year 6** class has been looking at formal use of language. During a walk around the local area, they have collected a variety of texts that make use of the passive voice, for example 'trespassers will be prosecuted' and 'dogs must be kept on leads'. The children discuss why the passive voice is used. They notice that the result is impersonal, hiding the identity of the writer and consequently making the message seem obligatory. The teacher later introduces a report from the local council on the closure of the local library and a newspaper article on the same issue. The children identify the use of passive in each text and discuss why the newspaper article makes more use of the active voice. Later, the children produce a statement from the school governors announcing the closure of the school snack shop.

Other activities that can promote understanding of grammar include:

- creating glossaries or dictionaries for words from local dialect, slang, a particular TV programme, topic-related vocabulary;
- finding as many words as possible to replace common words, for example 'nice', 'said', 'went' and discussing differences in meaning;
- cloze procedure and discussion of suggestions for appropriate words to fill gaps and comparison with original;
- highlighting particular types of words, such as connectives, and discussing their role;
- deleting particular types of words, such as pronouns, and examining the impact on the text.

# Punctuation

Punctuation plays a crucial role in conveying meaning. Note the difference in meaning between the following sentences from Rosen (1989: 40).

*The butler stood by the door and called the guests' names.*

*The butler stood by the door and called the guests names.*

In the first version, the inclusion of an apostrophe shows that the butler was performing his role appropriately. Its absence in the second version presents him as behaving far more rudely!

In the following example, the addition of two punctuation marks completely changes the meaning of this text from Waugh (1998: 14):

*Private. No swimming allowed.*

*Private? No! Swimming allowed.*

Punctuation is a feature of written text. In conversation, we use gestures, intonation and facial expression to make meaning clear. We supplement what is conveyed by our words, for example adding emphasis, suggesting nuances or inviting response. We use pauses to indicate that we have finished with a topic and intend to move on. In contrast, in written text, all these features are conveyed through the use of punctuation.

Punctuation, therefore, presents challenges for children. Their wide experience of spoken language will not have prepared them for its use (Kress, 1994). Writing depends upon the use of sentences (Kelly, 1998). However, providing an explanation of the nature of sentences is not so simple, even if we are intuitively able to recognize and reproduce them. References to 'making sense' or 'a complete unit of meaning' or 'where we take a breath' are problematic, as they tend to overlook that the same explanation can also be applied to clauses and phrases (Hall, 2001; Smith, 1982). In addition, the marks that are significant are small and easily overlooked (Hall *et al.*, 1996). Kress (1994) points out that many books written for young children present the text in such a way that the reader does not have to rely on the use of punctuation. By placing a single sentence on each page, or beginning each new sentence at the beginning of a line, the reader is encouraged to use the layout to indicate where a break is needed rather than the punctuation marks.

Very little research has explored the development of children's punctuation. However, Cazden *et al.* (1985 in Browne, 2001) and Hall (1999) have shown that children's early use of punctuation marks tends to reflect a desire to represent the mark, rather than any awareness of the meaning carried. Such placing of dots between words and at the end of each line is termed 'non-linguistic punctuation' by Wyse *et al.* (2001: 166). This is distinguished from the later stage of 'linguistic punctuation', which relates the use of punctuation marks (initially full stops) to the meaning of the text.

It is this understanding of the impact on meaning of the full stop which is crucial in the development of children's early understanding of punctuation. Hall *et al.* (1996) suggest that encouraging children from the earliest stages to write more than one sentence is useful. The traditional practice of asking children to write a single sentence encourages them to use the full stop simply as an indication of the completion of a piece of text. Writing a longer piece of text allows for more opportunities to become aware of divisions within the text.

The following activities encourage children to gain understanding of the nature and purpose of punctuation. They are relevant for use throughout the early and primary years, although clearly there will be increasing complexity in the type of punctuation in focus. Activities include:

- identifying the use of punctuation in shared texts and their impact on the text;
- modelling and discussing the use of punctuation marks in shared writing, exploring the impact on meaning when these are omitted or different marks are used;
- removing punctuation from a text, discussing impact on meaning and then deciding where punctuation is needed;
- using a text as a model for children's own writing;
- collecting examples of the use of a particular form of punctuation;
- producing guidance for others on using a particular form of punctuation;
- investigating ways in which the use of punctuation differs in different kinds of texts;
- preparing expressive reading of texts for performance.

The following scenarios show these activities being used with different age groups:

The **reception** teacher has read *Hallo! How are You?* (Watanabe, 1979) to the children. This is the story of a bear that meets many different animals and each time asks, 'How are you?' The teacher reads the story again and points to the words as the class join in with the repeated question. She then draws attention to the individual words and the children point out familiar letters. A child comments on the question mark and they discuss its role. The following day the class use this text as the model for their own story of a bear that meets different people and asks the same question. The teacher acts as scribe, writing the story and drawing attention to the use of the question mark.

The **year** 2 children are being introduced to the use of commas in separating items in a list. As a short activity, the teacher has returned to a familiar text: *The Very Hungry Caterpillar* (Carle, 1970). In this story, the caterpillar eats an increasing amount of food until one day . . . 'he ate through one piece of chocolate cake, one ice-cream cone, one pickle, one slice of Swiss cheese, one slice of salami . . .' The children have identified and discussed the role of the commas and have now been challenged to write the longest list of items that the caterpillar could consume in another day of feasting. The teacher frequently praises the children for remembering to include commas in their lists.

Groups of **year** 3 children work together to collect examples of the use of capital letters in texts within and beyond the classroom. They draw up a list of guidance on using capital letters for younger children.

The **year** 4 children are presented with the opening to *The Iron Man* (Hughes, 1968). All punctuation has been removed. In pairs the children annotate the text with punctuation, as they think necessary. They then compare their suggestions with another pair and discuss the impact on the text. As a class, the children then look at the original. They explore the impact of the use of short sentences in heightening tension.

The **year 6** children have been emailing children in a school in another country. They have also been collecting examples of emails used at home. They discuss the use of punctuation in email and compare its use in other texts. Later they produce a guide for people who are unfamiliar with writing emails, to show how punctuation is used.

In these examples the children are involved in recognizing and using punctuation in meaningful contexts. They are not simply practising the use of an aspect of punctuation in an abstract exercise which does not relate to their own use of language. As Bearne (2002) points out, the completion of such decontextualized exercises rarely has an impact on learning which transfers to the rest of their writing. Practice within meaningful use is far more likely to encourage application in the future.

Working with children on their own writing also provides a context for discussion about punctuation. Encouraging children to read their work aloud often helps them to identify where punctuation is needed and consider the needs of a reader. The motivation to punctuate work accurately is enhanced by activities that involve writing for a genuine audience and purpose.

In general, effective teaching of punctuation at every stage involves the following:

- an emphasis on the importance of punctuation in conveying meaning;
- encouraging interest in punctuation;
- modelling and discussing the use of punctuation;
- direct teaching about aspects of punctuation based on their use in texts;
- providing meaningful opportunities for reinforcing specific aspects of punctuation;
- individualized teaching where appropriate based upon a child's own writing.

# Spelling

Accuracy in spelling enables writing to be read easily by others, although, as discussed earlier, in everyday life the importance of accuracy in spelling varies according to our purpose and audience. It is therefore essential that children acquire spelling skills. However, we also need to maintain perspective. In responding to children's writing, as Bearne (2002) has pointed out, it is sometimes too easy to concentrate on spelling errors and to ignore content. This can give children an impression that spelling is the most important feature in successful writing. They may then devote less attention to the compositional aspects of the writing process and be cautious in their choice of vocabulary.

## Development in spelling

The development of spelling from the first stages of mark making through to competence and accuracy needs to be understood before we consider approaches to effective teaching of this area. Gentry (1981) suggests five recognizable stages:

- pre-communicative;
- semi-phonetic;
- phonetic;
- transitional;
- conventional/correct.

### Pre-communicative

As discussed earlier in this chapter, in the first stages of writing children engage in mark making, exploring and developing the manipulation of writing tools. As they gain control and move from producing lines and squiggles, they begin to experiment with finer shapes. In reproducing familiar letter shapes, they are taking the first steps towards learning to spell, even though these shapes have no correspondence with sounds. Children at this stage may be able to explain what they have written but a reader would not be able to make sense of it. The letter shapes may be divided into smaller groups, which begin to represent individual words.

Figure 5.3 illustrates the pre-communicative stage of development. This was produced by a child about to start nursery to indicate the things she liked to do. She clearly has a sense of script as carrying meaning. She conveys one idea at a time and arranges them as a list.

I like to:

drawing
singing
stories
playing outside
going home on my own
climbing

Figure 5.3. Sample showing pre-communicative writing

## Semi-phonetic

Children at this stage have gained some understanding of the correspondence between graphemes and phonemes. In their writing they are beginning to use graphophonic awareness, the ability to link letters with sounds. Individual words are represented using between one and three letters – generally consonants. Single letter names are used to represent words, such as 'r' for 'are'. Figure 5.4, a letter written to the tooth fairy, explaining the loss of a tooth while eating a chocolate biscuit, illustrates this stage of spelling development.

The note in Figure 5.4 reads: 'It fell out when I was eating my Penguin.' The child is able to represent initial sounds. She has also attempted to use some vowels and final consonants. (She may well have identified the 'g' in Penguin as the final consonant of a single word, followed by a second word beginning with 'w'.)

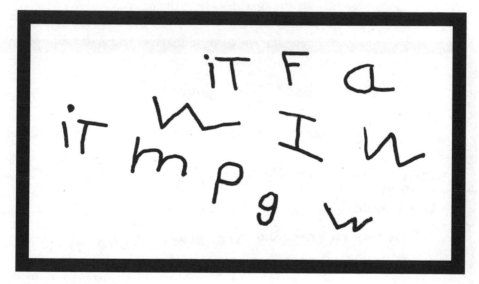

Figure 5.4. Sample showing semi-phonetic spelling

## Phonetic

Children at this stage recognize that all the sounds within a word can be represented by letters. In their spelling, they rely on the sounds of a word and use letters to represent each phoneme.

Figure 5.5 is a poem written about fireworks and reflects the phonetic stage of spelling development. All the sounds are now being represented. The first line has been copied.

I love Catherine wheels
I lac ol the difrt kols
I wev the sbocl arawd
I love the fay glwg
The nossis ov the bom fays krakl

Translation
I like all the different colours
I wave the sparkler around
I love the fire glowing
The noises of the bonfires crackle

Figure 5.5. Sample showing phonetic spelling

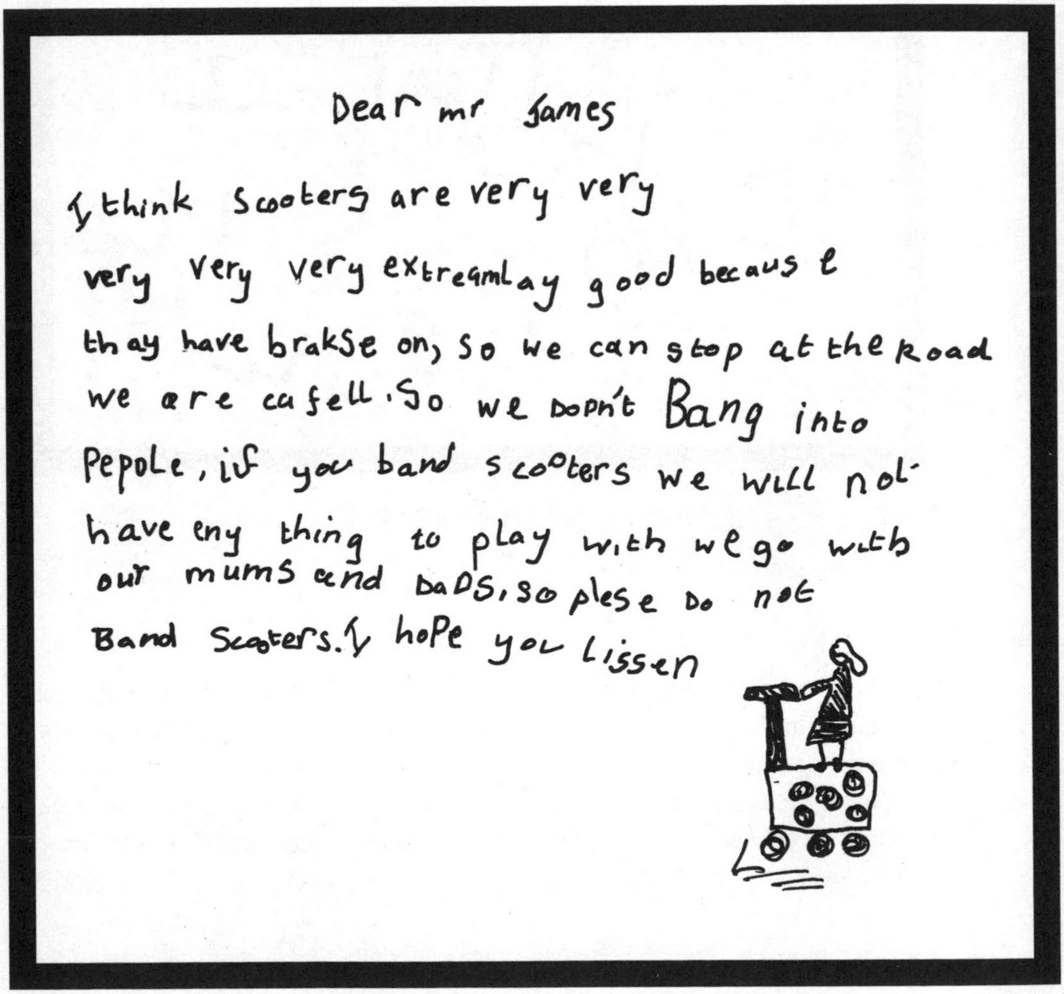

Dear mr James

I think Scooters are very very
very very very extreamlay good becaus e
thay have brakse on, so we can stop at the road
we are cafell. So we dopn't Bang into
Pepole, if you band scooters we will not
have eny thing to play with we go with
our mums and DaDs, so plese Do not
Band Scooters. I hope you Lissen

Figure 5.6. Sample showing the transitional stage of spelling.

## Transitional

At this stage, children cease to rely on phonetic representation of words and are aware that not all words are produced phonetically. This is an important stage. Children begin to rely on visual memory of language patterns and reproduce some familiar letter combinations that are not phonetic.

The writing shown in Figure 5.6 was produced in response to a letter arguing that children's scooters should be banned. It shows a move away from relying simply on the sounds of words. The writer is clearly aware of common letter combinations. The mistakes in spelling (for example 'extreamlay') show that the child has applied her knowledge of the language logically, even if she has not been accurate.

## Conventional/corrrect

Children at this stage are generally able to produce correct spellings by using a combination of strategies: their phonic knowledge, awareness of common letter combinations, memory of particular words and understanding of word structure.

An understanding of these stages of progression is useful for a number of reasons. It highlights that children's mistakes in spelling are not random but creative, systematic and logical. It also emphasizes the importance of children's phonic knowledge in the early stages (Goswami *et al.*, 1990; Bearne, 2002) as well as the need to develop alternative strategies for learning spelling as they reach the transitional stage.

# Strategies for learning spelling

Spelling can be learned using the following strategies:

- *Auditory* – focusing on sounds, for example splitting the word into syllables and saying the word as it is spelt.
- *Visual* – focusing on the appearance of the word, including looking carefully at the shape, length and image of the word.
- *Linguistic* – focusing on aspects of language, for instance comparing the word to other similar words, according to its root, identifying common affixes, and so on.
- *Kinaesthetic* – focusing on the physical movement of the hand to form the letters.

Research by Peters (1985) suggests that success in spelling generally depends on a combination of strategies. Learners often rely on one or more of these strategies more heavily than others. Given that every classroom includes children with different learning styles, it is therefore important to promote a wide range of approaches to learning spelling so that individuals are able to develop the combination of strategies most suited to them.

The following section presents a range of activities to promote the use of all of these strategies by children of all ages.

## Auditory strategies

As discussed earlier, through mark making children begin to recognize that writing represents language. Their early writing involves imitating the shapes they have seen in print around them. As discussed in Chapter 4, the development of graphophonic knowledge depends upon phonemic awareness (the ability to recognize sounds). Games and activities discussed in Chapter 4 are therefore relevant to the teaching of spelling in the early stages.

Activities that encourage children to segment words into phonemes are useful in preparation for spelling. This may involve the use of a puppet that needs to sound out or hear words as individual phonemes. Developing awareness of onset and rime and analogy (discussed in Chapter 4) is also important. Focusing on common patterns of letters (for example *h-ot*, *p-ot*, *l-ot*) can be used to encourage children to use this knowledge to spell a new word (such as *dot*). This use of analogy is a useful strategy for children at all levels because it encourages them to be systematic and self-reliant in tackling spelling.

Even at the later stages of spelling some children continue to find auditory learning useful. It can be helpful to draw attention to the link between the letters and the sounds of the word, by saying a word as it is written. A familiar example of this is to learn the spelling of 'Wednesday' as 'Wed - nes - day', emphasizing the frequently overlooked letters 'd' and 'e'.

Auditory learning can also be encouraged by spelling out a word by the letter names, drawing attention to the letters to be remembered, for example friend: 'f' 'r' 'I' 'e' 'n' 'd' or saying the letters in a rhythm, for instance useful: U-S . . . E-F . . . U-L.

Mnemonics can also be useful for common and challenging words. These are created by making a phrase, using words taking their initial letters from the spelling to be memorized. A popular example is '*B*ig *e*lephants *a*ren't *u*gly . . . they're beautiful', which helps children to remember the tricky beginning of the word *beautiful* or *they*: *t*eddies *h*ave *e*ars – *y*es! Children often enjoy creating their own mnemonics for words that continually cause them problems.

## Visual strategies

In the early years, visual discrimination can be developed through activities involving children in identifying similarities and differences in patterns and shapes, for example 'Snap', 'Odd one out', 'Spot the difference', and so on. Young children can also be encouraged to notice length and shapes of familiar words, height of letters and distinctive patterns.

At all ages, children can be encouraged to identify patterns created by letters and distinctive features of words which will help them to be recalled in the future. 'Snap shot' spelling – visualizing an individual word with eyes closed, can assist successful recall. The activity encourages children to focus on retaining the image of the word.

The use of visual strategies becomes increasingly important after a child reaches the transitional stage of development and has grasped that many words are not spelt phonetically. Visual memory can help them to retain letter patterns. Many adults also rely on the appearance of words and whether it 'looks right' to check their spelling. An emphasis on visual memory enables children to develop this ability.

Children can also be challenged to find smaller whole words within longer words. This activity reinforces memory of the spelling of the longer word: for example they – the; he; information – in; for; form; at; mat; formation and so on.

## Linguistic strategies

An interest in words, their meanings, uses, composition and origin is an asset in learning to spell and can be promoted as part of a general classroom ethos in which language is seen as interesting to explore.

An understanding of morphology, the way in which words are made up of smaller linguistic units, is particularly useful. The addition of these units at the beginning of the word, as a prefix, or at the end, as a suffix, change the meaning of the word. Examples include creating:

an opposite, for example agree – *dis*agree; happy – *un*happy.
a noun from a verb, for example agree – agree*ment*; act – act*ion*
an adverb from an adjective, for example careful – careful*ly*

Such understanding is helpful in spelling. For example, the awareness that the past tense is often conveyed by the use of '-ed' (as in 'walked', 'happened' or 'asked') is useful in predicting the spelling of other verbs with the same ending. Similarly, an understanding of the use of the prefix '*un-*' helps to reinforce that the word '*un*necessary' contains two of the letter n, whilst '*un*usual' has only one. Creating class lists of words with the common features (for example ending in '-ful' or '-ly' or beginning with 'un-') can draw attention to the focus feature.

### Activities for developing children's knowledge of spelling conventions

- investigating common patterns, for example:
  - sort the following list into groups and find a way to explain how to create plurals: toys, lorries, boys, seats, chairs, lawyers, worries, hats, fairies
  - make a list of as many words as you can that have 'c' in them. Find a way to explain when 'c' should be read as a soft sound and when it should be read as a hard sound;
- breaking compound words into their components, for example break/fast; class/room; under/ground; foot/ball, and so on;
- creating new compound words for inventions or alternatives for existing terms, such as cheekrest (hand) or timegiver (watch);
- developing awareness of roots of words in different languages, for example 'aqua' meaning 'water' (Greek) in 'aquatic', 'aquarium', and so on;
- collecting words with the same prefix, for example 'tele' as in telepathy, telephone, telegram, and so on, and suggesting possible meanings for it;
- building the longest possible word by adding a prefix or suffix at a time to the root, for example cover – discover – rediscover – rediscovery;
- playing 'Shannon's Game'. This is similar to 'Hangman' but children guess a specific letter

at a time, beginning with the first letter of the word. This is useful in encouraging children to use their knowledge of common spelling patterns. For example, if the word is THR _ _ _ _ , what possibilities are there for the fourth letter?

- discussing possible ways of spelling invented or obscure words.

### Kinaesthetic strategies

Reinforcement of the sense of movement required to write a word helps many children to learn spellings. Commonly needed words can be practised through miming the action of writing and then written in different sizes using a wide variety of implements and media, for example paint, chalk, in sand, on the ground, and so on. This draws attention to links in teaching spelling and handwriting, and handwriting practice can be used to practise common combinations of letters within familiar words. This has been the subject of increasing attention, particularly in relation to cursive (joined) writing. Ease in forming common joins in handwriting reinforces common spelling patterns (Cripps *et al.*, 1993). In some schools this has resulted in the introduction of cursive handwriting from the Foundation Stage.

## Learning spelling

The words most appropriate for children to learn are those which they use but cannot spell. Learning a small number of related words on a regular basis is more effective than long lists of unrelated words. Individualized lists are particularly appropriate (Daws *et al.*, 1997). The words for each child can be selected from their written work by the teacher or the child and kept in a spelling log or journal. Given that groups of children may have similar needs, group lists of spellings can be more efficient. Children may be given small collections of words to learn at home, but it is important to explain to parents and carers how words are chosen and learned.

The learning of spelling is often monitored by spelling tests, when children write down the words they have been given to learn. This is a stressful experience for many children. Such emphasis on skill in spelling can cause children to lose confidence and interest in writing. In addition, success in recalling spellings is no guarantee that they will be remembered in future writing. An effective alternative is a routine suggested by Peters and Cripps (1980) and widely promoted, commonly known as 'Look, Cover, Write, Check'. In order to make explicit each step of the routine we have presented it in six steps:

| | |
|---|---|
| *Look*: | look at the word, identify any noteworthy visual features. |
| *Study*: | consider any linguistic features, write the word out, underline any parts that seem problematic, spell or sound the word. |
| *Cover*: | cover the word up. |
| *Remember*: | recall the word in your mind. |
| *Write*: | write the word. |
| *Check*: | check if you have spelt it correctly. |

Repeat if necessary.

Setting aside regular brief slots for children to work on their spellings in this way can promote progress in spelling whilst avoiding anxiety. Modelling the process is important in drawing attention to the significance of each step and needs to be supported by activities that develop all children's awareness of the variety of strategies discussed earlier.

## Supporting children's spelling during the writing process

When children are engaged in the composing stages of the writing process, as discussed earlier, their attention needs to be focused on the content and structure of the text. If they feel that they need to ensure that their spelling is correct, the flow of ideas and creativity in the use of vocabulary are likely to be restricted. It is therefore useful to encourage children to 'have a go', rather than stopping to puzzle about a spelling. By writing a few letters and indicating the word with a wavy line, they can show that they need to return to it at a later stage.

Displaying commonly used words or vocabulary related to a particular topic is a useful way of supporting children in their writing. Their high visibility in the classroom provides a focus for discussion and familiarity may encourage visual recall. In the early years, laminated mats can be used to provide groups of children with easy access to high-frequency words. Children can also be encouraged to record common words that they find difficult to remember in spelling logs or journals.

This section has drawn attention to different learning strategies and how they can be promoted. In every classroom it is important to talk about spelling and make all the strategies available and familiar, encouraging children to reflect on and discuss their use. Children's belief in their ability to spell contributes to their success (Peters, 1985; Daws *et al.*, 1997). Such confidence enables them to be prepared to draw upon previous knowledge and experiment with the spelling of unfamiliar words. Children will only be willing and able to do this if they are encouraged to do so, if they expect they may be successful and if they are not inhibited by fears of making mistakes.

In conclusion, successful teaching of spelling requires the following:

- varied and interesting activities which promote an interest in language, discussion and experimentation;
- a focus on familiar vocabulary;
- an understanding that the need for accuracy in spelling depends upon the purpose and audience for writing;
- praise for experimentation with spelling as well as accuracy.

# Handwriting

As with other aspects of transcription, concern with quality of handwriting will depend upon the type of text and its intended audience and purpose. In a similar way, children need to be aware that they must write legibly in order to communicate. They also need to appreciate that others may make superficial judgements of the quality of their writing based on its presentation. Developing children's skills in handwriting is therefore important. The ability to write in a relaxed, comfortable manner enables children to devote attention to their composition and they will be more likely to be enthusiastic about writing.

On the basis of extensive research into the development and teaching of handwriting, Sassoon (1983) identifies three main features of successful handwriting: comfort, legibility and individual style.

In developing these aspects of children's handwriting it is therefore important to promote:

- correct posture, position of paper and pencil grip;
- the ability to form or/and join letters in specific ways;
- opportunities to develop individual style.

## Encouraging correct posture, position of paper and pencil grip

In encouraging children to feel comfortable and relaxed when writing it is important to ensure that:

- the chair and table are appropriate in height for the child;
- the child is not slouching over the table;
- there is sufficient light;
- paper is positioned to the right of the centre of the child's body in the case of right-handed children and to the left and slightly slanted for those who are left-handed;
- the pencil is held between the thumb and index finger in a firm but relaxed grip;
- children who are left-handed are seated to the left of right-handed children.

## Developing the ability to form or/and join letters in specific ways

In the early years, certain activities that do not directly involve writing help to develop the fine motor skills and visual sensitivity required for handwriting. Examples include finger rhymes, sorting objects and jigsaws. The provision of a wide range of writing implements and opportunities for writing will encourage children to experiment with and develop their mark making. Once conventional letter shapes begin to appear regularly in children's emergent writing, they are ready to be shown how to form letters. This involves copying a letter, following the letter formation by beginning the letter at the given 'entry point' and leaving at the 'exit point'. The selection of the letter to practise may come from the child's writing or from their name, so that it is familiar and meaningful to the child.

In teaching handwriting it is important to provide:

- specific patterns to copy which encourage pencil control and familiarity with strokes and direction of movement needed in the formation of letters;
- demonstration and explanation of the correct formation, which is imitated by the children;

- opportunities to copy, trace and practise the formation of letters in a variety of media, for example thick pen, chalk, sand and so on;
- praise for children's attempts to form letters correctly.

The specific style of handwriting and later sequence for teaching will depend upon the policy of the individual school. Many schools begin with the introduction of print.

Sassoon (1985: 34) divides the letters into the following 'stroke-related families' according to their common entry point and flow of movement.

- **itluyj** begin with a downward vertical line followed by an anti-clockwise arch
- **nmrh bpk** begin with a downward vertical line followed by a clockwise arch
- **cadgqoe** anti-clockwise movement beginning with the letter 'c'
- **sf vwxz** letters beginning with diagonal strokes from right to left and 's' and 'f'

Different models of handwriting may lead to differences in some of the letters included in the groups above. However, teaching the letters according to similarities in their formation reinforces the common movement.

Alignment of letters is also important in ensuring legibility. Children need to understand that:

- letters should be positioned on the line;
- ascenders should be the same height, on a level with capital letters;
- descenders should be the same length;
- small letters should also all be the same size;
- 't' is the only letter which reaches half way between small letters and tall letters;
- writing letters vertically enhances legibility.

Many schools introduce children to cursive (joined) handwriting after they have established the ability to write in print, introducing specific ways to join letters in a sequence dictated by the model of handwriting in use. A contrasting approach introduces children to cursive writing from the earliest stages. Cripps *et al.* (1993) point out that this avoids the difficulties of relearning established habits as a result of the change from print to cursive writing. They also argue that learning to join letters from the early years reinforces the use of common spelling patterns.

# Opportunities to develop individual style

Many children gain considerable satisfaction from spending time on their handwriting when they know that the product will be seen by others. They also enjoy experimenting with their handwriting and such opportunities need to be available if they are to develop a personal and comfortable style. Children are most likely to take care over their handwriting and presentation:

- when writing for real audiences;
- with a sense of purpose;
- after drafting and editing their own writing.

# Teaching writing

Earlier sections of this chapter have explored aspects of writing and have suggested activities that may be useful for engaging children in the writing process and developing transcription skills. This final section examines ways in which such activities can be used within the classroom.

## Shared writing

Shared writing often takes place as a whole-class session, but may also be used as a group activity. The teacher models the skills and strategies that are used in writing, whilst encouraging as much interaction as possible from the class or group. The writing is usually scribed on a large piece of paper, screen or whiteboard. Shared writing may focus on any aspect of the writing process (planning, drafting, composing, and so on). Over several days, shared writing may be used to model the different stages of producing a piece of writing.

The National Literacy Strategy (2001: 116) differentiates between three types of shared writing that provide different levels of support for children.

### Teacher demonstration

The teacher writes in front of the children and models the strategies used by a writer in composing a text, for example rehearsing sentences orally before writing, re-reading and altering the text. 'Thinking aloud' while writing enables the children to appreciate that writing involves making choices and considering the effect of the text upon the reader.

### Teacher scribing

The teacher writes, but using ideas and suggestions provided by the children. The teacher encourages the children to compose and helps them reflect on their composition.

### Supported composition

The children are given short pieces of writing (perhaps two or three sentences) to compose within the whole-class session. Often this is done in pairs, using mini-whiteboards or clipboards. The teacher can intervene and support individuals and make quick assessments about whether or not the children have grasped the objective that is being taught. Children are encouraged to share and evaluate what they write.

The following scenarios illustrate these different approaches. Note how the roles of the teacher and children vary:

### Reception (teacher scribing)

The children have been on a trip to a local city farm. A teacher sits down with a small group to word process some captions for the digital photographs they took. These will then be printed off for each child and made into a simple book for them to take home and share with their family. The teacher asks the children what should be written on the captions. She scribes their ideas.

### Year 2 (teacher demonstration)

A year 2 teacher wants to introduce her class to the idea of making notes. She asks the teaching assistant to read some information about the Fire of London. After each paragraph, the teaching assistant stops and the teacher models making notes to summarize the key points. She talks through the process as she does so: 'I think I'll use bullet points so that I can see the points I've written clearly . . . so what was the most important point there? How can I write that briefly? Which words do I need to write and which could I leave out? Actually I think I could use an arrow here to show . . .'

### Year 5/6 (supported composition)

The children have been investigating lifecycles. Each group has created a short animation of the lifecycle of a chosen animal, which will be used in a multimedia text to be published on the school Web site. They are now writing a passage to complement the animation and provide further detail. Following teacher demonstration and teacher scribing of explanation writing, the children are now working in pairs to write the opening sentence of their passage.

Evidently authorship varies between these different types of shared writing. In *teacher demonstration*, the teacher produces her own piece of writing. She is the author and the children observe her at work. In *teacher scribing*, authorship is shared, whereas *supported composition* allows the children themselves to write independently in a supportive context. By using a combination of these approaches, differing levels of support and guidance are provided. Decisions about which approach to use will be influenced by the degree of experience and confidence of the children in relation to the chosen focus.

## Guided writing

Like guided reading, guided writing involves teaching a small group of children who have similar needs. Again the learning objectives are closely matched to the needs of the children in the group. The activity may focus on any stage of the writing process. Generally, guided writing sessions are used to help children to apply what has been taught in their shared sessions within their independent writing, for example using principles for planning discussed during shared sessions. Alternatively the session may focus on an aspect of writing with which children in the group have had difficulties. For example, the teacher might notice that a particular group of children do not apply their knowledge of spelling strategies when writing independently and therefore work with them to reinforce this within the context of producing a piece of writing. Guided writing may also be used to extend the skills of more able writers. It is important to plan for guided writing sessions and consider how best to support the children in meeting the objective. This involves taking an active role in prompting children to think for themselves about how to tackle their task.

# Independent writing

Independent writing requires children to work without the help of the teacher. Opportunities are provided for children to use and apply skills learned in shared and guided sessions. Children are most likely to work well independently when tasks are motivating, relevant and achievable. (See Chapter 9 for discussion of differentiation.) A wide number of commercially produced schemes provide motivating contexts for real writing. However, there are others that suggest that decontextualized exercises are used to practise aspects of writing, for example writing in the past tense. These activities may have limited value in consolidating skills learnt, successful completion may have little impact on children's independent writing. Opportunities to use and apply skills when writing for real purposes and audiences are far more likely to motivate children to engage with activities and draw on their previous learning.

# Collaborative writing

Collaborative writing involves children working together on one piece of writing without the help of the teacher. They may decide to divide up parts of the writing task, or they may work together on a large piece of paper or a computer screen. An example of this involves a small group of children working together to present what they have learnt about magnetism in the form of a chart or diagram. Much of their learning will come about through discussing what to include and why. Clearly children who are unfamiliar with this approach will need to spend time discussing and evaluating their own skills in working together.

# Paired writing

Children may be paired for writing in the same way that they are paired for reading. Often, older children work with their younger peers to produce a piece of collaborative writing. Roles may be clearly allocated; for example the older children may scribe the ideas whilst the younger child provides illustrations. Alternatively each partner may scribe different parts of a text.

# Summary

This chapter has examined the writing process, the development of skills in composition and transcription and aspects of classroom organization. It has drawn attention to the importance of providing:

- meaningful contexts, real audiences and purposes for writing;
- opportunities to engage in the writing process;
- a variety of means to stimulate interest in writing;
- support in the planning stages including encouragement to talk and draw;
- explicit modelling of aspects of writing;
- opportunities for shared, guided, collaborative and independent writing.

The development of children's skills in transcription is clearly important. As children gain confidence and competence in these skills, they are freer to focus on composition and are also able to experiment with punctuation and layout and discover their impact on the text. They will also appreciate the changes in the role and conventions of spelling and punctuation resulting from developments in electronic communication as discussed in Chapter 1.

When teaching skills in transcription it is important to encourage:

- awareness of the value of such skills for effective communication;
- understanding that the need for a high standard of presentation and accuracy depends upon the purpose, audience and form of text;
- attention to be devoted to these aspects at the editing stage of writing;
- analysis of features of transcription in authentic texts;
- meaningful contexts for the application of learning.

# Reflective questions

1. Select an age range and a type of narrative text. Plan a series of activities that will take children through the writing process in order to produce their own text of this type for an audience.

2. 'My class won't want to be bothered with going through such a long procedure!' was a remark made by a teacher when discussing the writing process. What are your views on this? What strategies would you suggest she uses in order to engage and sustain children's interest?

3. A parent comments on a piece of written work you have marked, pointing out that you have not corrected some of the child's spelling mistakes. How would you explain this?

## FURTHER READING

Browne, A. (2001) *Writing at Key Stage 1 and Before*. Cheltenham: Stanley Thornes.

Provides useful guidance on teaching writing in the early years.

Evans, J. (ed.) (2001) *The Writing Classroom: Aspects of Writing and the Primary Child*. London: David Fulton Publishers.

An interesting collection of essays on various aspects of writing.

Graham, J. and Kelly, A. (eds) (1998) *Writing Under Control: Teaching Writing in the Primary School*. London: David Fulton Publishers.

Chapters cover the history of the teaching of writing, a useful explanation of the writing process, supporting composition and the teaching of transcription skills.

## REFERENCES

Barrs, M. and Cork, V. (2001) *The Reader in the Writer: The Link Between the Study of Literature and Writing Development at Key Stage 2*. London: Centre for Primary Education.

Bearne, E. (1998) *Making Progress in English*. London: Routledge.

Bearne, E. (2002) *Making Progress in Writing*. London : Routledge Falmer.

Browne, A. (1993) *Helping Children to Write*. London: Paul Chapman Publishing.

Browne, A. (2001) *Writing at Key Stage 1 and Before*. Cheltenham: Stanley Thornes.

Cripps, C. and Peters, M. (1993) *Collins Catchwords Teacher's Guide*. London: Collins.

Daws, P. with Smith, J. and Wilkinson, S. (1997) 'Factors associated with high standards of spelling in years R–4', *English in Education*, 31(1), 36–47.

Department for Education and Employment (DfEE) (1998) *National Literacy Strategy Framework for Teaching*. London: HMSO.

Department for Education and Employment (DfEE) (2000) *Grammar for Writing*. London: HMSO.

Gentry, J. (1981) 'An analysis of developmental spelling in GNYS AT WRK', *Reading Teacher*, 36, 192–200.

Goswami, U. and Bryant, P. (1990) *Phonological Skills and Learning to Read*. Hove: Lawrence Erlbaum.

Graves, D. H. (1983) *Writing: Teachers and Children at Work*. Exeter: Heinemann.

Hall, N. (1987) *The Emergence of Literacy*. London: Hodder & Stoughton.

Hall, N. (1999) 'Young people's use of graphic punctuation', *Language and Education*, 13(3), 178–93.

Hall, N. (2001) 'Developing understanding of punctuation with young writers and readers', in Evans, J. (ed.) *The Writing Classroom: Aspects of Writing and the Primary Child*. London: David Fulton Publishers.

Hall, N. and Robinson, A (1996) *Learning about Punctuation*. Portsmouth NH: Heinemann.

Hornsby, D. and Wing Jan, L. (2001) 'Writing as a response to literature', in Evans, J. (ed.) *The Writing Classroom: Aspects of Writing and the Primary Child*. London: David Fulton Publishers.

Kelly, A. (1998) 'Transcription: Spelling, punctuation and handwriting', in Graham, J. and Kelly, A. (eds) *Writing Under Control: Teaching Writing in the Primary School*. London: David Fulton Publishers.

Kress, G. (1994) *Learning to Write*. Second Edition. London: Routledge.

Kress, G. (1997) *Before Writing: Rethinking the Paths to Literacy*. London: Routledge.

Lewis, M. (1999) 'Developing children's narrative writing using story structures', in Goodwin, P. (ed.) *The Literate Classroom*. London: David Fulton Publishers.

National Literacy Strategy (NLS) (2001) *Shared Writing on School Placement: Key Stage 1 and Key Stage 2*. London: DfEE.

Peters, M. (1985) *Spelling: Taught or Caught?: A New Look*. London: Routledge & Kegan Paul.

Peters, M. and Cripps, C. (1980) *Catchwords: Ideas for Teaching Spelling*. London: Harcourt Brace Jovanovich.

Rosen, M. (1989) *Did I Hear you Write*? London: Deutsch.

Sassoon, R. (1985) *The Practical Guide to Children's Handwriting*. London: Stanley Thornes.

Smith, F. (1982) *Writing and the Writer*. London: Heinemann.

Vygotsky, L. S. (1962) *Thought and Language*. Cambridge MA: Harvard University Press.

Waugh, D. (1998) 'Practical approaches to teaching punctuation in the primary school', *Reading*, 32(2), 14–17.

Wells, G. (1985) *The Meaning Makers*. London: Hodder & Stoughton.

Wyse, D. and Jones, R. (2001) *Teaching English, Language and Literacy*. London: Routledge Falmer.

## CHILDREN'S LITERATURE

Browne, E. (1995) *Handa's Surprise*. London: Walker.

Burningham, J. (1970) *Mr Gumpy's Outing*. London: Cape.

Campbell, R. (1984) *Dear Zoo*. London: Puffin.

Carle, E. (1970) *The Very Hungry Caterpillar*. London: Hamish Hamilton.

Fine, A. (1990) *Bill's New Frock*. London: Mammoth.

French, F. (1987) *Snow White in New York*. Oxford: Oxford University Press.

Hughes, T. (1968) *The Iron Man*. London: Faber.

Medearis, A. (1995) *Too Much Talk*. London: Walker.

Rosen, M. (1989) *We're Going on a Bear Hunt*. London: Walker.

Scieszka, J. (1991) *The True Story of the 3 Little Pigs!* Harmondsworth: Puffin.

Tolstoy, A. (1968) *The Great Big Enormous Turnip*. London: Heinemann.

Tomlinson, T. (1997) *Meet Me by the Steelmen*. London: Walker.

Watanabe, S. (1979) *Hallo! How Are You?* London: Bodley Head.

# 6

# Language and Literacy across the Curriculum

In this chapter we focus on the relationship between English and the rest of the curriculum. We highlight the crucial role of speaking and listening, reading and writing in learning. We explore the nature of non-fiction texts and then move on to consider the process of reading and writing for information. The chapter demonstrates that talk, reading and writing have important contributions throughout the processes of information retrieval and production.

## Locating and making sense of information in everyday life

Chapter 4 drew attention to the fact that reading is often motivated by a sense of purpose, a need to gain information. As discussed, the kinds of texts used and the ways in which we read vary according to our needs and the nature of information required. Reading for information may involve scanning a television guide to check the time of a programme, skimming a Web site to check whether it offers products of interest, or reading in detail instructions for finding a location. The act of reading differs according to the purpose; we may read in depth, or skim to gain the gist of a text or scan for a specific piece of information.

In reading for information, speaking and listening and writing are also important. We may discuss with others what information is needed, where it may be found or to clarify understanding, and write notes of details we need to recall. Reading for information is rarely an isolated action; it often leads to further activity, the fulfilment of the purpose that precipitated the search for information. Each mode of language may be used in several different ways to support the process of locating and making sense of information. Through talk, questions are posed and comparisons, hypotheses, judgements and requests are made. Writing may be used to recall information in brief hastily written notes, or to provide a more formal record for another audience. Close, critical reading, skimming and scanning may all be involved.

Reading for information also offers opportunities for learning. A desire to explore a topic, for example an interest in a particular type of music, may involve an individual in watching television programmes and videos, lengthy searches on the Web and reading books and reviews over many years. The world today offers increasing sources of information and tremendous opportunities to satisfy personal interests and curiosity. This widespread access to information provides great potential for independent learning but also underlines the need for critical reading. It is essential that such access to information does not lead to passive acceptance of what is read. On the contrary it is important that texts are recognized for what they are: the products of writers who select their content according to their own interests, experiences and purposes.

This discussion highlights that reading for information in daily life is:

- motivated by a clear sense of purpose or personal interest;
- often supported by talk and writing;
- involves a wide range of texts and types of reading;
- supported by the ability to be critical.

Clearly, such factors have significance for the teaching of reading for information. Children need to be prepared to meet a wide range of texts, to locate, process and use information for a variety of purposes. They need to be aware of different ways of reading and have the ability to evaluate what they read. They should also be aware of the exciting and extensive opportunities to increase their knowledge of topics that interest or intrigue them.

# Reading for information

Significantly, as discussed in Chapter 4, children's earliest experiences of print include a wide range of non-fiction texts (Hall, 1987), including signs, notices and adverts in the street, magazines, reference papers and texts on the computer in the home. They will also be aware of how these are used. As children gain confidence and skills in their reading, it is likely that they will use the opportunities provided in and beyond the home for their own purposes, for example to pursue their own interests or explore subjects introduced in school (Burnett and Myers, 2002; Moss, 2000).

In developing children's ability to read non-fiction texts, it is clearly important to be aware of their experiences outside the classroom and the models of information retrieval in everyday life. However, reading non-fiction texts has a particular significance within the education system. As children move through and beyond the primary years, learning will increasingly rely on their ability to access information from texts. The ability to read for information is therefore important in supporting progress across the curriculum (Webster *et al.*, 1996).

In the past, the teaching of reading often focused on establishing children's skills in reading and writing through story. It was assumed that, as children became more fluent readers, they would be able to transfer their skills to non-fiction texts.

Such an approach tends to ignore key differences between fiction and non-fiction texts and the differences in ways of reading such texts. The following section therefore considers the nature of non-fiction texts and ways in which they are read, before moving on to consider the development of children's skills and understanding in reading for information.

## Non-fiction texts

The terms 'fiction' and 'non-fiction' can be misleading in appearing to present contrasting categories, distinguished by whether or not they present 'facts' and 'truth'. Such distinctions are not so simple. Although non-fiction purports to provide information, its validity cannot be assumed. Equally, in writing fiction, authors inevitably draw upon their experience, the reality they know and may also include actual events, settings or characters. Fiction can therefore sometimes provide opportunities for learning, for example offering an insight into a historical period or geographical setting. Merchant *et al.* (2001: 7) suggest that the key distinction between fiction and non-fiction lies in their purpose: 'Non fiction aims to instruct us, to provide facts or information about the real world.' As readers of non-fiction we expect the text to inform, although we have a responsibility to question its reliability. In contrast, fiction aims to entertain. As readers of fiction we accept imaginary characters and events even if, as in the case of historical fiction, these may be based on real events or characters.

Narrative, the telling of a sequence of events, is a feature of most fiction texts, for example stories, novels, plays and ballads, and is also used in some forms of non-fiction, for example historical accounts, newspaper reports of events, biographies and autobiographies. Such texts are chronological, organized around a sequence of time, as discussed in Chapter 4. However, non-fiction also includes a wide range of texts that are not chronological, for example Web sites, leaflets, books about science and geography, explanations of cause and effect and how systems work. These incorporate a wide range of illustrations: pictures, diagrams, tables, maps, photographs and so on, to supplement or support the information provided in the written text. Web sites and CD-ROMs also often offer moving images and sound. As such texts are not organized around a sequence of time, they do not have to be read from beginning to end. Readers have an active role to play in exploring and making sense of the information. Retrieval devices, such as an index, contents pages and section headings, enable readers to select the appropriate part of the text to find the information required. This non-linear approach to reading is even more apparent when using the Internet, as links and hyperlinks allow the reader to move around a Web site and into other sites at the click of a mouse. This experience is very different from that of reading fiction, where the chronological organization demands that the text is read from beginning to end

A further difference between these texts relates to the use of language. When reading fiction, children often meet familiar use of language, written in an informal, conversational style. In contrast, as highlighted by Mallett (1992), non-fiction is frequently presented more formally, using longer and more complex sentences. Arnold (1992) points out that texts written by experts of the subject matter can fail to accommodate children's linguistic and conceptual development and consequently the information offered is inaccessible to them. In order to overcome such problems, texts for children are sometimes written by non-specialists, who use more familiar language. However, by avoiding specialist terminology, they may produce simplistic texts lacking in inspiration or challenge, or overlook key concepts that are necessary for understanding (Neate, 1992). The language and terminology associated with a subject are crucial aspects of the subject itself. The knowledge of a scientific process depends upon the understanding of the relevant vocabulary. For example, understanding the meaning of words like 'cycle' in a scientific sense is crucial to the understanding of the process of change resulting in the transformation of frogspawn to tadpoles, to frogs that lay spawn.

Non-fiction can offer children a range of exciting opportunities for satisfying curiosity, extending their interests and independent learning. However, children's difficulties with accessing information have been acknowledged for some time (Lunzer *et al.*, 1979, 1984). Children may find such reading challenging as a result of aspects of its nature and use. Such features include:

- varied organization, format and presentation;
- dependence on understanding of a diverse range of illustrations, photographs, tables, maps, diagrams and so on to supplement information carried by the written text;
- unfamiliar concepts and content;
- subject-related use of vocabulary and use of language;
- dependence on the use of retrieval devices.

# Teaching reading for information

Children of all ages need opportunities and encouragement to explore, use and enjoy non-fiction and to gain understanding of its potential to answer their questions, satisfy curiosity and provide endless scope for independent learning. Such experience can be provided through:

- regular reading aloud of non-fiction – including a range of text types;
- encouragement to read non-fiction books during independent reading time;
- opportunities to share and discuss a wide range of non-fiction texts in paired and group reading;
- using non-fiction as a focus for guided and shared reading;
- providing and recommending non-fiction texts relevant to the children's interests and hobbies.

Reading for information is appropriate for all ages irrespective of levels of fluency and experience in reading. The increasing use of visual text in the form of photographs, pictures, diagrams, and so on, offers a valuable source of information. Support from an adult or a more fluent peer can provide the least confident readers with access to written text. Modelling by the teacher is also useful in demonstrating the use of retrieval devices and ways of reading: skimming, scanning and close reading.

Teaching has sometimes focused on the use of retrieval devices or approaches to reading non-fiction without providing a purpose or context for such activities. As a result, children often fail to transfer these skills to genuine research or appreciate their relevance or value. More successful approaches involve using the wider curriculum to provide meaningful opportunities for enquiry and the development of skills in information retrieval. Through various subjects, children of all ages can gain experience of using a range of texts and developing their knowledge, skills and understanding in reading for information. Rather than practising such skills in isolation, they can develop and use them in the context of finding answers to questions that are meaningful and relevant to them and contribute to their learning.

## The learning process

An in-depth discussion of the nature of learning is beyond the scope of this chapter. However, it is useful to highlight some key points that have arisen from constructivist theories of learning. One of the most important insights is that learning is a process of interaction between new knowledge and what is already known. In order to make sense of new information, we relate it to our prior knowledge. Constructivist theories regard knowledge as patterns or schemas of thought stored in our minds. New information may be absorbed or assimilated within existing schemas. On the other hand, at times it may challenge the existing understanding and cause schemas to alter (Nutbrown, 1999). Learning therefore involves changes in understanding. As Henre *et al.* (2000: 3) point out: 'Learning is about understanding things differently – not just about remembering more information'. Consequently, effective teaching requires 'mediation' (Webster *et al.*, 1996: 28), helping children to construct such new understanding by supporting them in making sense of their experiences.

As mentioned in Chapter 3, talk plays an invaluable role in the learning process. It offers the possibility to explore ideas, to gain insights into one's own opinions, and it allows for tentativeness and hypothesis. Talk also provides insight into others' opinions. Through collaboration, children develop a shared understanding which is likely to be at a higher level than would be possible independently (Vygotsky, 1962).

## Supporting children's research

Various frameworks have been created to show how children can be supported in their research and learning. They present information retrieval as a process involving different types of activities, which encourage collaborative learning. These activities are designed to motivate and support children in building on their existing knowledge, finding and making sense of information. A particularly influential example is the EXIT (extending interactions with non-fiction texts) model created by Wray *et al.* (1997), which outlines a detailed process for engaging children's interest in research and supporting them through locating and processing information to a final stage of presentation of findings to an audience. Their term 'interactions' is important, because it draws attention to the active role of readers in bringing and applying their own knowledge, experience and understanding to making sense of a text.

The framework presented below draws from the EXIT model and a similar sequence suggested by Mallett (1992). Like the EXIT model, it incorporates the presentation of findings, as children are motivated by a sense of a purpose and audience for their research. The process is not to be seen as a linear series of steps. Stages may occur in a different order or take place simultaneously. In addition, as Riley and Reedy (2000: 145) point out, 'It may be the discovery of a new piece of information that makes us reflect on our previous knowledge and thus raise questions that need to be answered.'

## A framework for supporting children's research

- **Exploring previous knowledge;**
- **gaining new experiences;**
- **asking questions and deciding what information is needed;**
- **finding information;**
- **interaction with texts;**
- **recording information;**
- **presentation of information.**

It is not assumed that children's research will always include every stage of the process presented. Sometimes it involves a more focused activity. However, what is crucial is that, as Mallet (1999) points out, children's curiosity is excited. If learning is to take place, children need to be motivated to make sense of information, to relate it to existing knowledge and to create new levels of understanding. Arnold (1992: 133) comments:

> We learn best when our heart and head are engaged. It is important to be able to use reading as a knowledge resource, but for most children (as well as for me most of the time) reading for learning is primarily a means of triggering and satisfying curiosity, of helping to make sense of a constantly changing non-factual world.

Her words serve to emphasize that development of skills in information retrieval must take place in a context that is meaningful to children. It is important to develop a classroom community in which the exploration of questions is shared and valued as a means for learning.

The scenarios below illustrate this model in practice in different settings. Notice how children's existing understanding is used as a starting point for further learning and how their interest is engaged. Consider the ways in which the search for information is structured and focused.

> A **nursery** group has been playing outside. A group of children is intrigued by a caterpillar they have found in the grass. As they watch it, they discuss its features and

ask questions about where it lives and what it eats. The teacher finds a relevant book and models the process of finding answers to these questions. Later, when all the children are sitting inside, he asks members of the group to tell the rest of the class about what they have found out.

Minibeasts are the topic for this **year 2** class. The class has already visited a local natural history museum and has searched for minibeasts in the local environment. The teacher has now introduced some categories of minibeasts: woodlice, spiders, worms and snails. The children are keen to know more about each of the examples. The teacher divides the class into groups and each group is given a type of minibeast to research. As a class, they draw up a chart for each group to complete (Table 6.1). This focuses children's attention on the information required and makes limited demands on writing. In the plenary each group reports on their findings.

**Table 6.1. Minibeast chart**

| | |
|---|---|
| Type of minibeast: | |
| What do they look like? | |
| Where do you find them? | |
| What do they eat? | |
| Do they have legs? How many? | |
| Do they have wings? | |
| Other interesting information: | |

The **year 3** class is involved in a topic on the Tudors and is to visit a local Tudor house. Before the trip, the children draw pictures to show how they anticipate the house will look and create a list of questions they hope to answer. During the visit they find answers to these questions through observation, listening to a guide and reading labels and display boards. They also take digital photos. After they return, the class is asked to produce a guide on Tudor life for other children visiting the house. They discuss different aspects of life, including food, travel and clothing, and groups of children explore a different topic through CD-ROMS, books, artefacts and fact sheets provided by the local library. Using desktop publishing and incorporating their photos, each group then prepares a section of the leaflet.

A speaker from Friends of the Earth has visited a **year 5** class to talk about conservation. After the talk, the children reflect on what they have learned and create a concept map (a collection of topics relevant to the main subject, in which related issues are linked). They annotate this with questions that they still want answering. They then watch a video on the subject but feel that it does not answer all of their questions. They also find its presentation very formal and inaccessible. The teacher suggests that they could create an alternative video on the same subject to be shown to the rest of the school. The children are excited by this prospect and discuss additional information which is needed. A list is created to identify key topics for research. The search for information involves children sending emails and letters to local and national organizations, as well as finding information from key Internet sites, CD-ROMs, books and leaflets.

All these scenarios show children engaged in reading for information in meaningful contexts for purposes that are relevant and appropriate to them. Their activities are generally linked to a final goal, involving the presentation of the results of their research to an audience. In each case, but in very different ways, the children move through the framework presented above. Existing knowledge is made explicit through the use of drawing, concept mapping, lists and discussion. A stimulus is used to provide a new experience, generate interest or invite questions. The children are actively involved in planning their research. Their search for information requires a variety of different types of reading and this is supported through the use of questions, tables and graphic organizers (explored later in the chapter). The activities encourage children to make sense of their findings and provide many opportunities for collaboration.

The scenarios also show how talk and writing support information retrieval. In the early stages, talk enables children to explore and make explicit their existing understanding and to formulate questions for investigation. As they search for information, talk enables children to support each other in locating relevant texts and identifying information that will be useful. It facilitates interaction with texts, providing opportunities to make sense of findings. It also offers an important mode of presentation.

Writing also contributes at different stages of the information retrieval process. In the early stages writing lists, notes, drawings and questions serves to focus children's attention, engage interest and stimulate curiosity. Writing makes existing knowledge explicit and encourages the identification of questions and hypotheses. It also supports interaction with texts. Creating notes, lists and tables can help children to record and categorize information. Annotating texts with questions makes them monitor their own level of understanding and focuses attention on areas where more information is needed. Writing is often the means of publishing and presenting the results of research and its role at this stage in supporting learning is discussed in greater depth later in the chapter.

## Activities for supporting children's research

Depending on the situation, it is often appropriate to engage in a single stage or part of the research process. The following list presents some examples of activities that may be used.

### Exploring previous knowledge

- Mind mapping/concept mapping;
- drawing a picture to show what is understood;
- using a picture/photograph/artefact/discussion to generate what children already know.

### Gaining new experiences

- For example, visit, video, artefacts, story, observation, photograph, picture.

### Asking questions and deciding what information is needed

- Devising questions based on what has been generated through brainstorming/concept mapping/a visit or experience;
- using a photo/map/diagram/illustration/text to generate questions;
- providing question 'starters' (when, what, why, where);
- listing ten questions and then selecting three to investigate.

### Finding information

- Selecting from a variety of sources (interview, Internet, email, letter, video, document, CD-ROM, and so on);
- teacher modelling use of organizational features in a big book, such as contents page or subheadings. Discussion about which type of reading is appropriate – skimming, scanning or close reading;
- creating class flow charts, for example how to find a book;
- comparing/evaluating information texts;
- text marking (such as highlighting/underlining key words, annotating text with notes in margin, numbering).

### Interaction with texts

- Drawing a diagram to represent information;
- labelling – children label a diagram using information presented in the text;
- creating/completing a grid using information from a text;
- underlining key points/crossing out irrelevant points;
- producing a summary;
- making lists and tables;
- restructuring (for example represent content as a flow chart);
- generating further questions for investigation;
- note making;
- evaluating information, comparing different sources;
- DARTs activities (discussed in Chapter 4).

### Presentation of information

Findings from research may be presented as:

- newspaper articles;
- letters;
- diary entries;
- reports;
- leaflets;
- fact-files;

- advertisements;
- information texts for younger children;
- posters;
- board games;
- radio/TV programmes;
- drama.

Audiences for presentation include other children in the class or school, parents or visitors. Children can be encouraged to evaluate the success of their presentation.

In developing children's skills in research, two elements may present particular challenges: note making and critical reading.

## Note making

Note making involves the selection and recording of relevant aspects of a spoken, written, visual or audio-visual text. As Neate (2001) has pointed out, many adults and children have difficulty writing notes, finding it hard to decide what should be recorded, and in making use of them at a later stage. Crucially, children need to be taught how to take notes and they need to do this when there is a clear purpose involved. Such a purpose provides a focus for collecting information and a means to distinguish what is relevant from what is not. An example of this would be the need to use information provided in a video or talk in research or to inform parents or other children. Notes can also be taken from audio tapes, pictures, diagrams and CD-ROMs as long as there is a reason for such records to be kept.

Modelling of note making by the teacher during shared writing offers a valuable means to demonstrate how decisions are made and ways of recording. Further examples of activities designed to develop children's ability to identify key points include:

- underlining/highlighting relevant points;
- deleting irrelevant parts of a text;
- compiling lists such as lists of points or features;
- collaborating with others in note making;
- comparing notes created individually.

Such activities can be used throughout the primary age range, with modelling and scribing being particularly valuable for the least confident readers. At every stage, the challenge of the task is affected by the demands of the text and the level of support provided.

## Critical reading

Chapter 4 raised the importance of critical reading of literature. In reading non-fiction, it is also important that children are encouraged to recognize that a text is produced and its content, presentation and validity are affected by the purposes and prejudices of the producer. The following scenarios show children of different ages engaged in activities which encourage them to develop such awareness:

The **reception** children have been asked to collect examples of texts that they see in their lives outside school. A class 'text box' has been created, containing tickets, leaflets, sweet wrappers, adverts, cards, timetables, and so forth. During a shared reading session the children look closely at a crisp packet, projected onto a screen. The teacher asks the children to predict what the main words say and she then reads them aloud. They explore the information conveyed by the smaller print and discuss why the lettering and font are different. They also talk about the use of bright colours in attracting attention.

The **year 2** children are working in pairs, looking at descriptions of toys in a catalogue. They have been told to highlight any words that they believe are used to make people want to buy the items. They later discuss the kinds of words found and make a class collection. This is used in shared writing to provide suitable vocabulary for a description of a particular toy. The children then work in pairs to create their own descriptions of items for a class catalogue.

The **year 5** teacher has collected two contrasting newspaper reports about a summer festival. One describes the good weather, the happy, friendly atmosphere and high standard of entertainment. The other is less enthusiastic and mentions the excessive heat, the litter and congestion in the area. The children discuss differences between the texts and common points. Later they produce contrasting reports on the school summer fair.

Such activities enable children to appreciate that the production of a text involves deliberate choices and decisions and to be aware of the intentions of the writer (Wray *et al.*, 1997).

### *Teaching reading for information – key points:*

- reading for information requires an understanding of non-fiction texts, the use of retrieval devices and different ways of reading;
- the knowledge and skills required to read for information can be taught most effectively within research that is meaningful and relevant to the children;
- subjects across the curriculum and children's own interests provide meaningful contexts for research;
- children at all stages and levels of ability can be involved in locating and making sense of information; those who are unable to read independently may use sources of information other than written text or be supported by a more able reader or adult;
- the initial stages of the information retrieval process are vital in generating children's interest and curiosity;
- interaction with texts is important in encouraging children to make sense of what they read;
- talk and writing are valuable throughout the process;
- informal or formal presentation of results validates children's findings and efforts and provides a valuable goal for their research.

# Writing non-fiction

Attention has long been drawn to the value of writing in organizing thinking and helping the writer to make sense of experience (Britton, 1970). Bereiter *et al.* (1993) identify a 'knowledge transforming' model of writing. This refers to the use of writing to clarify thoughts and make new ideas and information part of the writer's own understanding. The process of organizing ideas, required in order to write, leads to a greater depth of understanding. Composing a written presentation of research findings therefore encourages children to make sense of the information they have gathered and make the knowledge their own.

Writing therefore provides:

- a highly effective means to support and facilitate learning;
- a valuable tool to aid information retrieval and interaction with texts;
- a powerful means to organize thinking and make sense of experience.

The next section of the chapter explores in more depth the nature of non-fiction genres and then considers ways in which children's writing of such texts can be supported and developed.

# Non-fiction genres

The relevance of genre theory, discussed in Chapter 1, for the teaching of writing was first reflected in the First Steps programme of the Education Department of Western Australia (1997). There has been some discussion over the identification of written genres. However, the following range, proposed by Wray *et al.* (1995) and based on work by genre theorists including Martin *et al.* (1987), is intended to reflect those most frequently required in school-based writing across the curriculum. These six non-fiction genres have also gained prominence and recognition through their use in the National Literacy Strategy (DfEE, 1998):

- recount;
- report;
- explanation;
- persuasion;
- discussion;
- procedure/instructions.

## Features of non-fiction genres

As discussed in Chapter 1, texts within a genre share a common underlying purpose, as well as similarities in terms of organization and language features. This is exemplified by considering a range of procedural/instructional texts, which might include recipes along with instructions for playing a game, constructing a DIY cupboard or topping-up a mobile phone. These texts share common features.

## A procedural/instruction text

Purpose:      tells a person how to do something.

Organization:    chronological texts which often include:
a simple title – usually the name of the final product or goal;
a list of ingredients or requirements, with quantities and equipment;
a series of numbered steps;
diagrams or pictures.

Use of language often includes:
sequenced sentences or numbered steps;
imperatives at the beginning of sentences such as 'take' or 'join';
many simple sentences;
temporal connectives, such as 'then' or 'after';
the present tense.

Vocabulary:    technical language, for example in recipes, 'simmer', 'marinade', 'sauté'.

Consider, as a contrast, a range of non-chronological reports: a non-fiction book for children on spiders, a report on the state of housing in an area of the country and an extract from an encyclopaedia on stringed instruments. In contrast with the procedural texts discussed above, none of these texts would be likely to include lists, imperatives or many temporal connectives. Their purpose and content necessitate a very different structure and use of language.

## Features of a (non-chronological) report

Purpose:      to describe the way things are.

Organization:    non-chronological texts presented in paragraphs which often include:
an opening sentence which introduces a general category, for example minibeasts, or provides context, such as location of country;
classification into types of minibeasts: molluscs, insects, and so on;
description of features or qualities of the main subject;
illustrations.

Use of language is often impersonal and includes:
simple, compound and complex sentences;
the present tense.

Vocabulary:    subject specific language.

116

It is important to note that texts do not comply rigidly with such formats. A single text may follow many of the conventions of a single genre but also deviate in other ways. An example of this is the following comment taken from a recipe by the well-known cookery writer, Jamie Oliver (2000: 272). Following a series of concise numbered instructions on how to make smoothies, he comments: 'If you haven't got a liquidiser you can do what I have been known to and place the ice into a clean tea towel and bash the hell out of it with a rolling pin . . . It's good but not quite so good.'

Such a comment is unusual in an instruction text in its use of a complex sentence, slang, personal tone and use of the personal pronoun. However, it does not in any way reduce the effectiveness of the writing. If anything it adds a sense of individuality and humour. Significantly, the rest of the recipe does follow the conventions of the genre in providing a list of ingredients and clearly sequenced steps, and the use of imperatives to provide concise instructions. Such aspects are necessary for the text to fulfil its purpose.

A text may therefore follow the conventions of a genre, but it is still individual in nature. Indeed texts used and found in everyday life often contain a combination of different genres. Language is dynamic and existing genres change in their features and scope and new text types are created. Teaching about genres, therefore, should not attempt to provide fixed formulae for children or encourage simple reproduction of given forms (Czerniewska, 1992) as this presents writing as a process of 'imitation' rather than 'authorship' (Wyse *et al.*, 2001: 129). Instead, the teaching of writing should make children aware of the conventions they will need to follow, in order that their communication is understood and valued. It should not limit their capacity for originality and creativity.

Children will develop awareness of the features of a genre as a result of experience and analysis of real texts. This can be achieved through the teaching sequence for narrative texts described in Chapter 5. Children can then apply their understanding to writing for relevant purposes and audiences. In promoting 'authorship', children therefore need to have content to handle that is appropriate to the specific genre. They also need to be involved in making decisions about which genre suits their purpose. This highlights again the relevance of making links between literacy and the wider curriculum, because other subjects provide the concepts and content for children to handle in their writing, as well as reading.

### *Teaching non-fiction writing – key points:*

- genres are not rigid; new genres are created and existing genres change their features;
- individual texts within a genre do not necessarily conform in every way;
- a single text may include features of different genres.

The teaching of non-fiction writing needs to provide:
- experience of authentic texts;
- opportunities to examine authentic texts to identify common organizational and linguistic features of specific genres;
- meaningful contexts and motivating purposes to apply this knowledge and produce their own texts.

# Teaching non-fiction writing

The following scenarios provide a range of examples of the teaching of non-fiction writing at different levels. Note in each case how the context for writing is created, how children's writing is supported and how their motivation is engaged.

During a visit to a local bakery, the **nursery** teacher draws the children's attention to the print they can see. They notice the shop name, the list of prices, notices on the door, leaflets and labels on the different kinds of bread and cakes. On their return, the children discuss what is needed to create a bakery in the classroom and, over the next few days, they are encouraged to produce items for the shop. In addition to baking a range of products, they create labels for the food on display, a list of sandwiches, an open and closed sign for the door and a note to tell customers to check their change!

The **year 1** class has been studying plants and growing seeds as part of a science topic. Through experiments and discussion they have become aware of the need for sun, light and water and have successfully grown a range of seeds. The literacy focus for the week is instruction writing. The children look at a range of seed packets and identify common features. As a class they create an outline which they will use for the seed packets (Figure 6.1) and the teacher scribes for the children as they complete an example as a class. The children are then asked to create their own seed packets for sunflower seeds which will be used in the nursery role-play garden centre.

| ............................ ....seeds | How to grow the seeds |
|---|---|
| Picture | You will need: _____ _____ _____ |
| These seeds grow into.... | 1. Get ... 2. ... 3. |
| Price | |

Figure 6.1. Writing frame instruction writing (seed packets)

The **year** 2 children have been learning about Florence Nightingale. They have created a time line and identified key events in her life. The teacher tells the children about Mary Seacole who has received less attention although she also made a highly significant contribution to medical care at that time. The class discuss the lack of information available about Mary Seacole and agree that they could produce books on her life for the school library. The children create a simple time line and use the Internet, CD-ROMs, fact sheets and encyclopaedias to collect the information they need. Before they begin writing the books, the class children prepare a storyboard to show main events. They also discuss common features of the books on Florence Nightingale.

In **year** 5, work in design technology, art, maths and geography has focused on biscuits: their production, marketing and the source of their ingredients. The children have created their own recipes and packaging. They are now expected to advertise their biscuits. They collect a range of packaging and adverts and list common features. The children then prepare their own advertisements, which are displayed around the school in preparation for a biscuit sale.

In **year** 6, the history topic is Ancient Greece. The children have been asked to work in groups to produce a television documentary on life at this time for children's television. In preparation for this project, they watch a number of extracts from television documentaries and note common features and differences. At the end of the project the children show their documentaries to the rest of the school.

In each scenario, the content and context for writing are provided by a subject area other than English and the children have a clear purpose and audience. They gain experience of authentic examples of a particular text type, before being encouraged to identify its distinctive structural and linguistic features. The next stage of the process is to prepare for writing in that genre. For most children, support is needed to apply the knowledge they have gained of the features of texts to their own composition.

In teaching non-fiction writing, the various forms of classroom organization and teaching strategies included in the final section of Chapter 5 are relevant. Shared writing provides opportunities for demonstrating an aspect of writing, scribing for the children or encouraging the children to apply their learning through focused pieces of composition. Guided writing is useful in supporting or extending the writing of children with particular needs, whilst independent writing offers opportunities for the analysis and production of texts. In supporting children's independent writing, graphic organizers and writing frames are useful and these are discussed below.

## Graphic organizers

As explained in Chapter 4, graphic organizers (Moline, 2001) provide visual structures for recording information. However, organizers are also useful in supporting writing, because their presentation reflects the structure of the original text. When a child is using a particular type of text for research and is expected to produce the same type of text to present their findings, a graphic organizer provides a framework for recording and preparing for writing. Examples include: using a time line or storyboard to record information represented in a recount; using a tree diagram to record categories and details included in a report; using a flow diagram to represent the process presented in an explanation text.

## Writing frames

The idea of writing frames has been widely promoted by Wray and Lewis (1995, 1997) as a means to provide children with a structure to organize their non-fiction writing. The frames are designed to support the writing of specific text types. Use of the writing frame is intended to help children to write in a specific genre. A frame may consist of sentence starters, as suggested by Bereiter *et al.* (1993), or grids (see Tables 6.2 and 6.3), which encourage children to organize and present their own content appropriately.

Table 6.2 provides an example of a frame to prepare for writing a discussion text (Wray *et al.*, 1997). Table 6.3 provides an example of a frame to support the writing of a discussion text (Wray *et al.*, 1997).

**Table 6.2. Planning for discussion writing**

| The issue we are discussing is . . . | |
|---|---|
| Arguments for:<br>1.<br>2.<br>3. | Arguments against:<br>1.<br>2.<br>3. |
| My conclusion: | |

**Table 6.3. Writing frame for discussion text**

| |
|---|
| There is a lot of discussion about whether . . . |
| The people who agree with this idea such as . . . claim that . . . |
| They also argue that . . . |
| A further point to make is . . . |
| However, there are also strong arguments against this point of view.<br>. . . believe that . . . |
| They say that . . . |
| Furthermore, they claim that . . . |
| After looking at the different points of view and the evidence for them I think that . . . because . . . |

It is clear that an appropriate structure and language use is encouraged by such support. The frames include cohesive ties to link parts of the text and encourage the appropriate use of tense, style, vocabulary, and so on. However, the danger is that such frames are presented to children without explanation and are completed as little more than a worksheet activity. Such an approach also tends to present a view of genres as rigid, whereas they are flexible and open to innovation as discussed earlier. Without a context or purpose, children are unlikely to relate this activity to other texts, make any decisions about their writing or develop their individuality as writers. Wray *et al.* (1997) therefore emphasize that frames are to be used flexibly and in meaningful contexts.

Writing frames can support the development of children's writing as long as they understand its origin and relevance. The most effective way of using such a frame is to involve children in its production. After gaining experience of authentic examples of relevant texts, children of all ages can be encouraged to look for common features. Given the motivation to produce such a text themselves, with support from the teacher, they will then be able to produce an appropriate frame. Even in this case, it is essential that children recognize that the frame provides guidance rather than a prescription for how the text should be written; they should be encouraged to change and adapt it for their own uses. The aim is to encourage children to become independent of support.

# Summary

In conclusion, this chapter has demonstrated how the development of children's ability to read and write non-fiction cannot be taught effectively in isolation. The wider curriculum provides the contexts, purposes and texts for such learning, but the relationship is more complex than this. The use of language and the organization of texts are essential features of each subject and the effective teaching of non-fiction reading and writing depends upon this understanding.

It is interesting and perhaps sobering to note an observation made by Webster *et al.* (1996: 148) from their research in the classroom. They noted that it was the teachers, not the children, who spent most time engaged in 'identifying problems, negotiating learning routes, constructing writing, exploring reading sources, analysing and reflecting on literacy processes'. By assuming responsibility for these activities, teachers deny children opportunities for engaging in meaningful, relevant research and taking ownership of their learning. In an environment in which the process and results of such research are shared, valued and discussed, children see reading as offering opportunities to satisfy their curiosity and writing as a powerful means to communicate information to others.

In planning to develop children's use of language and literacy across the curriculum, it is therefore important to:

• provide support for children to develop the skills required for information retrieval within the context of meaningful research;

- engage children's interest in research through providing stimulating topics;
- encourage the use of talk, reading and writing at all stages of research;
- include opportunities for the presentation of findings;
- use discussion and analysis of authentic texts to develop understanding of features of non-fiction genres;
- encourage children to apply their understanding of genres through their own purposeful writing.

# Reflective questions

1. Select a topic from across the curriculum and plan how you can take children through the stages of locating, selecting, processing and using information to present their findings to an audience.

2. Try to collect a range of authentic texts from each of the listed non-fiction genres. Note common features of organization, use of language and vocabulary. (For support with this activity, refer to Merchant *et al.*, 2001.)

3. Collect a range of leaflets advertising local attractions, theme parks and so on. Different extracts of these texts often reflect different genres. Identify which genres are represented and then consider how you would use these as a stimulus and model for children's writing.

## FURTHER READING

Mallett, M. (1999) *Young Researchers*. London: Routledge Falmer.
  A detailed overview of relevant research combined with case studies illustrating use of non-fiction texts from nursery to Key Stage 2.

Merchant, G. and Thomas, H. (2001) *Non-Fiction for the Literacy Hour*. London: David Fulton Publishers.
  Practical ideas for reading and writing non-fiction in the classroom. Particularly helpful in its analysis of features of non-fiction genres and clear annotation of example texts.

Riley, J. and Reedy, D. (2000) *Developing Writing for Different Purposes: Teaching about Genre in the Early Years*. London: Paul Chapman Publishing.
  Chapters 7 and 8 provide a clear explanation of genre theory and a range of examples of classroom practice, including young children's writing.

Wray, D. and Lewis, M. (1997) *Extending Literacy: Children Reading and Writing Non-Fiction*. London: Routledge.
  A detailed account of the EXIT model with suggestions for using it in the classroom.

## REFERENCES

Arnold, H. (1992) '"Do blackbirds sing all day?" Literature and information texts', in Styles, M., Bearne, E. and Walsh, V. (eds) *After Alice: Exploring Children's Literature*. London: Cassell.

Bereiter, C. and Scardamalia, M. (1987) *The Psychology of Written Composition*. Hillsdale NJ: Lawrence Erlbaum.

Bereiter, C. and Scardamalia, M. (1993) 'Composing and writing', in Beard, R. (ed.) *Teaching Literacy: Balancing Perspectives.* London: Hodder & Stoughton.

Britton, J. (1970) *Language and Learning.* London: Penguin.

Burnett, C. and Myers, J. (2002) '"Beyond the frame": exploring children's literacy practices', *Reading: Literacy and Language*, 36(2), 56–62.

Czerniewska, P. (1992) *Learning about Writing.* London: Blackwell.

Department for Education and Employment (DfEE) (1998) *National Literacy Strategy Framework for Teaching.* London: HMSO.

Education Department of Western Australia (1997) *First Steps: Writing Resource Book.* Port Melbourne, Victoria: Rigby Heinemann.

Hall, N. (1987) *The Emergence of Literacy.* London: Hodder & Stoughton.

Henre, S., Jessel, J. and Griffiths, J. (2000) *Study to Teach: A Guide to Studying in Teacher Education.* London: Routledge.

Lunzer, E. and Gardner, K. (1979) *The Effective Use of Reading.* London: Heinemann.

Lunzer, E. and Gardner, K. (1984) *Learning from the Written Word.* London: Oliver & Boyd.

Mallett, M. (1992) *Making Facts Matter: Reading Non-Fiction 5–11.* London: Paul Chapman Publishing.

Mallett, M. (1999) *Young Researchers.* London: Routledge Falmer.

Martin, J. R., Christie, F. and Rothery, J. (1987) 'Social Processes in Education: A reply to Sawyer and Watson (and others)', in Reid, I. (ed.) *The Place of Genre in Learning.* Victoria and Sydney: Deakin University.

Merchant, G. and Thomas, H. (2001) *Non-Fiction for the Literacy Hour.* London: David Fulton Publishers.

Moline, S. (2001) 'Using graphic organizers to write information texts', in Evans, J. (ed.) *The Writing Classroom: Aspects of Writing and the Primary Child 3–11.* London: David Fulton Publishers.

Moss, G. (2000) 'Raising boys' attainment in reading', *Reading*, 3(34), 101–6.

Neate, B. (1992) *Finding out about Finding Out.* London: Hodder & Stoughton.

Neate, B. (2001) 'Notemaking techniques for young children', in Evans, J. (ed.) *The Writing Classroom: Aspects of Writing and the Primary Child 3–11.* London: David Fulton Publishers.

Nutbrown, C. (1999) *Threads of Thinking: Young Children and the Role of Early Education.* Second Edition. London: Paul Chapman Publishing.

Oliver, J. (2000) *The Return of the Naked Chef.* Harmondsworth: Penguin.

Riley, J. and Reedy, D. (2000) *Developing Writing for Different Purposes: Teaching about Genre in the Early Years.* London: Paul Chapman Publishing.

Vygotsky, L. S. (1962) *Thought and Language.* Cambridge MA: Harvard University Press.

Webster, A., Beveridge, M. and Reed, M. (1996) *Managing the Literacy Curriculum.* London: Routledge.

Wray, D. and Lewis, M. (1995) *Developing Children's Non-fiction Writing: Working with Writing Frames.* Leamington Spa: Scholastic.

Wray, D. and Lewis, M. (1997) *Extending Literacy: Children Reading and Writing Non-Fiction.* London: Routledge.

Wyse, D. and Jones, R. (2001) *Teaching English, Language and Literacy.* London: Routledge Falmer.

# 7 Preparing to Teach English

The previous four chapters have explored reading, writing, speaking and listening. Here we consider some *generic* aspects of English teaching and discuss the knowledge needed to teach this subject. This chapter therefore begins by showing how curriculum documents may be interpreted in the light of the principles for effective practice outlined in Chapter 2. Particular attention is given to the literacy hour as this influences the organization and management of much reading and writing teaching for primary pupils in England. This is followed by an investigation of ways in which teachers may stimulate discussion among children in whole-class, group and individual contexts. Finally, the chapter explores the role of teacher's subject knowledge and outlines some key aspects of subject knowledge that new and beginning teachers need to develop.

## Curriculum requirements

As explored in Chapter 2, requirements for teaching speaking, listening, reading and writing in England are contained in the 'Communication, Language and Literacy' section of the *Curriculum Guidance for the Foundation Stage* (QCA, 2000) and *National Curriculum for English* (DfEE, 2000). Whilst these documents address the needs of children at a different stage of development, both are underpinned by an approach to language and literacy provision that emphasizes:

- opportunities to communicate for a variety of audiences and purposes;
- experience of a range of spoken and written texts (including children's literature) in meaningful and practical contexts;
- the development of language to support learning;
- reflection on their language use;
- plenty of interaction between children, their peers and adults;
- recognition of, and reflection on, linguistic diversity.

# Linking speaking and listening, reading and writing

As explored in the previous chapter, reading, writing, speaking and listening are closely linked and meaningful activities in the classroom usually involve all these areas. Table 7.1 lists three literacy activities alongside a range of reading, writing, speaking and listening tasks that children might engage in as they tackle each one.

**Table 7.1. Linking speaking, listening, reading and writing**

| Task | Speaking and listening | Reading | Writing |
|---|---|---|---|
| | *(Each task is numbered, to suggest the sequence in which they might take place.)* | | |
| *Nursery* Shared writing of a letter in response to an invitation to a teddy bears' picnic | 2. Deciding whether to respond 3. Talking through what should be written | 1. Reading invitation 5. Re-reading it to check that their letter has responded to all parts of the invitation | 4. Writing the letter 6. Making any agreed changes 7. Writing the envelope |
| *Year 2* Making a class book about minibeasts | 1. Discussing what children already know about minibeasts and asking further questions 5. Discussing what has been found out 6. Planning organization and layout | 3. Searching for information 8. Reading book to a neighbouring class | 2. Noting questions 4. Writing notes 7. Writing sections of the book |
| *Year 6* Participating in a newsroom simulation and producing a newspaper | 1. Discussing plans for issue 5. Discussing editorial decisions 8. Discussing layout | 2. Reading information supplied by reporters 3. Critically evaluating reports | 4. Writing notes 6. Editing 7. Drafting headlines 9. Compiling reports into newspaper |

## Opportunities for linking speaking and listening, reading and writing:

- use oral work to reflect on and refine their writing;
- read widely to help broaden awareness of vocabulary and language structures;
- analyse texts which can then provide models for writing;
- discuss texts to deepen response and enhance comprehension;
- compare language in oral and written modes in order to reflect on the appropriateness of language use;
- use reading, speaking and listening (including drama) as stimuli for writing;
- use notes as a way of sequencing ideas for a formal talk or presentation;
- write notes following reading to refine a response to a text or summarize what has been read.

Whilst common principles underpin effective teaching and learning for all pupils, some particular considerations are relevant to teachers in different phases. Below we discuss:

- interpreting the 'Communication, Language and Literacy' strand of the Foundation Stage Curriculum;
- considerations for using the National Literacy Strategy (NLS) Framework (DfEE, 1998) and literacy hour.

# Interpreting 'Communication, Language and Literacy'

As explored in previous chapters, English is inevitably cross-curricular. In the early years, development in language and literacy does not occur in isolation but feeds into, and is enhanced by, learning in other areas. Importantly, learning opportunities need to build on children's own experiences and needs. Drake (2001: 45) suggests seven ways in which practitioners in the early years can intervene in children's learning. They can:

- stimulate interest;
- provide high quality resources;
- listen and respond to children's talk;
- question children to extend learning;
- work alongside children, modelling skills and use of key vocabulary;
- encourage, reassure and praise children;
- value and celebrate their achievements.

The following series of activities demonstrate how 'Communication, Language and Literacy' can be integrated with other areas of learning in meaningful contexts. Note how the teacher uses a range of the strategies listed above to promote learning.

The children have been reading *Jasper's Beanstalk* (Butterworth *et al.*, 1993) and used props to retell the story. Some children are keen to grow beans themselves and plant broad beans in jars to grow in the classroom. Every couple of days they take digital photographs to record the beans' progress. One child brings in a sprouting potato and the teacher suggests that they plant it and see what happens.

During a visit to a local garden centre, the children look at a range of plants, discuss their preferences and buy some seeds and plants. The garden centre manager shows them some trade catalogues and shows them how she uses them to place orders. She gives them some old catalogues to take away.

Some children plant the seeds in a flowerbed in the corner of the outside play area. With the teacher, they look at the seed packets to choose what to plant and find out what conditions the seeds need to grow.

The children are keen to set up their own garden centre in the role-play area, part of which extends into the outside play area. They include a desk, complete with order book, catalogues and a telephone. There is an area for potting and labelling plants, some plastic plants and a tray of seed packets. A small trolley is available for collecting purchases, which can be paid for at the till. The teacher asks a parent to visit the garden centre and ask for some advice on what to plant in her garden.

Planning and organization are more subject-focused in Key Stages 1 and 2, but English is still closely linked with the rest of the curriculum: language provides the means of accessing, developing and recording information in all subjects and other subjects provide meaningful contexts for developing knowledge, skills and understanding in English.

# Interpreting the National Literacy Strategy (NLS) Framework

In interpreting the NLS framework, teachers must find ways of interpreting NLS objectives. These are sorted into three strands: text, sentence and word level:

- *Text level objectives* relate to writing composition and reading comprehension.
- *Sentence level objectives* relate to grammar and punctuation.
- *Word level objectives* relate to spelling, phonics, handwriting and vocabulary.

It is evident that within any real-life reading or writing activity these three levels are closely related. As explored in Chapter 4, successful reading involves orchestrating a range of strategies to make meaning. These operate at text level (semantic), sentence level (syntactic) and word level (graphophonic). When we write, we make decisions about how to use text, sentence and word level features to have the desired effect on the reader. This is because our response to texts is affected by the overall structure and organization of texts (text level), grammatical features and punctuation (sentence level) and vocabulary choices (word level).

Effectively, our comprehension and composition of whole texts depend on us accessing, interpreting and evaluating a variety of text, sentence and word level features. This means that, in planning learning experiences for children, we need to find ways of linking text, sentence and word level objectives. If sentence- and word level objectives are taught separately, then it is likely that children will not see the relevance of what they are learning for their independent reading and writing. Indeed it has been found (Wray *et al.*, 2002) that the most effective teachers of literacy find ways of linking text, sentence and word level work in meaningful ways in the context of texts.

Note how the teachers in the two scenarios that follow successfully draw on features at each level. The children increase their understanding of how whole texts work through exploring these different features.

## Shared writing: year 1

The children have been on a trip to a local farm and made a chart of the animals, plants and machinery they saw. They are now writing a recount of their trip during a shared writing session. (This will go in the parents' newsletter along with some digital photos they took.) They have already looked at other recounts and explored the way that temporal connectives such as 'first', 'next', 'after' and 'when' are used. As the teacher works with the children to create the recount, he encourages them to use these temporal connectives to signal the order of events. He also draws the children's attention to the use of capital letters at the beginning of sentences and full stops at the end. Once finished the recount is read through. The children then make a couple of changes; they realize they have not told parents much about what the farm itself was like and add in some further description.

## Shared reading: year 5

During a shared reading session, a year 5 class is looking at 'The Hairy Toe', a bizarre narrative poem that is part traditional tale and part horror story. An old woman finds a 'hairy toe' out in a field and takes it home. She is then pursued by the toe's owner, a 'thing' who is never named. The poem ends as the 'thing' finds the woman and confronts her. The following excerpt shows how the suspense builds as the 'thing' approaches.

*. . . The woman scrooched down,*
*way down under the covers,*
*and about that time*
*the wind appeared to hit the house,*

*smoosh,*

*and the old house creaked and cracked*
*like something was trying to get in.*
*The voice had come nearer now,*
*And it said,*
*'Where's my Hair-r-y To-o-oe?*
*Who's got my Hair-r-y To-o-oe?' . . .*

(Traditional, in Harrison and Stuart-Clark, 1990)

Having read and enjoyed the poem, the children comment on the way that suspense is created. They notice the use of personification ('the wind appeared to hit the house') and simile ('like something was trying to get in') that seem to suggest that the environment itself is closing in on the old woman as the 'thing' approaches. They also discuss the layout of the poem, noting how the breaks at the end of each line prompt the reader to pause at key moments. They are particularly interested in the placing of 'smoosh' in a line on its own – they feel this strengthens the impact of the word. Together they rehearse reading it with and without pauses at the end of each line and notice that pausing at the line breaks helps to enhance the tension. They also note the use of alliteration and onomatopoeia ('creaked and cracked') and practise reading the poem in a way that echoes the sounds the house is making. They refine their reading for performance in a class assembly, deciding how to allocate parts to different readers and discussing how to use their voices to maximize the sense of tension that the poem creates.

The National Literacy Strategy Framework is designed so that the majority of text, sentence and word level objectives can be integrated. Even when objectives are taught discretely (for example, some spelling and phonics objectives), children need opportunities to apply their skills within a context involving reading and writing. Working on these three levels in an integrated way through texts can:

- be motivating and enjoyable and ensure that children know that reading and writing are purposeful and worthwhile;
- develop children's awareness of how texts are constructed and help them evaluate the effect of different writing decisions on the way a reader responds to a text;
- increase children's ability to analyse critically the texts they encounter and produce;
- provide varied examples of language in use and help them understand the relevance of what they are learning to their independent reading and writing.

# The literacy hour

The NLS provides specific guidance on how literacy should be taught, suggesting a four-part daily literacy hour that includes:

- approximately 15 minutes' whole-class shared text work (shared reading or writing);
- approximately 15 minutes' whole-class focused word or sentence level work;
- approximately 20 minutes' independent group work during which the teacher works with a group on guided reading or writing;
- approximately 10 minutes' plenary.

These elements are used flexibly and timings will vary according to the specific focus. For example, the first and second parts are often combined or reordered and many schools sometimes lengthen the independent session to allow for more extended reading and writing. Other schools move activities, such as guided reading, to other times during the day. In reception, the different elements of the hour (shared and guided reading and writing and phonics teaching) can be integrated with other activities and taught throughout the day although it is assumed that children will have some experience of whole literacy hours prior to entry to year 1.

Table 7.2 lists the kinds of activities that take place during different parts of the hour.

**Table 7.2. Literacy hour activities**

| Shared text work (whole class) | Word/sentence work (whole class) | Independent group /guided work | Plenary (whole class) |
|---|---|---|---|
| Shared reading with a focus on text, sentence or word level | Grammar investigations | Guided reading (teacher focus) | Sharing and celebrating |
| Shared reading of a range of digital and print texts | Phonics games | Guided writing (teacher focus) | Reflecting |
| | Spelling investigations | Small world play | Reviewing |
| Analysis of the structure and language features of a range of texts | Editing and proofreading shared writing | Role play | Comparing and evaluating children's responses |
| Shared writing (teacher demonstration, teacher scribing, supported composition) at any stage of writing process | Exploring word and sentence level features within context of texts | Storytelling and puppet play | Generating questions to be explored in future sessions |
| | | Bookmaking | |
| | | Using writing table | Playing games that reinforce key objectives |
| | | Investigations at text, sentence and word level | |
| Discussion of examples of children's work | | DARTs activities | |
| | | Independent writing | |
| | | Independent reading/ book browsing | |
| | | Group/paired reading | |
| | | Collaborative writing | |
| | | Writing response partner activities | |
| | | Reader response activities | |
| | | Spelling games | |
| | | Work on spelling and reading journals | |

The literacy hour structure is designed to scaffold children's learning. New skills and concepts are modelled during whole-class work and children are encouraged to apply them during guided work and consolidate them during independent activities. There is a strong emphasis on encouraging children to reflect on and review their learning during the plenary. The introduction of the literacy hour has seen an increase in whole-class and group teaching prompted by research into school improvement, which suggested that structured teaching has a positive impact on pupil achievement (Mortimore, 1998).

Many have expressed concerns that such tightly structured and teacher-directed sessions leave little room for individual pupil autonomy and restrict teachers from responding to children's needs and enthusiasms (Marshall, 1998; Meek, 1998; Hall, 2001). However, literacy hours can be used creatively and flexibly and take place within a context that emphasizes choice, ownership, independence and meaningful use of language. In achieving this, it is particularly important to ensure that whole-class sessions are interactive and motivating. Guidelines on how to facilitate discussion during these and other teacher-led sessions are provided below.

# Facilitating discussion during teacher-led activities

Vygotsky (1978) argued that children's ability to arrive at new understandings is stimulated through interactions with those more experienced than themselves. In the classroom, these 'experienced others' may be teachers or peers. Discussion can encourage children to engage with texts and reflect on reading, writing, speaking and listening in different contexts. Ironically, some of the least productive classroom talk has been found to take place during interactions between teachers and children (Corden, 2000; Skidmore *et al.*, 2003). The following transcript illustrates the possible limitations of a teacher-led discussion:

Teacher [*holding up a picture of a four-poster bed*]: Can anyone tell me why the bed's called a four-poster?
Child [*putting hand up and answering immediately*]: Because it's cold.
Teacher: Put up – wait a minute. Put your hand up and I'll ask you. Stephen?
Stephen: Because it's got four posts.
Teacher: Four po- **Why** has it got four posts? Can anyone – Put your hand up if you want to say. **Why** has it got four posts? Where's Sean?
Sean: Here. [*Sean has not put his hand up.*]
Teacher: Why has it got four – Why has it got the four posts, do you think? [*To Sean*] Can you think? [*To whole class*] Think hard inside your heads everybody and –
Child 2: I know. Because it –
Teacher: Wait a minute. Wait a minute. Wait a minute.
Child 3: I know.
Teacher: I want the little ones to try and answer. Try and think hard. Linda, can **you** think why it's got four posts? [*Linda stares, then shakes her head.*] Think hard inside your head. Can you, Stella? [*Stella shakes her head.*] Think. Can you, Karen? [*Shows Karen the picture of the bed.*]

Karen: Um –

Child 4: I know.

Teacher: All right I know the big ones probably know. Let's see if the little ones have got the answer first.

Child: Angela's got her hand up. [*Angela is one of the 'little ones'.*]

Teacher: Well, I know Angela has. But – We'll ask Angela if nobody else can say . . . why it had four posts. [*Looking at Stephen*] Have you got any ideas why it might have four posts? [*Stephen shakes his head.*] Let's come back to Angela, then. [*Holds book up in front of Angela.*]

Angela: 'Cause it's got curtains. [*The children laugh.*]

Teacher: Yes, it's got to hold the curtains, hasn't it? What else has it got that needs four posts? [*Some children put their hands up; she selects one.*] Paula?

Paula: To hold it [*pointing to roof of bed in picture*].

Teacher: Yes, it's got a sort of roof – flat roof to it, hasn't it.

(Wells, 1985: 89–90)

This teacher is so intent on getting the answer she wants and managing the children's contributions that she fails to listen and respond to what the children say. Although her initial question is ostensibly open (inviting a range of answers) it is, in effect, closed – she ignores all answers except those she deems acceptable. Such closed questioning will do little to develop children's learning and is likely to inhibit children's contributions as they become wary about giving 'wrong' answers. Significantly, all responses are directed through the teacher. She does most of the talking and the children do not offer any questions themselves.

More effective interactions occur when teachers act as 'active participants in the construction of knowledge' (Mercer, 1995: 74) and help children engage with concepts or processes that they would find difficult on their own. By entering genuinely into 'sustained shared thinking' with children (Siraj-Blatchford *et al.*, 2002: 1), teachers can help children arrive at new understandings. One of the most powerful strategies that teachers can use involves demonstrating and making explicit their own use of exploratory talk and attentive listening. This helps children understand that it is acceptable to contribute to discussions with suggestions that are not fully formed; it helps them realize that there is no fixed answer and that their ideas matter. Edwards (1992) stresses the importance of encouraging children to 'think aloud' in this way and advises teachers to focus on 'more problem-posing and less solution-giving' (Edwards 2003: 40). Table 7.3, which is based on a National Literacy Strategy handout (DfEE, 1999), includes many of Edwards' suggestions for ways in which teachers can model and facilitate effective talk.

**Table 7.3. Facilitating discussion**

| Strategy | Examples of what teachers may say or do |
|---|---|
| Model tentative 'thinking' talk. | 'Hmmm . . .' <br> 'I wonder if . . .' <br> 'I'm not sure about . . .' |
| Playing devil's advocate. | 'But what about . . .?' <br> 'But surely . . .?' |
| Inviting children to elaborate. | 'Go on . . .' <br> 'Hmmmm . . .?' <br> 'Can you tell me more about that . . .?' |
| Encourage children to summarize. | 'So what have we said so far . . .?' |
| Encourage children to respond to each other's suggestions. | 'Do you agree?' <br> 'Does anyone have anything to add?' |
| Give children time. | Wait 5 seconds before responding. <br> Let children discuss ideas with a partner before reporting to the whole group. |
| Encourage children to justify suggestions. | 'What tells you that . . . ?' <br> 'Why do you think that . . . ?' |
| Be encouraging. | Use eye contact to invite children to respond. <br> Smile and nod. <br> 'That's interesting . . .' |
| Encourage children to ask questions for others to answer. | 'What would you like to know?' <br> 'What would you like to find out?' <br> 'Are there any parts that you find confusing?' |

Note how the two teachers in the following examples promote discussion.

Having just returned from a school trip to the seaside, a **year 2** teacher uses shared writing to create a descriptive poem about the sea. The class begins by looking at an enlarged photograph of the beach they visited (taken during the visit and projected onto the whiteboard). She invites the children to describe the photograph and then shut their eyes and imagine that they are standing on the shore again. She prompts them to try to create a picture of the scene in their minds and consider the kinds of sounds they hear and how they feel as they stand there. Afterwards the children tell their talk partners what they saw and felt and then share words and phrases to describe the scene with the whole class. The teacher scribes their suggestions onto the picture and encourages the children to extend and build on each other's ideas. Next she works with them to order some of the phrases into a poem. She asks two children to use the 'drag and drop' facility on the whiteboard to move the phrases around following suggestions from the rest of the class. As they experiment, they often reread what they have written. The teacher encourages the children to suggest changes and evaluate the impact of their poem on a reader.

A **year 4** class is reading *Wreck of the Zanzibar* (Morpurgo, 1995). The book, set in the 1900s, tells the story of a young girl, Laura, and her family who live an isolated life on the Scilly Isles. The story is told through a series of extracts from her diary. The teacher wants the children to explore how setting is developed and they read the first diary extract to establish where the story is set and consider Laura's attitude to her surroundings. The teacher sits the children in a semi-circle around the extract. She uses open-ended questions. (What do you think it was like? Can you tell me anything about the place where she lived? How would you feel living in a place like that?) She frequently invites them to justify their ideas with reference to the book (which bit makes you think that?) and use what they have discussed to predict what will happen next (what do you think could happen in such a place?). She often pauses to give the children time to think and uses eye contact to encourage children who are reluctant to contribute.

These two teachers avoid the 'guess what's in my head' approach (Alexander, 1995) used by the teacher in the earlier transcript and manage to generate real discussion. This is achieved partly by establishing an environment where children are encouraged to talk through their emerging ideas within an atmosphere of mutual trust. Each teacher has also thought carefully about the context for the session. The first gives the children time to explore a stimulus and the second sits the children in a semi-circle to ensure that they can all see each other as well as the teacher. This encourages them to respond to each other's suggestions rather than directing all their responses through the teacher.

The kinds of questions that a teacher uses will inevitably vary according to the objectives s/he is trying to teach. However, it is useful to be aware of a range of questions that can be used to prompt different levels of response. Questions can be used to encourage children to:

- Recall (Can you remember what the sea was like?)
- Infer (What sort of place is the Scilly Isles?)
- Deduce (What do we know about Laura?)
- Evaluate (Would a reader get a sense of what the sea is like from our poem?)
- Empathize (What would it be like to live on the Scilly Isles?)
- Predict (What could happen in this desolate place?)
- Picture (What does this place look and feel like?)
- Apply (Can we find a way of ordering these phrases to create a sense of what the sea is like?)
- Synthesize (Try and write your own opening to establish the setting for your story.)

### *Summary of guidelines for stimulating discussion:*

- model tentative learning talk and encourage discussion between children rather than responding to all suggestions yourself;
- ask a range of open and closed questions;
- ask questions that require children to infer, deduce and evaluate;
- give children an opportunity to talk about what they already know and understand before moving on to new areas.

- provide opportunities for the children to ask their own questions;
- give children enough thinking time before expecting an answer or give children time to discuss ideas in pairs/groups before contributing to whole-class discussions;
- make sure you are genuinely interested in what children have to say.

# The importance of subject knowledge

## Teachers' knowledge about language and literature

Teachers in primary or early years settings need sound subject knowledge of English. This involves knowledge about texts and language features along with an understanding of how children, including those with English as an Additional Language, develop as language and literacy users. Teachers need to be clear about how spoken and written language differ and know how ICT can be effectively integrated into English teaching. This knowledge informs planning and teaching and enables teachers to identify children's strengths and areas for development. Consider the subject knowledge needed to support children effectively in the following situations:

A **nursery** teacher is chanting action rhymes with a group of children. Every now and then she pauses and lets the children say the rhyming words. Together the teacher and children enjoy a series of rhymes from different cultures.

*The teacher uses her understanding of phonology to develop the children's awareness of onset and rime. Her knowledge of a range of poetry and rhymes helps her select suitable rhymes to share with the children.*

A **year 1** teacher is working with a guided reading group. She notes that one of the children is relying heavily on phonic cues when he reaches an unfamiliar word. This often results in him misreading a word and consequent loss of meaning.

*The teacher's awareness of the reading cueing systems helps her diagnose this child's difficulties. This will inform her future planning for this child.*

The **year 4** children have been comparing a series of fiction and non-fiction texts: *Dear Greenpeace* (James, 1993), *Oi! Get Off Our Train* (Burningham, 1991) and *Where the Forest Meets the Sea* (Baker, 1998) and have also visited the Greenpeace Web site. During a shared reading session they compare the different ways in which each text explored environmental issues. They discuss which had the most impact.

*The teacher's knowledge of the features and purposes of a range of texts enables her to support children through an open-ended discussion.*

The **year 5** children are participating in drama work exploring the impact of building a new supermarket. Different groups are in role as town planners, local residents, council members, environmentalists and supermarket owners. The children are now writing formal speeches to be presented at a meeting to discuss the plans. The teacher notices that some children are having difficulty in using standard English and facilitates a discussion about the different grammatical features used in formal and informal language.

*The teacher's knowledge of the grammatical features of standard English enables her to draw attention to contrasts between formal and informal language.*

An understanding of how texts work helps teachers integrate text, sentence and word level features in meaningful ways and gives them the confidence to let children investigate language for themselves. This can, in turn, help cultivate a fascination for English that assists children in becoming independent and literate language users. Knowledge about language also helps teachers diagnose problems that children may be having and plan appropriate opportunities for addressing these.

In developing their subject knowledge, teachers need to become familiar with a range of specialist terminology to support their teaching, such as 'phonemes' and 'graphemes', 'compound and complex sentences', 'recounts' and 'reports'. Teachers need to be able to do more than simply define and locate linguistic features. They need to be aware of the kind of texts in which those features are common and be able to analyse the use of language critically in a range of fiction, poetry and non-fiction. This includes exploring the impact on the reader of:

- layout of texts, for example use of images, bullet points;
- specific features of fiction and non-fiction such as character, setting, structure, index and contents pages;
- use of formal and informal language;
- word order;
- cohesion within sentences, such as use of conjunctions such as 'and' and 'but';
- cohesion within texts, for instance use of connectives to link sentences and paragraphs such as 'first', 'second', 'finally';
- use of paragraphing;
- different types of sentences, for example questions, exclamations, simple, compound and complex sentences;
- punctuation, such as full stops, commas, semi-colons, colons, speech marks.

## Developing children's knowledge about language and literature

Subject knowledge is also important in helping children to expand their own knowledge about language and literature. This enables them to reflect on their own language use and understand how speech and writing can be structured in different ways. It is helpful to encourage children to use appropriate terminology when discussing texts. Just as it is difficult to explain why a ball falls to the ground when dropped without using 'gravity', 'force' or 'pull', so it may be hard to discuss possible improvements to a piece of writing or analyse how a text works without referring to linguistic terms. Importantly these terms are *only* useful to children as a vocabulary with which they can discuss texts. Simply teaching children the meaning of words, such as 'noun' or 'verb', will do little to support their development. Knowledge and understanding of terminology relating to language and literacy gives children a *metalanguage* (or language used to describe language) with which they can:

- talk about how texts are put together;
- critically analyse what they read;
- evaluate their own and others' written and spoken language more confidently and precisely;
- become more aware of the choices they have when writing and speaking;
- discuss what they intend to do in their writing.

Children who can use this kind of metalanguage will also be better equipped to reflect on *how* they approach reading, writing, speaking and listening. As they become more aware of the processes they use, they are more likely to take control of their own reading and writing development (Quick *et al.*, 1994; Hall *et al.*, 1998; Williams, 2000). This awareness, known as 'metacognition' (or knowledge about learning), can enable children to find ways of tackling new problems or identify more effective ways of overcoming difficulties. Children can be encouraged to reflect on their reading, writing, speaking and listening before, during or after an activity.

### Before

- Prompt children to discuss how they will approach a task or what they will do if they face a difficulty: for example, how they will tackle spelling.
- Model being a reflective language and literacy user, for instance by talking through your own decisions when writing or talking through why you have a certain opinion about a book.

### During

- As children work (for example in guided reading or writing sessions), ask them to talk through the way they are approaching tasks, such as how they are accessing information on a Web site.
- Invite children to share work in progress with a group/rest of the class and ask for comments or help.

### After

- Ask children to describe how they tackled a task, compare different approaches and discuss which methods were most effective.
- Ask children to devise charts or guidelines for tackling a literacy/language activity, for example the writing process.
- Use literacy and language conferences to provide an opportunity for children to reflect on the way they have used language.

The following list suggests the kinds of questions that children can be encouraged to ask themselves as they reflect on their learning:

### Questions for children to ask about their use of language and literacy:

- Did I structure my story/speech/instructions in a way that was helpful to my listeners? If not, why not?
- What could I have said to move the discussion forward?
- Is this making sense? What can I do if it's not?
- What do I do when I get stuck on a word when I'm reading?
- What do I think about this character? What's prompting me to think like this?
- How can I locate the information I need from this Web site?
- What can I do when I can't think of an idea?
- How should I approach planning this?
- What kind of language would be appropriate here?
- How is writing different on screen from on paper?
- What do I do when I can't spell a word?
- Does the piece of writing have the effect I want it to have? If not, why not?
- How would a reader react at this point of my writing?

# Reflective questions

1. Consider the literacy hour structure. What are the advantages and possible drawbacks? How can you ensure that children's learning does not become fragmented as a result of the four-part structure?

2. Evaluate your own skills in promoting discussion. How effectively do you enter into 'learning conversations' with children? When might it be appropriate to direct or give children information rather than helping them discover it for themselves?

3. Consider your recent experiences of delivering/observing literacy teaching. What subject knowledge was necessary? How was the focus of each lesson linked to children's independent reading, writing, speaking and listening? You can begin to audit your subject knowledge in relation to:

- your ability to *define and identify* word, sentence and text level aspects of language and literature;
- your understanding of how this knowledge is *relevant* to planning, teaching and assessment;
- your ability to *apply* this knowledge in learning, teaching and/or assessment contexts.

## FURTHER READING

Beard, R. (1999) *National Literacy Strategy: Review of Research and other Related Evidence*. London: DfEE.

Provides references to research underpinning the approaches adopted by the National Literacy Strategy.

Bunting, R. (2000) *Teaching About Language in the Primary Years*. London: David Fulton Publishers.

Links an analysis of linguistic and textual features with practical suggestions for classroom activities.

Crystal, D. (1988) *Rediscover Grammar*. London: Longman.

Accessible support for understanding grammatical conventions.

Gamble, N. and Yates, N. (2002) *Exploring Children's Literature: Teaching the Language and Reading of Fiction*. London: Paul Chapman Publishing.

An accessible guide to the features and genres of children's fiction.

Mercer, N. (1995) *The Guided Construction of Knowledge: Talk Amongst Teachers and Learners*. Clevedon: Multilingual Matters.

An exploration of teacher/pupil interaction.

## REFERENCES

Alexander, R. (1995) *Versions of Primary Education*. London: Routledge.

Corden, R. (2000) *Literacy and Learning Through Talk*. Buckingham: Oxford University Press.

Department for Education and Employment (DfEE) (1998) *National Literacy Strategy Framework for Teaching*. London: HMSO.

Department for Education and Employment (DfEE) (1999) *Training Modules: Teaching and Learning Strategies*. London: DfEE Publications.

Department for Education and Employment (DfEE) (2000) *The National Curriculum for English*. London: HMSO.

Drake, J. (2001) *Planning Children's Play and Learning in the Foundation Stage*. London: David Fulton Publishers.

Edwards, A. D. (1992) 'Teacher talk and pupil competence', in Norman, K. (ed.) *Thinking Voices: The Work of the National Oracy Project*. London: Hodder & Stoughton.

Edwards, T. (2003) 'Purposes and characteristics of whole-class dialogue, in *New Perspectives on Spoken English in the Classroom*. London: QCA, pp. 38–40.

Hall, K. (2001) 'An analysis of primary literacy policy in England using Barthes' notion of "readerly" and "writerly" texts', *Journal of Early Childhood Literacy*, 1(2), 153–65.

Hall, K. and Myers, J. (1998) 'That's just the way I am: metacognition, personal intelligence and reading', *Reading*, 32(2), 8–13.

Marshall, B. (1998) 'English teachers and the third way', in Cox, B. (ed.) *Literacy is Not Enough*. Manchester: Manchester University Press.

Meek, M. (1998) 'Important reading lessons', in Cox, B. (ed.) *Literacy is Not Enough*. Manchester: Manchester University Press.

Mercer, N. (1995) *The Guided Construction of Knowledge: Talk Amongst Teachers and Learners*. Clevedon: Multilingual Matters.

Mortimore, P. (1998) 'Effective Schools for Primary Students', in *The Road to Improvement: Reflections on School Effectiveness*. Lisse: Swets & Zeitlinger, pp. 49–68.

Qualifications and Curriculum Authority (QCA) (2000) *Curriculum Guidance for the Foundation Stage*. London: QCA.

Quick, J. and Winter, C. (1994) 'Teaching the language of learning: towards a metacognitive approach to pupil empowerment', *British Educational Research Journal*, 20(4), 429–45.

Siraj-Blatchford, I., Sylva, K., Muttock, S., Gilden, R. and Bell, D. (2002) *Researching Effective Pedagogy in the Early Years*. London: DfES.

Skidmore, D., Perez-Parent, M. and Arnfield, S. (2003) 'Teacher-pupil dialogue in the guided reading session', *Reading: Literacy and Language*, 37(2), 47–53.

Vygotsky, L. S. (1978) *Mind in Society*. Cambridge MA: Harvard University Press.

Wells, G. (1985) *The Meaning Makers: Children Learning Through Language and Using Language to Learn*. London: Hodder & Stoughton.

Williams, M. (2000) 'The part that metacognition can play in raising standards in English at Key Stage 2', *Reading* 34(1), 3–8.

Wray, D., Medwell, J., Poulson, L. and Fox, R. (2002) *Teaching Literacy Effectively in the Primary School*. London: Routledge Falmer.

## CHILDREN'S BOOKS

Baker, J. (1998) *Where the Forest Meets the Sea*. London: Walker.

Burningham, J. (1991) *Oi! Get Off Our Train*. London: Red Fox.

Butterworth, N. and Inkpen, M. (1993) *Jasper's Beanstalk*. London: Hodder Children's Books.

Harrison, M. and Stuart-Clark, M. (1990) *The Oxford Book of Story Poems*. Oxford: Oxford University Press.

James, S. (1993) *Dear Greenpeace*. London: Walker.

Morpurgo, M. (1995) *The Wreck of the Zanzibar*. London: Mammoth.

# 8 Planning to Teach English

In this chapter, we investigate planning for English to support effective teaching and learning. An overview of different types of planning is followed by practical guidance for planning for English in the Foundation Stage and primary years. Planning will be informed by sound subject knowledge, which was explored in the previous chapter.

In this book so far, we have established some principles for effective teaching and learning, emphasizing the importance of:

- providing opportunities for children to increase their understanding of linguistic diversity;
- recognizing and valuing the language(s) that children bring with them to school;
- treating children as independent, active and autonomous language users whilst at school;
- providing opportunities for children to read, write, speak and listen for a variety of purposes so that they develop their ability to use language appropriately in different contexts;
- providing meaningful contexts for language and literacy use;
- providing opportunities for children to read and write in new ways and encourage them to be flexible enough to respond to future change;
- developing children's awareness that people's values, perspectives and prejudices influence the way they use language in speaking and writing;
- providing activities in which reading, writing, speaking and listening are integrated;
- providing opportunities for children to engage in a variety of texts, including children's literature, everyday texts, popular culture and a range of digital and print-based sources of information;
- recognizing and preparing children to meet the demands on literacy and language made by different subjects.

Through careful planning, teachers can find imaginative ways to interpret the curriculum and put these understandings of effective teaching and learning into practice. This can be a creative and empowering process.

As children move through school it is clearly important to ensure that they make progress. Bruner's concept of a 'spiral curriculum' is helpful here (Bruner, 1966). Progression in English involves revisiting the same skills, knowledge and understandings with greater degrees of complexity and depth. This means that planning needs to be influenced by a consideration of children's needs to ensure that learning opportunities build on what they already know and what has gone before. As they develop, children are introduced to a greater variety of audiences for their language and literacy and a widening range of texts. They are expected to be able to read, write, speak and listen in these different contexts with growing autonomy, expertise and appropriateness. This may involve using and encountering increasing degrees of complexity and formality.

Careful planning is therefore necessary to ensure:

- **progression** so that children face increasingly challenging experiences that build on those that have gone before;
- **continuity of approach** so that children consolidate and build on their understandings of language and literacy;
- **breadth and balance** so that children develop a range of skills and concepts, encounter diverse texts and experience a variety of teaching approaches and learning opportunities.

## The planning process – an overview

Planning takes place at a number of levels, long term, medium term and short term, which are described in Table 8.1. As can be seen, planning at each stage is informed by knowledge about the children. Practical guidance on gathering this knowledge through a range of assessment procedures is provided in the next chapter.

## Planning for 'Communication, Language and Literacy' in the Foundation Stage

Practitioners in the Foundation Stage need to plan to ensure that children encounter a range of experiences that address all areas of learning, while maintaining the flexibility to respond to their interests, enthusiasms, needs and prior experiences. Planning in the area most closely related to English is based around the 'Communication, Language and Literacy' area of learning from the Curriculum Guidance for the Foundation Stage. Planning for children in Reception is also informed by the NLS objectives (which are in line with the ELGs).

Long-term plans provide an overview of the way that skills and concepts will be developed in relation to different themes throughout the year. They need to ensure that children in a setting for more than a year do not repeat the same series of activities. Plans identify how the indoor and outdoor learning environment will be used and suggest stimuli that could provide starting points for learning, such as special events,

**Table 8.1. Levels of planning**

| | Description | Planning decisions | What do we need to know about the children in order to make these decisions? |
|---|---|---|---|
| **Long-term planning** | | | |
| (*Time scale*: period during which children attend the school or early years setting) | Outlines what will be taught in each term of each year throughout the school or early years setting. | How can we meet the needs of the children in our school? How can we ensure balance, breadth, continuity and progression *during the time children are at the school or early years setting*? | What are the needs of *the children in our school or early years setting*? |
| **Medium-term planning** | | | |
| (*Time scale*: half term or term) | Draws objectives from the long-term plan and provides more detail on the contexts in which these objectives will be taught. | How shall we interpret the long-term plan in a way that is meaningful, relevant and appropriate to this cohort of children? How can we ensure balance, breadth, continuity and progression *during this half-term or term*? | What are the needs and interests of *this cohort of children*? What do termly or half-termly assessments tell us about their progress? |
| **Short-term planning** | | | |
| (*Time scale*: day, week or unit) | Maps out activities over a day, week or more (through session, weekly or unit planning) and specifies precise intentions about what children and adults will do within each activity. | How shall I sequence these activities in a meaningful way? How can I ensure balance, breadth, continuity and progression *over a day or week*? Which strategies and activities shall I use? Do I need to adapt the plan in any way as a result of assessment? | What are the emerging needs and interests of *groups or individuals*? How are the children in my class responding to this unit of work? |

stories, visits or visitors. In some settings, a medium-term plan is also produced that provides more detail on precise activities and experiences. Compiling a medium-term plan involves selecting a theme that will provide a motivating context for learning. Relevant ELGs are selected from all areas and then learning intentions are devised to meet the needs of children at different stages of development.

Short-term planning often takes place during a weekly or daily review where staff share their observations of children's experiences and decide which activities to use to encourage progress. Teachers specify 'learning intentions' (QCA, 2001: 4) for each activity, which are based on the Early Learning Goals or 'stepping stones'. These may be drawn from the long-term or medium-term plan or developed as a result of assessment in order to respond to children's interests and needs.

**Table 8.2. Foundation Stage weekly plan**

THEME: **Plants/growth**          Garden Centre          w/b 6 April

| | What do we want the children to learn | How will we enable this learning to take place? |
|---|---|---|
| | **Learning intentions (based on stepping stones/ELGs)** | **Vocabulary** |
| **Personal, social and emotional development** | • Take turns<br>• Show caring for living things<br>• Select and use resources independently | 'Please can I have a turn?' |
| **Communication, language and literacy**<br>Objectives from the literacy framework | • Listen and respond to stories<br><br>• Take part in role play<br>• Write for different purposes<br><br>• Use sequence words<br><br>• Hear/say phoneme 'g', 's', 't'<br>• Recognize letters 'g', 's', 't' | <br><br><br><br><br>first, then, after that |
| **Mathematical development**<br>Objectives from the mathematics framework | • Use number names<br>• Count objects<br>• Recognize numerals<br>• Use vocabulary to compare size | Numbers 1–10<br>More than<br>Less than<br><br>Bigger, smaller, more |
| **Knowledge and understanding of the world** | • Identify features of plants<br>• Show awareness of change<br>• Recognize everyday use of ICT | Stem, leaf, leaves, root<br>Grow/n<br>Longer, taller<br>More, fewer<br>scan, till |
| **Physical development** | • Explore malleable materials<br>• Handle tools with care | Spade, fork, trowel, dig, plant |
| **Creative development** | • Explore colour and texture | Rough, smooth |

| How will we know who has learned what? | | What next? |
| --- | --- | --- |
| **Activities/routines** | **Assessment** | **Notes on how assessments will inform future plans** |
| Garden centre role play – roles – customer/assistant | Note which children take on roles | |
| Plant seeds<br>Care for seedlings | | |
| *Jasper's Beanstalk* (Butterworth and Inkpen)<br>*Titch* (Hutchins)<br>Songs: Oats, Peas, Beans and Barley grow<br>Action rhyme: Growing flowers | | |
| Customers/assistants in garden centre<br>Make labels and notices for garden centre | Note use of language in role | |
| Show others how to prepare cress for planting | Collect example of labels created | |
| Find objects beginning with sounds<br>Sort letters and objects<br>Group objects | | |
| Count plant pots, bulbs and seeds | List children who know and can use numbers to 5 | |
| Organize different sizes of plant pots | List children who know 5–10 and above | |
| Sketches/paintings of plants<br>Plant seeds in garden and inside<br>Sow cress<br>Use till, computer and price scanner in role-play area | Observation: can describe plant or painting using appropriate vocabulary | |
| Outside area – earth/water<br>Planting seeds and seedlings | Record children who dig – can hold spade and control | |
| Collect and compare leaves<br>Collage | Use of different textures | |

Learning intentions specify what practitioners hope the children will achieve through an activity, although the children themselves may take the activity in an unexpected direction that actually develops learning in a different way. At the planning stage, practitioners make decisions about their own role within each activity. They may work alongside children, start them off and then withdraw, or leave them to play independently. At other times they will plan opportunities for observation and intervene only if they feel they can extend children's engagement with a task or activity. Short-term planning needs to be flexible enough to achieve a balance between adult directed and child initiated tasks.

Sample weekly and activity plans are included in Tables 8.2 and 8.3. These plans are linked to the series of activities based on a garden centre trip discussed in the previous chapter. Note how 'Communication, Language and Literacy' is not addressed discretely but integrated with learning in other areas.

**Table 8.3. Foundation Stage session plan**

**Activity:**

Planting beans

Grouping of children: 3–4 children

| Main learning intentions: | Key vocabulary/questions |
| --- | --- |
| Show care for living things (PSED) | Cover |
| Write label (CLL) | Bean |
| Use number names (MD) | Water |
| | Rough, dry, soft, smooth |
| | Numbers: 1–10 |
| | What will it need to make it grow? |
| | What will you write? |
| | What does it feel like? |

| Resources: | Adapting the activity for the individual children |
| --- | --- |
| Garden | Children may: |
| Trowels | • need additional help with digging |
| Watering can | • need support with counting |
| Bean | • count out beans for self |
| | • count out beans for next group |
| | • need encouragement to write |

**Children for whom this activity is particularly appropriate**

Morning:     Sam, Ranjit, Tom (counting to five)
                Sofia, Ayesha, Sam (encourage writing label)

Afternoon:    Katy and Naima (counting to 10) Luke, Hannah (counting to 5)
                Joanna, Jasdeep, Samina (encourage to write names)

# Planning for English at Key Stages 1 and 2

Most primary schools in England use the National Literacy Strategy Framework for Teaching (DfEE, 1998) as the basis for their long-term planning for reading and writing teaching. This specifies a wide range of text, sentence and word level objectives to be taught in each term within a specified range of texts. The National Literacy Strategy (NLS) has produced sample plans for medium- and short-term planning (DfES, 2003a, 2003b) and there are currently many published schemes available that supply detailed plans and suggested activities for literacy teaching.

These can provide valuable support for teachers lacking in time or confidence, but the most effective planning is usually done by teachers who know the needs of the children in their class. The process of creating their own plans enables teachers to:

- familiarize themselves with and gain ownership of what they will teach;
- interpret guidelines in response to the needs of the children;
- find motivating and meaningful contexts for learning.

Here we begin by exploring the process of planning from the NLS Framework and then consider other aspects of planning for English.

# Medium-term planning from the NLS Framework

At the medium-term planning stage, teachers find ways of sequencing, linking and contextualizing the objectives within the Framework. The level of detail within medium-term plans varies from school to school. Regardless of the school's expectations for recording planning, it is important to think through ideas thoroughly at the medium-term planning stage. This means that different options can be considered and resources prepared. A four-stage process for devising detailed medium-term plans from the NLS Framework is outlined below.

## Step 1: Identifying learning objectives

The first stage of the planning process involves becoming familiar with the range of objectives that will be taught during the half term or term. Often the teaching objectives are fairly broad and need to be broken down into more focused learning objectives. At this stage it is helpful to refer to the whole NLS Framework to see whether objectives build on those from previous years or introduce new concepts or skills.

Teachers aim to address all of the objectives in the appropriate term, but certain *key objectives* will inevitably be prioritized. These key objectives will be identified as a result of assessment or may reflect a particular focus for the school. Objectives may also be supplemented by those that relate to other skills or concepts that are pertinent to the children.

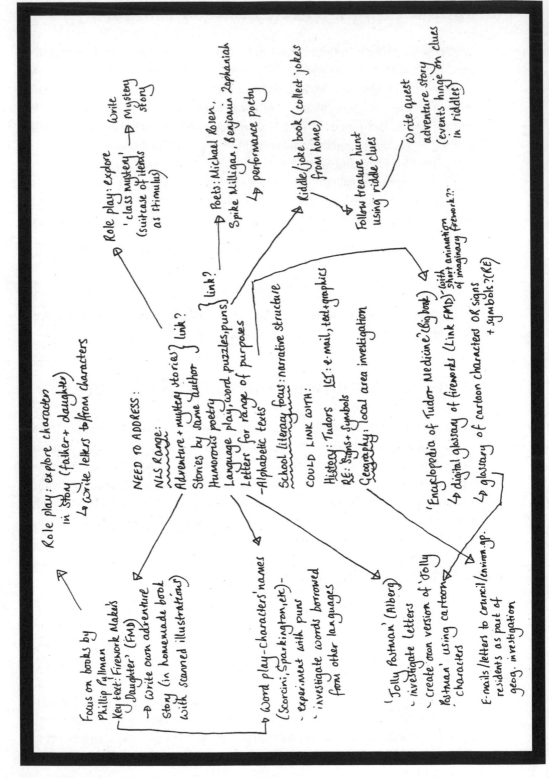

Figure 8.1. Ideas for medium-term planning

## Step 2: Identifying continuous objectives

Some objectives will need continual reinforcement. These may be ongoing objectives, such as 'to reinforce word level skills through shared and guided reading' (which occurs throughout Key Stage 1) or may relate to a concept or skill that the children have found difficult or of which they have previously had little experience. These objectives are known as *continuous objectives* and will be taught during the entire period of the medium-term plan.

## Stage 3: Identifying blocked objectives

Other objectives may be linked together and taught during a specified period of time (perhaps two or three weeks). These are known as *blocked objectives*. At this stage teachers consider objectives that may fit together and generate activities within which they could be taught. This involves choosing suitable *texts* and *contexts* through which objectives can be met and considering possible *outcomes* that children may produce, such as pieces of writing, presentations, performances and Web sites. Reading and writing activities should be purposeful, motivating and meaningful to the children and close links should be made between different areas of learning. This means integrating:

- reading, writing, speaking and listening;
- text, sentence and word level objectives;
- different subjects within the curriculum.

Many teachers find it helpful to begin by generating lists of possible texts and contexts that could be used and outcomes that children could produce (see Figure 8.1).

It is common practice to devote one set of blocked objectives to each text type identified in the range for a particular term (for example, letters, adventure stories, humorous poetry) and link objectives relating to reading and writing this kind of text. Often, however, links can be made between different types of texts (for instance using a focus on narrative as a stimulus for letter writing) and so a set of blocked objectives could include work on two or more text types.

## Stage 4: Planning units of work

Once ideas have been generated, a series of *units of work* can be planned. Each unit of work will contain a set of blocked objectives and associated activities. In planning a unit of work, teachers place activities and objectives in the probable order in which they will be addressed in the classroom. At this stage, many schools simply identify a sequence of objectives that will be taught (see Table 8.4) whereas others specify learning activities, assessment opportunities and resources (see Table 8.5). The time spent on each unit of work will vary to reflect the number of objectives addressed and the complexity of the focus.

**Table 8.4. Extract from medium-term plan**

This shows continuous objectives and one set of blocked objectives linked to adventure stories. A complete plan would include further sets of blocked objectives related to other units.

Objectives are drawn from year 3, term 3 of the NLS Framework (DfEE, 1998).

**Key objectives are written in bold.**

| Week(s) | Word level objectives | Sentence level objectives |
|---|---|---|
| **Continuous objectives** | | |
| | Revise and consolidate:<br>1 the spelling of words containing long vowel phoneme<br>2 identify, blend and segment phonemes<br>3 read and spell high-frequency words from KS1<br>4 discriminate syllables in reading and spelling<br>5 identify misspelt words, keep individual lists and learn to spell them<br>**6 use independent spelling strategies**<br>**7 practise new spellings using look-say-cover-write-check**<br>17 practise correct formation of basic joins in handwriting | 1 use awareness of the grammar to decipher new or unfamiliar words |
| **Blocked objectives** | | |
| | 8 identify short words from long words as an aid to spelling | 7 become aware of the use of commas in marking grammatical boundaries within sentences<br>6 investigate through reading how words and phrases can signal time sequences |
| | | 6 investigate through reading how words and phrases can signal time sequences |
| | 13 collect synonyms which will be useful in writing dialogue exploring effect on meaning | 4 use speech marks and other dialogue punctuation appropriately in writing and use conventions which mark boundaries between spoken words and rest of the sentence<br>3 ensure grammatical agreement in speech and writing of pronouns and verbs |

| Text level objectives | Text |
| --- | --- |

5 discuss characters' feelings, behaviour, relationships
3 distinguish between first- and third-person accounts
12 write a first-person account
16 read examples of letters
20 write letters
22 experiment with recounting same event
in variety of ways

Adventure stories: *The Firework-Maker's Daughter* (Pullman)

1 re-tell points of story in sequence
4 consider the credibility of events
**10 plot a sequence of episodes modelled
on a known story**
2 refer to significant aspects of the text, e.g. opening,
build-up, atmosphere and know how language is used
to create these
13 write more extended stories based on
a plan of incidents
11 write openings to stories or chapters linked to or
arising from reading; focus on language to create effects

**Table 8.5. Extract from detailed medium-term plan**

This is an extract from a more detailed plan based on the blocked set of objectives. It shows planning relating to a unit on adventure stories.

T = text level objective; S = sentence level objective; W = word level objective

| Subject unit planning sheet: English | |
| --- | --- |
| **Learning objectives:** | **Assessment of outcomes criteria: mode:** |
| T1 to be able to re-tell points of story in sequence<br>S6 to be able to use temporal connectives (words and phrases to signal time sequences), e.g. first, then, after, meanwhile, once, when | Can they retell the main points of the story in sequence using appropriate temporal connectives?<br>Mode: Observation of retelling<br>(Focus group: whales) |
| **T13 to write an extended story based on the plan**<br><br>T10 to plot a sequence of episodes as a plan for writing<br><br>S6 to be able to use temporal connectives (words and phrases to signal time sequences), e.g. first, then, after, meanwhile, once, when<br><br>To be able to establish a 'back story' for their main character (what happened to them before the story started) | Can they use an appropriate range of temporal connectives<br>Mode: Observation<br>(Focus: Sharks) |
| T2 to be able to describe way that exposition is used to establish character and setting in opening of *The Firework-Maker's Daughter* (Pullman) | |

| Subject: | | Class: | |
| --- | --- | --- | --- |
| **Activity and organization (include differentiation)** | **Pupil outputs** | **Special resources needed** | **Links (inc. literacy, numeracy and ICT)** |
| Work in pairs to draw map of the main events of the story<br>Model retelling of story using words such as 'first', 'then', 'after' to signal time sequences<br>Paired work: retell the story<br>Plot Lila's journey onto map to identify key events and what motivates them. Discuss how Lila feels at different points in the story – when is she most afraid? Discuss opening, build-up, climax, resolution<br>Investigate narrative structure of guided reading texts and compare structures (using graphic organizers)<br>Each group to plan and give two-minute sales pitch for book read during guided reading<br>Display graphic organizers and ask children to add titles of books which fit similar structures | Map | *The Firework-Maker's Daughter* (Pullman)<br><br>Saved copies of chosen extracts to be used on electronic whiteboard<br><br>Guided reading texts | |
| **Write adventure story in chapters, involving the following activities:**<br><br>Use map to create plan for quest based on structure of FMD (child wants something that parent won't let them have, goes on quest to find it, then returns to help parent who is in trouble as result of what happened) – mark on events that will happen in key places<br>Talk through main events of story with a partner (using map to support) and using words and phrases to signal time sequences<br><br>Use freezeframes/hotseating to explore 'back story' for their own stories (i.e. how have their characters arrived where they are at the start of the story)<br><br>Discuss information given about Lila in opening to story and analyse structure<br>Discuss openings in guided texts<br>Compare openings | **Handmade book to be word processed, laminated and presented to infant class**<br><br>Plans for own story (collated in planning folder)<br><br><br>Poster: ideas for story openings | Bookmaking equipment | Combining text and graphics |

**Table 8.5.** Extract from detailed medium-term plan (continued)

T = text level objective; S = sentence level objective; W = word level objective

| Subject unit planning sheet: English | |
|---|---|
| **Learning objectives:** | **Assessment of outcomes criteria: mode:** |
| S6 to be able to use temporal connectives (words and phrases to signal time sequences), e.g. first, then, after, meanwhile, once, when <br> T11 to use language to establish character and setting in a story opening | |
| T13 to use paragraphs to organize the narrative | |
| S4 to use speech marks and other dialogue punctuation appropriately in writing <br> W13 to use synonyms for 'said' in writing dialogue | |
| T2 to describe how language is used to create tension in the build-up | |
| T11 to use language to build tension in the build-up in their own story | |
| T2 to describe how language is used to create atmosphere in establishing setting | |
| T11 to use language to create atmosphere in establishing setting | |
| | Can they write a story that contains: <br> • paragraphs <br> • sequence of episodes <br> • appropriate use of temporal connectives <br> • opening that establishes character and setting <br><br> Mode: Analysis of story |

154

| Subject: | | Class: | |
|---|---|---|---|
| **Activity and organization (include differentiation)** | **Pupil outputs** | **Special resources needed** | **Links (inc. literacy, numeracy and ICT)** |

155

Analyse use of temporal connectives in opening passage

Use temporal connectives in own story
Write own opening


Analysis of use of paragraphs story and apply to own

Improvise scene between own main character and parent to explore relationship: at moment when character tells parent what s/he wants
Write dialogue based on this scene using accurate speech punctuation and considering effect of using synonyms for 'said'

Focus on pp. 43–8
Discuss build up of tension and note role of illustrations in enhancing tension
Read drafts to response partners. Stop at key points and see if they can predict what will happen. Share ways of increasing tension in whole class

Pairs: draw the cave of *Razvani the Fire-Fiend* (pp. 55–7) based on description in book
Create found poem about the cave using descriptive words and phrases from the passage
Use drama (freezeframe and thought tracking) to explore children's own reactions to entry to the cave and then compare these to Lila's – what does this tell us about her?
Use drama to explore key place in own story. Give guided tour of place to a partner
Write passage establishing setting at key moment of story

Draft, revise own story and publish in book

Collection of synonyms for 'said' collected earlier in term

Guidelines on working with response partners devised earlier in term

Found poem — Art materials

PLANNING TO TEACH ENGLISH

The planning extract in Figure 8.5 includes some common features of effective literacy planning:

- activities are sequenced so that they build on those that have gone before;
- the children will work towards an outcome (making a book);
- opportunities for speaking and listening are integrated with those for reading and writing;
- some objectives are repeated during the unit;
- texts, sentence and word level objectives are linked;
- NLS teaching objectives are broken down into focused learning objectives.

## Planning for mixed-age classes

Teachers with mixed-age classes need to find ways of using the NLS Framework flexibly. Some schools use the objectives on a two-year rolling programme: for example, in a year 3/4 class, the teacher may use objectives for year 3 during one year and those for year 4 the following year. In each year he or she may use objectives from other years to support or extend the learning. In other schools, the class works from one set of key objectives that combine objectives from two or more years. It is evident that careful long-term planning to ensure continuity and progression for different cohorts of children is vital in these situations.

# Short-term planning from the NLS Framework

Detailed medium-term plans provide a bank of suggestions for learning activities that are then used in *short-term plans*. Short-term plans may include *weekly or unit plans* and *session plans*.

## Weekly/unit plans

Weekly planning involves deciding how the unit of work will be mapped onto a series of literacy hours and how whole-class, guided and group work will be used. A series of literacy hours can all too easily become fragmented if work on different objectives is not integrated. This can be avoided by developing ideas and concepts over a series of hours, gradually building towards one or more significant outcome. When the literacy hour was first introduced, most teachers planned using a weekly planning format but current NLS guidance suggests that it is more helpful to create detailed planning for the whole period of the unit. This enables teachers to plan for continuity within and between weeks, but it must be stressed that plans will need to be adapted in response to children's needs. Table 8.6 contains an example of a weekly plan taken from the unit on adventure stories outlined in Table 8.5.

**Table 8.6. Weekly plan/extract from unit plan**

SR = shared reading      GR = guided reading      SLW = sentence level work
WLW = word level work    FMD = *Firework-Maker's Daughter* (Pullman)

| 3RN W/b: 2 June | Shared text | Focused word/ sentence level work | Guided work | Independent work | Plenary |
|---|---|---|---|---|---|
| Monday | SR Recap on main points of story using illustrations from book as prompt<br><br>SLW Use temporal connectives (first, then, next) to signal sequence of events in retelling | | | GR: Seahorses group Read final chapter of guided reading book. Plot main events of story on map and compare to structure of FMD. | Work in mixed-ability pairs to create map of places in story and then begin to rehearse an oral retelling using time connectives to help sequence events. | Ask one pair to retell events whilst others listen for similarities/ differences to their own version. Discuss reasons for differences. |
| Tuesday | SR Discuss structure of FMD by marking Lila's journey onto map: i.e. child goes away from home on a quest and returns to use what she knows to help parent<br><br>WLW Strategies for learning words from own spelling lists | | | GR: Whales group Read and discuss structure of guided reading book. Plot main events on map and compare to structure of FMD. Complete graphic organizer. | Ability groups: learning spellings using look-cover-remember-write-check. Playing spelling games to consolidate spelling of personal word list. | Discuss and share strategies used to learn how to spell words on list. |
| Wednesday | SR Ask guided groups to report on structure of stories they have read. Compare to that of FMD. Compare graphic organizers. Use structure of FMD to plan story. Mark ideas onto map using time connectives to sequence ideas | | | GW: Sharks group Planning story | Mixed-ability pairs: create own skeleton plan and then draw map of the places visited. Put in planning folder for adventure story. | Ask two pairs to share plans for stories: how are they similar to/different from FMD? |
| Thursday | Drama: session to help children develop main characters for their own stories.<br>Use hotseating to explore character and freezeframes to show how they react at key moments in the story.<br>Use freezeframes as starting point for retelling planned story to rest of the group.<br>Next create three freezeframes representing the character's life up to the point where story begins.<br>Record what is known about character on an outline of the person. Put in planning folder.<br>Map character's thoughts at different points of story onto maps prepared yesterday. | | | | | |
| Friday | SR Discuss exposition in opening: what kind of information is provided? How does it relate to what follows in rest of story?<br>Explore use of temporal connectives in passage: once, many a time, when, soon. How does their use affect reader?<br>SW Use structure of FMD to write own opening. | | | GW: Dolphins group Planning story | Write own story opening using ideas explored through drama and structure used in FMD. Seahorses/Sharks groups: use FMD as model. Turtles: use FMD as model (support: Mrs Lloyd). Whales group: encourage originality in opening. | Read openings. Rest of class evaluate: what do they learn about character? How does the opening hint at what will happen in rest of story? |

A number of observations can be made about this plan:

- There is continuity during the week. Activities build on one another and the children use their experience of reading and analysing texts to feed into their writing.
- Some tasks relate to the continuous spelling objective.
- Many of the activities are introduced during whole-class sessions before they are explored in independent work.
- Some activities, such as the use of writing response partners, are not modelled in this way. (This is because the children are already confident with the processes involved. If they had not been, then the teacher would have planned to spend time discussing the process of using response partners.)
- Work on sentence and text level work is closely linked.
- There are many opportunities to use speaking and listening to support reading and writing.
- Whilst most drama work usually takes place outside the literacy hour, the teacher has decided that it is appropriate to use one hour of this week as an extended drama session to explore ideas to be used in Friday's session.
- Sometimes children work in mixed-ability groups and sometimes tasks are differentiated. (Further guidance on differentiation is provided in Chapter 11.)

When planning, it is important to consider the role of other adults within the classroom. Other adults can provide valuable support for learning, but it is important that children do not come to rely on the adults they work alongside. Adult support should be used to promote independence rather than solve problems for children. Teachers therefore need to plan to ensure that the support offered by these colleagues is deployed effectively. Other adults will participate in learning activities in different ways. They may:

- support a group or individual children, for example by encouraging them to apply what has been learned or priming them for shared work by visiting texts or ideas before whole-class sessions;
- carry out observations of children for assessment purposes, for instance monitoring and noting contributions during whole-class sessions or observing and recording children's response to activities;
- take part in whole-class sessions, for example presenting ideas jointly with the teacher, leading sessions to release the teacher to observe or enabling children to access an activity through translation or interpretation.

## Session plans for adult-led activities

Whilst the weekly plan outlines the activities in which children will be involved (including references to differentiation), session plans are used to support adult-led activities and are based on clear, precise learning objectives. A session plan may be written for a *complete lesson* (for example a whole literacy hour), a *complete activity* (such as guided writing) or a *part of a lesson* (such as shared writing or the plenary). The process of compiling a session plan is particularly useful for student and beginning teachers. At this stage it is important to identify a precise objective for each session.

A sample session plan is presented in Figure 8.2. This relates to the highlighted section of the weekly plan in Table 8.6.

Session plans usually follow a three-part structure that includes an introduction, development and conclusion. The purpose and planning decisions involved in each of these are outlined below.

## Introduction

*Purpose*:

- to ensure that children are clear about what they will learn and why it is relevant;
- to motivate children to participate.

*Planning for the introduction will involve deciding*:

- how to capture children's interests, for example through use of puppets, drama, images;
- how to encourage children to recap on prior learning or previous relevant experiences (gained in or out of school);
- on key questions to address;
- how to encourage interaction and discussion, for instance through modelling tentative talk, using talk partners, individual whiteboards or games;
- how to make expectations clear to children;
- how to organize children, use other adults and manage resources.

## Development

*Purpose*: to engage children in learning, through working alongside an adult, with other children or individually.

*Planning for the development will involve deciding*:

- on an activity that is purposeful and motivating;
- how to differentiate activities (for instance, through objective, grouping, task, resources, input, outcome);
- what children will do once they have finished;
- how to make expectations clear to children;
- how to organize children, use other adults and manage resources.

## Conclusion

*Purpose*: to enable children to reflect on and review what they have done and make links to future learning.

**Figure 8.2. Session plan**

Session plan:    Thursday

Session Title:    Story openings
Class: 3RN

**Resources:**    **saved copy of opening extract**
**electronic whiteboard**

**class plan of new story**
**individual whiteboards and pens**

**Objectives:**    T2 to be able to describe way that exposition is used to establish character and setting

**Assessment of outcomes:**
**Criteria:** can children describe the way that character and setting are established in the opening of FMD?
**Mode:** oral (focus on Sharks)

L/A = questions for least able children
M/A = questions for most able children

| What will you do/say | What will the children do? |
|---|---|
| **Shared Reading** | |
| **Introduction** | |
| Remind children they will be writing own adventure story based on characters and stories explored through drama | |
| What is the purpose of a story opening? (Scribe ideas on poster: 'ideas for story openings') | Talk partners: share and report back initial thoughts |
| Outline aim of lesson: to look at opening of FMD to get some ideas for our own opening (and add further suggestions to poster) | |
| **Development** | |
| L/A Having already read the whole story, what do we know about Lila? Record suggestions | Talk partners: share and report back ideas |
| Read story opening What do we learn about Lila just from the opening? | Talk partners: reread and discuss what the reader learns from this part (family, poor, firework-maker's daughter, passion for fireworks and talent for making them, shows initiative, etc.) |
| | Report back ideas and highlight relevant parts of text |
| L/A Use 'role on the wall' to collect information about Lila: What do we know about her? How do we know it? How does this compare with what we know about her from reading whole story? | Compare ideas on 'role on wall' with earlier brainstorm based on whole story |
| M/A Why did Philip Pullman decide to tell us this information at the beginning? | Suggestions (hinting at events to come, creating expectations . . .) |

| What will you do/say | What will the children do? |
|---|---|

### Conclusion

What does this story opening tell us?
Return to 'story openings' poster – add suggestions based on discussion of this opening
Signal that similar ideas can be used for own story opening

Talk partners: summarize what Philip Pullman achieves through this opening in a sentence to be added to poster: 'A story opening can . . .'
Children share and evaluate summaries and one is chosen to add to poster

### Sentence level work

### Introduction

Recap on temporal connectives discussed earlier this week and add to class list. How were they useful when telling a story?

List connectives
Explain how they were used to help sequence story

Aim: have a closer look at *how* Philip Pullman writes his opening by focusing on how temporal connectives are used

### Development

Look at opening sentence: 'A thousand miles ago, in a country east of the jungle and south of the mountains, there lived a Firework-Maker called Lalchand and his daughter Lila.'
What does the reader learn from this?

Highlight information given in opening sentence in different colours to show which parts of sentence give information on time, place, character

Locate temporal connective
M/A What's strange about this?
Why do you think he chose to use this?

Identify 'a thousand miles ago'

Suggest reasons for this choice

Teacher demonstration: write sentence to start story based on class plan using similar structure
Set up brief supported writing activity (scribe for least able)

Supported writing: use individual whiteboards to write similar opening sentence for own story in pairs (to establish time, place and character)

Can you spot words in the passage that help us to sequence what we learn about Lila? Reread

Identify temporal connectives: once, many a time, when

Try swapping these around or experimenting with other time connectives from class list – what is the effect on the meaning?

Reread paragraph with connectives in different places
Discuss effect on reader

Teacher scribing: complete class story opening

L/A Read back what is written
Recap on main character and 'back story'
Suggest ways of writing this using connectives to help sequence

### Conclusion

Return to 'story openings' poster'

Paired discussion and report back

Outline paired task: writing story opening based on own plans

Summarize how temporal connectives can be used and add to story poster

*Planning for the conclusion will involve deciding*:

- how to encourage children to report back and summarize what has been learned;
- how reflection will be promoted (through whole-class/group or paired discussion or individual note making, and so on);
- how to clarify how future learning will build on what children have learned;
- how to make expectations clear to children;
- how to organize children, use other adults and manage resources.

## Planning independent tasks

It is important to provide opportunities for children to read, write, speak and listen without adult support. Of course 'independent' activities may not necessarily be individual. As explored earlier, children need to collaborate and interact with their peers, for example during group reading, paired writing or play-based activities. Within the literacy hour, planning for children to work independently also releases the teacher to provide focused support for particular groups through guided reading and writing. However, many teachers have found it difficult to organize independent literacy activities and either abandon guided work so that they can supervise the whole class or resort to planning 'safe' tasks that they know the children can complete without their help. The following guidelines are useful in planning effective independent activities.

### Guidelines for planning independent activities:

- the activity itself should be purposeful, motivating and well matched to the children's needs;
- grouping should be carefully considered. Remember that collaborative tasks offer rich opportunities for learning and that children can be grouped in many different ways;
- decide how the activity will be introduced during shared sessions. Effective stimuli should be used to motivate children to tackle the task and help them develop ideas. Careful modelling of what is expected can ensure that children are clear about what the task involves and how they could approach it. Guidelines for the task may then be devised with children;
- make sure that children know what they can do once they have finished. This may mean allocating each table a game or extension task, or providing a list of ongoing activities from which children can select (for example reading, writing dialogue journals, adding to interactive displays, learning individual spellings);
- discuss expectations for the activity with children. This may involve devising criteria that they can use to check or evaluate their own work;
- consider how resources and the classroom environment can be used to support the activity. Ensure that children have access to everything they need or know where they can get it;
- make sure that children know what to do if they have a difficulty. Encourage them to support one another and develop the confidence to try and overcome problems themselves. If the children lack confidence in certain areas (such as in spelling unknown words), then use teaching time to discuss and model strategies that can be used.

Often teachers feel pressurized into ensuring that all independent activities result in a recorded outcome. However, many valuable learning opportunities can arise from open-ended activities, such as investigations, games and book browsing. Opportunities for play are also important and can be used throughout early years and primary settings. Through play, children explore their ideas and understandings; they practise skills and learn to co-operate with one another. Play-based activities, involving puppets, role-play areas, toy figures and so on, can provide powerful opportunities for children to explore aspects of reading and writing during literacy lessons. Importantly the classroom ethos is key to successful independent work. Practical guidance on creating an environment that supports and encourages independence is contained in Chapter 10.

## Planning plenaries

In Chapter 7, we explored the importance of encouraging children to review and reflect on their learning. Plenary (or review) sessions provide a valuable opportunity for such reflection, enabling children to revisit what they have done, discuss what they have learned and begin to make links between this and other knowledge. The plenary also provides an opportunity to celebrate what children have done and for teachers to give feedback. Key questions to guide planning for plenaries include:

> What did we do?
> How did we do it?
> What did we learn?
> How can we use or apply what we have learnt?
> What shall we do next?

There are many ways of organizing plenaries and it is important to be clear about their purpose. Note the function and organization of each of the following sessions. The first, third and fourth examples involve the children in consolidating their understandings whilst the second concentrates on helping children articulate the processes they used.

> A group of **reception** children has been working with a classroom assistant to create their own skipping rhymes. They share their rhymes with the rest of the class who spot the rhyming words. They are challenged to try and think of other words to rhyme with those identified.

> A group of **year 2** pupils has been using a variety of sources (Web sites, different non-fiction books, and so on) to collect information in response to questions linked to the class topic on plants. In the plenary, the children are asked to explain how they accessed these different sources. The teacher scribes a list of tips for locating information based on their ideas.

> Having read the opening chapters of *The Angel of Nitshill Road* (Fine, 1992), a class of **year 4** children has recorded their thoughts on the main character, Celeste, in their

reading journals. One group present their thoughts to the rest of the class, who are invited to agree or disagree. Any challenges must be justified with reference to the text. The children then have two minutes to jot down any new thoughts about Celeste. These will be revisited the next day when they read the next chapter.

A group of **year 6** children has been devising arguments to persuade the council to build a skate park in the local area. In the plenary, the teacher takes on the role of the councillor and invites the children to persuade her to adopt the proposal. Following some attempts at persuasion, the teacher comes out of role and the class discusses what effective persuasion involves.

## Planning for speaking and listening

Importantly, the National Literacy Strategy was never intended to address all aspects of English and most notably did not provide guidance for teaching speaking and listening. In planning for speaking and listening, many schools use the document *Speaking, Listening, Learning* (QCA, 2003), which specifies aspects of speaking and listening that can be taught in different terms from year 1 to year 6 and provides some sample lessons. Suggestions for each term of each year are organized under four headings that reflect the different aspects of the speaking and listening Programmes of Study:

- speaking;
- listening;
- group discussion and interaction;
- drama.

Tables 8.7 and 8.8 show how aspects of speaking and listening can be linked to literacy and other subjects (and provide a possible model for planning these links).

**Table 8.7. Planning speaking and listening in Year 1, term 1**

| Speaking and listening objective (QCA, 2003) | Possible link objective (From NLS framework or other subject) | Learning opportunity through which both objectives could be met |
| --- | --- | --- |
| **Speaking** To describe incidents or tell stories from own experience, in an audible voice | **Literacy: Y1 T1T3** To notice difference between spoken and written forms through telling stories and comparing oral version with text | Create story map to represent the places visited during 'Talk Talk' (traditional story from Ghana which tells the story of people's reactions to a series of talking objects) and retell the story using map as a prompt |
| **Listening and responding** To listen with sustained concentration | **Literacy: Y1 T1T6** To recite stories and poems with predictable and repeating patterns | Listen to a reading of 'Too Much Talk' (Medearis, 1996) and 'Farmer Duck' (Waddell, 1995) and join in with repetitive refrains and phrases |
| **Group discussion and interaction** To ask and answer questions, make relevant contributions, offer suggestions and take turns | **Science: Light and Dark** To be able to group materials together and make a record of groups | Selecting materials to be used as reflective strips on their bags |
| **Drama activities** To explore familiar themes and characters through improvisation and role-play | **Literacy: Y1 T1T7** To be able to re-enact stories through role-play | Role-play involving giving advice to teacher in role as farmer from 'Farmer Duck' who wants to start up a new farm having been chased away from his old one |

**Table 8.8. Planning speaking and listening in year 4, Term 2**

| Speaking and listening objective (QCA, 2003) | Possible link objective (from NLS Framework or other subject) | Learning opportunity through which both objectives could be met |
|---|---|---|
| **Listening** To listen to a speaker make notes on the talk and use the notes to develop a role-play | **History: Children in 2nd World War** To find out about the feelings and experiences of evacuees (Using a range of sources) | Interview visitor who was evacuee during WW2. Use interview as stimulus for role-play exploring experiences of evacuees. |
| **Drama activities** To develop scripts based on improvisation | See above | Create a docudrama about evacuees to be presented to parents. |
| **Speaking** To respond appropriately to the contributions of others in the light of alternative viewpoints. | **Literacy Y4 T2 T12** To collaborate with others to write stories in chapters, using plans and particular audiences in mind. | Work in small groups to create interactive, web-based adventure story set in imagined world. Discuss and agree on characters and alternative plot developments. |

# Additional English planning

As explored in Chapter 6, language and literacy are integral to learning in all subjects and there will be many opportunities for reading, writing, speaking and listening across the curriculum. Various other specific reading and writing activities may also be provided outside the literacy hour. These may include: extended writing; handwriting; library visits; and USSR (Uninterrupted Sustained Silent Reading) or ERIC (Everyone Reading In Class). Teachers need to give particular consideration to the role of ICT in English.

# Planning to use Information and Communication Technology (ICT)

As explored in Chapter 1, we encounter a range of digital texts in our everyday life. Children can be encouraged to use, evaluate and create these varied texts in school and observe and discuss the value of using ICT in school.

Using ICT in English involves using computer-based activities as well as other technology, such as tape recorders, television, overhead projectors and video equipment. Interestingly, there are few references to ICT in the National Literacy Strategy Framework although a variety of documents have been circulated to schools suggesting ways of using ICT to enhance literacy teaching (DfES, 2001, 2003c). Guidance on using ICT in the Foundation Stage is particularly sparse. However, just as the most effective English teaching is generally that which takes place within meaningful contexts, so ICT is probably most valuable when integrated within play-based activities. Children may gain more from using items such as telephones, tape recorders, walkie-talkies and computers in role-play areas than from using some specifically designed educational software (O'Hara, 2004). Children may be encouraged to not only develop their ICT skills, but observe and discuss the value of using ICT in different contexts. In Chapter 10, we explore the range of ICT resources available in the classroom. Table 8.9 summarizes ways in which ICT may be used within English teaching to:

- support composition;
- find new audiences for children's writing;
- introduce children to a variety of texts;
- capture evidence of speaking and listening;
- stimulate language use;
- support teaching.

**Table 8.9. Using ICT within English teaching**

| ICT application | Possible uses/advantages |
| --- | --- |
| **Supporting composition** | |
| Desktop publishing packages | Easy to redraft and manipulate text |
| Word processing | Can experiment with layout and produce to professional standard<br>Can import images, moving images captured from web cam,<br>alter layout and presentation to create multimedia text etc.<br>Spellchecks and thesauruses can provide on-screen support<br>Can add hyperlinks between pages to create interactive books with children |
| Talking word processors | Computer will 'read back' writing |
| Electronic whiteboard | Easy to draft work and manipulate texts |
| Tape recorders/dictaphones | Can record ideas, for example on a trip, words to describe a place<br>can be recorded and then used in a poem on return to school<br>Can record and listen to drafts before making revisions |
| Writing frames | Can save frameworks developed through shared and guided<br>writing and children can write directly onto these |
| Digital video and<br>editing equipment | New software makes it relatively easy for children to create their own films<br>Can make and discuss film sequences in preparation for<br>writing a print narrative |
| PowerPoint | Can create presentations incorporating animation and images |
| Concept keyboards | Children can click on images to create words on screen<br>Programs such as Clicker enable teachers to produce<br>wordbanks for children to use |
| **Finding new audiences for children's writing** | |
| Desktop publishing and<br>word processing | Easy to reproduce multiple copies of texts (newspapers,<br>leaflets) etc. for distribution to parents, other classes |
| Web sites | Can publish own work on Web site designed by children or on existing sites |
| Email and fax | Can contact people and organizations around world<br>Can email teacher in role as character from fiction |
| **Accessing a variety of texts** | |
| Web site and CD-ROMS | Can explore strategies for accessing information using digital texts<br>Can reflect on difference between digital and print texts<br>Can use split screen to display a Web site and make notes alongside it<br>Can copy and paste key words from digital texts into own notes |

168

| ICT application | Possible uses/advantages |
| --- | --- |
| Talking books and living books | Can help children access texts |
| Taped stories in English or other languages | |
| Television, film, computer games, animation, etc. | Can develop ability to critique moving image texts |
| Online dictionaries | Access to meanings and pronunciation of unfamiliar words |

**Capturing speaking and listening**

| | |
| --- | --- |
| Audio recording | Can record radio plays, storytelling and so on<br>Can record discussions to be evaluated |
| Video recording | Can record drama work/storytelling/presentations to be evaluated |

**Stimulating language use**

| | |
| --- | --- |
| Using video | Can explore differences between way narrative/character etc. is presented through print and moving image text |
| Images and Web sites | Can use as stimulus for writing or drama |
| Using Adventure programs and simulations | Can stimulate collaborative work and learning talk<br>Images can be projected onto wall of role-play area |
| Creating video, Web sites, PowerPoint, etc. | |

**Use as a teaching aid**

| | |
| --- | --- |
| Electronic whiteboard and remote keyboard and mouse | Easy to manipulate, highlight and mark text during shared reading and writing<br>Remote keyboard and mouse can make it easier for children to write on whiteboard during whole-class sessions |
| Digital images | Can create digital images of children's activities, visits, etc., for sequencing/discussion/assessment |
| Drag-and-drop facilities | Can use for sorting and categorizing words with different spellings, DARTs activities, sequencing lines of a poem, and so on |
| Overhead projector | Children can present work to class that has been written onto transparencies<br>Easy to manipulate and mark text during shared reading and writing |

# Planning homework activities

Since 1997, schools have been advised to provide an hour of homework a week for children in the first years of primary education and half an hour a day for children at the top of Key Stage 2. Different schools have interpreted this guidance in their own ways and individual teachers need to ensure that they follow school policy. Setting homework provides an opportunity to support and extend children's learning. Probably the most effective activities are those that capture children's interests and involve them in open-ended activities that will feed back into learning in the classroom.

### Sample open-ended activities for homework:

- collect a range of leaflets that are designed to persuade you to buy something. Now create a leaflet to advertise your own imaginary product;
- collect rhymes and greetings in different languages to add to the class display;
- make a glossary of words linked to your favourite hobby, TV programme or sport;
- make a collage of labels from your favourite foods. Now create a label for an invented food;
- write a fact file on a cartoon character, pop star or sports personality. Use this as the basis for writing a brief biography of their lives;
- collect jokes containing homonyms for compilation in a class joke book. Can you make up any of your own?
- write the final draft of your story in a home-made book. You can use flaps, pockets and pop-up features. Think carefully about where these should go;
- select three books to recommend for the school library;
- collect words and phrases in local and other dialects to be linked to appropriate regions of the map on the classroom wall.

There has been a long tradition of encouraging children to take home books to read with parents or siblings. This can be a valuable opportunity for children to share and enjoy books out of school. It is important, however, that teachers, children and parents all have a shared understanding of the purpose of this activity so that it does not deteriorate into a frustrating routine. Books should be motivating and varied and parents may need advice on how they can best support their children. Schools often send out leaflets of guidance to parents or invite them to workshops at the beginning of the school year. Many schools also provide pupils with lists of words to learn how to spell. This can be useful as long as the words are meaningful and relevant and the children are clear about what they can do to learn how to spell them (for example, using approaches described in Chapter 4).

# Summary

The process of planning involves considering:

- knowledge about the children's strengths, weaknesses and interests;
- national expectations for the curriculum;
- breadth, balance, continuity and progression;
- knowledge of effective practice.

Effective planning will identify:

- precise learning objectives;
- meaningful and motivating texts, contexts and activities;
- specific outcomes for children;
- links to other curriculum areas (including ICT) when appropriate;
- links between text, sentence and word level aspects;
- links between reading, writing, speaking and listening;
- differentiation;
- how other adults will be involved;
- ways in which children will be grouped;
- opportunities for children to reflect on their learning.

With experience, planning becomes easier as teachers build up banks of successful activities and gain a greater understanding of how children learn. However, perhaps most importantly, planning needs to be flexible enough to respond to children's needs: areas may be consolidated, revisited or even missed if teachers feel this is appropriate for the children in their class. Such professional judgements need to be made in the light of careful and frequent assessments of children's learning. Guidance on conducting such assessments is contained in the following chapter.

# Reflective task

Look back at the principles identified at the beginning of this chapter. Consider the implications of these principles for planning. In the light of this, evaluate examples of medium- and short-term planning you have used or seen.

## FURTHER READING

Gamble, N. and Easingwood, N. (2000) *ICT and Literacy: Information and Communications Technology, Media, Reading and Writing*. London: Continuum.
   Explores the relationship between English and ICT.

O'Hara, M. (2004) *ICT in the Early Years*. London: Continuum.
   Discusses issues relating to integrating ICT in early years settings.

Qualifications and Curriculum Authority (QCA) (2001) *Planning for Learning in the Foundation Stage*. London: QCA.
   Provides detailed guidance on planning in the Foundation Stage with plenty of exemplification material.

## REFERENCES

Bruner, J. S. (1966) *Towards a Theory of Instruction*. Cambridge MA: Belknapp Press.

Department for Education and Employment (DfEE) (1998) *National Literacy Strategy Framework for Teaching*. London: HMSO.

Department for Education and Skills (DfES) (2001) *ICT in the Literacy Hour: Whole Class Teaching*. London: DfES Publications.

Department for Education and Skills (DfES) (2003a) *An Example of NLS Medium Term Planning*. London: DfES Publications.

Department for Education and Skills (DfES) (2003b) *Planning Exemplification:* http://www.standards.dfes.gov.uk/literacy. Accessed 30/07/03.

Department for Education and Skills (DfES) (2003c) *ICT in the Literacy Hour: independent work and guided reading*. London: DfES Publications.

O'Hara, M. (2004) *ICT in the Early Years*. London: Continuum.

Qualifications and Curriculum Authority (QCA) (2000) *Curriculum Guidance for the Foundation Stage*. London: QCA.

Qualifications and Curriculum Authority (QCA) (2001) *Planning for Learning in the Foundation Stage*. London: QCA.

Qualifications and Curriculum Authority (QCA) (2003) *Speaking, Listening, Learning*. London: QCA.

## CHILDREN'S BOOKS

Ahlberg, A. and Ahlberg, J. (1999) *The Jolly Postman: or Other People's Letters*. London: Viking Kestrel Picture Books.

Butterworth, N. and Inkpen, M. (1993) *Jasper's Beanstalk*. London: Hodder Children's Books.

Fine, A. (1992) *The Angel of Nitshill Road*. London: Mammoth.

Hutchins, P. (1997) *Titch*. London: Red Fox.

Medearis, A. (1996) *Too Much Talk*. London: Walker.

Penrose, J. (1999) *Encyclopedia of Tudor Medicine*. Oxford: Heinemann.

Pullman, P. (1996) *The Firework-Maker's Daughter*. London: Corgi.

Waddell, M. (1995) *Farmer Duck*. London: Walker.

# Assessing English

In this chapter, we focus on the role of assessment in teaching English in primary and early years settings. The nature of assessment in English is described and practical guidance provided on conducting assessments in reading, writing, speaking and listening. The importance of self-assessment is examined alongside effective strategies for giving feedback to children and setting targets. National requirements and guidelines on assessment are discussed.

## An overview of assessment

Assessment is a necessary part of day-to-day teaching. When you are teaching you will notice that some children find the tasks you have set easy whereas others find them difficult. Similarly some children will respond readily to the questions you ask and engage confidently in learning discussions; others may be reticent or demonstrate misconceptions. As you teach you will make adjustments to your planned lesson, perhaps recapping on key points, providing direct support to particular individuals or missing out activities. When you return to the same focus, you may decide to revisit certain aspects for some children or provide further challenges for others. These everyday interactions will help you form an overview of each child's development and are crucial in ensuring that teaching is closely matched to children's learning needs. Such intuitive judgements, however, need to be complemented by more systematic approaches that provide detailed insights into children's strengths and weaknesses. This information about children's progress and attainment can then be communicated to a range of audiences. These include:

- pupils themselves;
- parents/carers;
- other teaching staff, teaching assistants and nursery nurses;
- school managers, English co-ordinators, Special Needs Co-ordinators and governors;
- external agencies, such as educational psychologists, LEAs, OFSTED, DfEE.

Assessment can also be used to help schools and individual teachers evaluate the effectiveness of their provision. Insights into pupils' particular strengths and weaknesses may prompt a review of teaching methods or the relative emphasis placed on different parts of the curriculum. Assessment can be:

- **Summative**: used at the end of a phase of learning, for example a term, year or Key Stage. It involves judging overall competence and sometimes assigning grades, levels or scores to individual pupils.
- **Diagnostic**: used to provide an in-depth analysis of a child's difficulties and needs in a specific area and is often conducted by or following guidance from external agencies, such as an educational psychologist or special educational needs support service.
- **Formative**: used to form a picture of children's attainment in order to inform planning for teaching and learning. A number of studies have shown that formative assessment has a strong impact on children's progress in primary and early years settings (McCallum, 2000; Siraj-Blatchford *et al.*, 2002) and 'assessment for learning' (Assessment Reform Group, 1999) is now a focus for development in many schools.

The recursive process of planning, teaching and assessment is summarized in Figure 9.1.

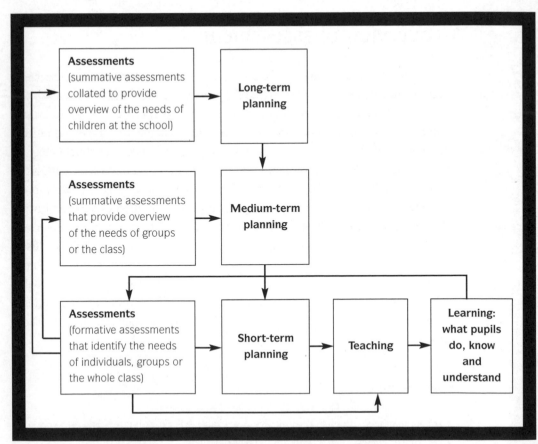

Figure 9.1. Planning, teaching and assessment

# Issues in the assessment of English

Making judgements about progress in English can be difficult as concepts of successful language use are often subjective. What is good reading? Effective writing? Successful speaking and listening? Discussions about favourite films or books reveal how closely judgements are influenced by individual preferences, interpretation and personal experience. Similarly, individual style and intentions are reflected in both writing and speaking. Of course, children need to develop the skills to spell accurately, use standard English and know how to do the kinds of reading and writing necessary to make progress academically. However, as explored in previous chapters, children also need to develop new and varied ways to express themselves and explore the world around them. The scope and range of assessment should reflect this. Before exploring practical methods for assessing reading, writing, speaking and listening, we therefore highlight some considerations for effective assessment in English. These are listed in Table 9.1 (overleaf), linked to the key points about language and literacy use identified in Chapter 2.

Assessment in English needs to be carefully planned to achieve a balanced view of children's language and literacy development. This means that it is important to collect evidence in a *range of contexts*. The scope of this can be illustrated by exploring what can be learnt about a child's writing from a single piece of evidence and considering other types of information that it would be useful to collect.

The story below was written by Haseena, a child in year 5. The children had been exploring myths and legends and were asked to create their own local myth. Haseena's myth grew from the idea of a single rose growing in a bare patch of earth in wintertime. As the story unfolds the reader meets the mythical creature who planted the rose. Just the opening of Haseena's story is presented here. The original was written in red font upon a green background.

There was once a beauty and a beast
formally known as the hit Disney film
Beauty and the Beast. The magic rose has
reminded me of my great, great, great
Grandma's death, as we had a familiar Rose
lay on her chest.
One night, I thought about it, but
something was distracting me; it was some
banging on my window. I drew the curtains
nervously back but there was nothing there.
But then something caught my eye; it was a
big rapid scrape on my window.
The next morning, I went to my garden to

get the post and I saw nothing but bare
grass (as it was winter,) but a blood red
mark caught my eye. It wasn't blood, it
wasn't paint, but right in front of my eyes
was a red Rose. Now this doesn't seem
right. As this was the same rose my
Grandmother was holding when she died and
the same as when it was laid on her chest.
I felt a shiver down my spine and the hairs
on my neck pricked up, as I entered the
house with the post still on the doorstep.
That night I lay awake. As the clock turned
12 an ear- splitting scream struck the air.
I quickly got my dressing gown and got my
torch and ran downstairs and swung the door
open to find a giant footprint with 4 toes.
Shocked, in my slippers, I moved to find no
more. I ran as fast as possible up the
winding stairs, got in my bed and flung the
covers over and went fast to sleep.
The next morning I woke up not surprised
too see... THE DREADED ROSE!

By examining this piece of writing we can learn a great deal about Haseena as a writer:

- She clearly feels that the visual appearance of her writing is significant: she has centrally justified the story and seems to have chosen colours that reflect those of the rose.
- She is able to use word-processing skills to draft, revise and present her writing.
- She is able to use several techniques to create tension; for example, she does not describe the beast but hints at who or what it is by recounting the sounds it made and marks it left and by using repetitive phrases to entice the reader to keep reading: 'It wasn't blood, it wasn't paint, but right in front of my eyes was a red Rose.' Her use of first-person narration enables her to give the reader direct insights into her feelings and thoughts and so create a vivid and compelling impression of events.
- She is familiar with the language used to structure narrative, using temporal connectives, such as 'One night' and 'The next morning' to help signal time sequences within her story.
- She structures her sentences effectively. Short simple sentences, 'Now this doesn't seem right', provide commentary on events, whilst compound sentences create a sense of rapid activity: 'I quickly got my dressing gown and got my torch and ran downstairs and swung the door open to find a giant footprint with 4 toes.' Complex sentences help her juxtapose

**Table 9.1. Considerations for English assessment**

| Key point | Implications for scope and process of assessment |
| --- | --- |
| **We need to recognize that:** | **In response to this we need to:** |
| Our society is linguistically diverse | Recognize that understanding of texts can be conveyed without accuracy in speaking or writing. Select texts carefully to ensure that content is accessible. |
| Children use language(s) and literacy in a variety of ways beyond the classroom | Talk to parents and children to find out what children know, understand and can do in relation to language and literacy. Ensure that assessment contexts are meaningful and relevant to children. |
| Children are active and autonomous language users | Involve children in their own assessment to enhance their sense of ownership of their own development. Provide opportunities for children to reflect on work and consider how it matched their intentions. |
| Language and literacy are used for a variety of purposes outside the classroom and vary widely within different contexts | Provide a range of contexts for assessment. |
| Outside the classroom, language and literacy are motivated and affected by specific purposes | Ensure that assessment tasks are purposeful and motivating to children. |
| The nature of language and texts is constantly evolving | Expand the scope of assessment to focus on skills and processes involved in using, producing and interpreting language in new ways. |
| Texts reflect the purposes, values and experiences of the people who create them | Recognize the purposes, values and experiences that children bring to their literacy and language use. Be clear about children's intentions in relation to the assessment task. |
| Speaking, listening, reading and writing are often interlinked | Recognize that it is difficult to separate assessments in these different areas. Select assessment modes carefully, e.g. avoid assessing comprehension through a written task if a child lacks fluency in writing. |
| Written texts vary in nature and provide us with a breadth of opportunities for pleasure, gaining information and broadening understanding | Use a wide range of texts as contexts for assessment acknowledging that children have different interests. |
| Confidence and competence in language and literacy underpin effective learning | Recognize that English can be assessed in any curriculum area as long as assessment focuses on speaking, listening, reading or writing rather than knowledge of another subject. |

the strange events with the normality of everyday life: 'I felt a shiver down my spine and the hairs on my neck pricked up, as I entered the house with the post still on the doorstep'.

- She can use punctuation and capitalization in conventional ways but also knows that they can be used creatively for effect, for example '. . . THE DREADED ROSE'.
- She also seems to be drawing from her experience of previous texts. We can see this explicitly in the opening sentence – the film of 'Beauty and the Beast' seems to be her inspiration for the use of the rose as symbol and the phrase 'formally known as' seems derivative. It is interesting that the story does not reflect the mythic qualities evident in the classical myths explored in class.

This brief analysis highlights some of Haseena's strengths as a writer. However, several questions remain unanswered in relation to both composition and transcription.

## Composition

Did she collaborate with other children and was this process productive? How effectively and confidently did she tackle different stages of the writing process? Where did she get her ideas? Has she written anything similar before? Is she equally skilled in producing other types of writing, for example non-fiction or a more typical myth?

## Transcription

Why did she decide to present her story in this way? How effective is her spelling when she is unable to use a spellcheck? What is her handwriting like? Was she satisfied with her story? What did she feel was successful? Did she enjoy writing it? Is she able to write in other languages?

Answers to these questions would be important in helping the teacher plan for Haseena's future development. It is clear from this that assessment in English needs to be used to investigate a variety of aspects of children's language and literacy development and use. In planning assessment that will address the full breadth of the English curriculum we need to investigate:

- **Skills, knowledge and understanding**: relevant to the child's stage of development.
- **Range**: assessing children in a range of contexts enables teachers to plan balanced experiences and use children's existing experience of language and literacy at home and school as the springboard for new learning.
- **Process**: an insight into the processes children engage in when they use language and literacy can help teachers decide how best to support them and identify reasons for any difficulties they may be having. This kind of assessment may reveal that children are relying too heavily on one strategy when several are required (for example, in reading) or trying to do too much at a first attempt (for example, in writing).
- **Attitudes**: children's perceptions about English and themselves as language and literacy users will influence how they read, write, speak and listen. Understanding how a child conceives reading, writing, speaking and listening may help teachers identify why they are

having difficulties. Similarly insights into which aspects of language and literacy children enjoy and feel confident in can help teachers find ways of motivating them.

# Practical approaches to assessment in English

In the next section, we explore a range of practical approaches for collecting information on children's skills and attitudes, the processes they use and the range of language and literacy in which they engage. This assessment can involve observing children as they read, write, speak and listen, analysing the outcomes of their language and literacy use or discussing their development with them. These assessments may be *formal* or *informal*.

*Formal* assessments are planned for and include tests. It is impractical to conduct formal assessments of all children all of the time and assessment and recording procedures should be manageable. School policy usually dictates how frequently formal assessments are conducted and how they are recorded. Many teachers focus on a selected group of children each week who can be monitored in whole-class, group and/or individual situations. In some schools, formal assessments are carried out on a half-termly basis and samples of evidence are collated in individual pupil portfolios.

*Informal assessments* use a variety of unobtrusive methods for collecting information and are not necessarily planned as they arise naturally out of work with children. Some schools have policies for recording informal assessment, whereas in others, individual teachers devise their own systems. Of course children's progress does not necessarily run parallel to the sequence of objectives within teachers' planning. Open-ended activities may present unexpected opportunities for assessment and children often demonstrate abilities that are significant even if not related to the planned focus. Teachers need to recognize these achievements and use them to inform their planning.

Table 9.2 provides an overview of possible sources of assessment evidence listing those that could be used to support assessment of the three attainment targets in relation to range, process, attitudes and skills, knowledge and understanding. Key approaches are then described in the following section.

**Table 9.2. Approaches to assessment**

| | Speaking and listening | Reading | Writing |
|---|---|---|---|
| **Knowledge, skills and understanding** (What does the child know and understand? What can s/he do?) | Observation Analysis of outcomes Interviews with children Speaking and listening conferences | Observation Listening to children read individually or during guided reading Discussing responses to texts Analysing recorded responses, for example to DARTs activities, answers to comprehension questions Reading conferences Reading journals Standardized reading tests | Observation Analysis of writing/ mark-making Writing conferences Spelling journals Spelling tests |
| **Range** (What kinds of reading/writing/ speaking and listening does the child do?) | Observation Conferences | Observation Reading diaries/journals Conferences | Observation Overview of written outcomes Conferences |
| **Process** (How does s/he do it?) | Observation Conferences | Observation Miscue analysis/ running record Discussion about process during guided reading sessions | Observation Analysis of plans and drafts Discussion about process during guided writing sessions Spelling journals |
| **Attitudes** (How does s/he feel about it? Which aspects does s/he enjoy?) | Observation Conferences Talk diaries | Observation Conferences Reading diaries | Observation Conferences |

Clearly, assessment modes should be suited to the needs and development of the child; for example, whilst a running record can be very useful in assessing the development of early and developing readers, it is not very helpful for those who are reading fluently. Observations and conferences offer a valuable tool for assessment in all areas of English and these are discussed below. Specific guidance relating to the assessment of speaking, listening, reading and writing follows.

## Observation 181

A great deal about children's literacy and language development can be learned through careful analysis of what they do in different contexts: in whole-class sessions, group work, play or independent reading and writing. Insights can be gained into their understanding of the purpose and nature of language and literacy, their approaches to different tasks and their attitudes and interests.

Observations may be general or tightly structured with a pre-planned focus. They may involve:

- noting significant events;
- noting behaviours at short time intervals, for example every minute;
- using checklists to monitor particular behaviours.

Observations can concentrate on how particular children participate in a range of activities or look at how different children tackle the same activity.

The following scenarios illustrate the use of observation for assessment purposes. Consider what could be learned about children's language and literacy from each of the following situations and note how this might be used to inform planning. (Notice how two of the examples arise from planned observations whereas the other is incidental.)

The **nursery** teacher spends time observing a small group of children in the book corner. One child is 'reading' a big book that has previously been shared by the teacher. She notices how the child holds the book the right way up, points at the pictures and repeats the repetitive refrain that runs through the book.

A **year 3** teacher conducts some focused observations of children as they work in pairs to design and make a torch. She notices that one of the children makes helpful suggestions that are ignored by the more dominant child.

A **year 6** teacher observes a group of children during 'golden time' at the end of the week (a period in which children are rewarded for good behaviour during the week by being allowed to select their own activities). A pair of children are using the computer to create a simple animation using Flash. This is a skill they have clearly learnt at home.

Much assessment will be carried out through interactions with children during whole-class, group or individual learning activities. As explored in Chapter 3, the organization of collaborative activities will affect children's participation, so careful consideration should be given to group size and make-up. Moreover, as highlighted in Chapter 5, teachers must facilitate such sessions in a way that encourages rather than inhibits talk. Well-planned questions can help gain insights into what children know and understand and will prompt them to reflect on their own learning.

### Conferences

Conferences provide more formal opportunities to discuss children's language and literacy with them. These involve teachers working with children to make detailed assessments about their progress and find out about their interests and attitudes inside and outside school. Time for individual conferences may be limited, but they can easily be held as group sessions, for example during guided reading or writing. A conference may focus on reading and/or writing and/or speaking and listening and involve any or all of the following:

- listening to a child read (possibly conducting a running record), discussing the text and the way they approached the reading;
- discussing samples of writing;
- evaluating their use of talk in different situations;
- talking about their reading, writing, speaking and/or listening outside school;
- discussing their thoughts on their own progress and their attitudes towards literacy;
- identifying targets for future development.

## Assessment in speaking and listening

Assessments of children's talk can take place in any curricular area as long as talk is essential to the task in hand and children understand the kind of talk that is expected. Importantly, the teacher must make sure that children will be not inhibited by a lack of knowledge about the subject. Moreover, as discussed earlier, grouping must be carefully considered to give children lacking in confidence an opportunity to work with those with whom they feel comfortable. Drama is particularly useful for assessing children's speaking and listening as it can be used to create motivating contexts, which require children to speak and listen in different ways. In conducting assessments of children's ability to use formal language, it is important to be clear about the difference between dialect and accent. Remember that a child speaking in a regional accent can still be using standard English.

The following situations each provide an appropriate context for assessing speaking and listening. Consider the aspects of speaking and listening in focus as well as possible advantages and drawbacks of each assessment opportunity.

A group of **year 4** children are trying to piece together what happened to some evacuees during World War II, using a selection of documentary evidence (letters, newspaper reports, school reports and diary entries). The teacher makes notes on the way they use exploratory talk.

The teacher is working with a group of **reception** children to set up a doctor's surgery in the corner of the classroom. She consults with them on how the surgery should be laid out and asks a teaching assistant to use a structured observation form to make notes on the way they explain and negotiate their ideas.

A **year 2** class is making a children's television programme. The children have worked in groups to prepare slots on making toys and puppets. The teacher videos their presentations and replays them for the children to evaluate. This enables her to both revisit and assess the presentations and review the children's ability to reflect on their talk.

Speaking and listening are usually assessed together but teachers may decide to conduct specific assessments in listening if they have particular concerns about a child or group of children. Insights into children's listening can be gained by:

- Observing their body language: are they focused on what is being said?
- Listening to what they say in response to others' contributions: do they build on what others have said? Are their contributions relevant?
- Giving them a task to complete as a result of listening, for example summarizing what has been said, following an instruction, explaining a process to another child.

Collecting evidence of children's progress in speaking and listening is problematic due to the transience of talk. However, teachers can capture talk by writing notes or making audio or video recordings which they can return to later for analysis. (Video can be particularly useful as it records facial expression, gesture and tone of voice.) Evidence from speaking and listening assessments can be compiled into a record, such as the one in Table 9.3, to provide an overview of a child's progress in using different types of talk in different situations.

**Table 9.3. Speaking and listening record**

| Rebecca W. | | Class 3B | | | |
|---|---|---|---|---|---|
| Date | Social context | Place | Activity | Purpose | Observations |
| 10.09.03 | small group friendship self-selected | playground | skipping game | talk for organizing, chanting | R. organizes who is skipping and who is holding rope – 'it were fun yesterday' use of dialect; rhymes/language play |
| 11.10.03 | ability group | classroom | history investigation – pyramid building | questioning – hypothesizing | R. generates several questions – e.g. who built pyramids? Why? |
| 27.10.03 | pair teacher-selected | computer desk | rewriting collaborative story on screen | tentative suggestions – e.g. 'perhaps we could . . .' | R. listens to partner and accepts changes. Builds on partner's suggestion about opening – 'yeah that'd be good and we could . . .' |
| 03.12.03 | whole class | book corner | telling story to class | narration | Used facial expression and tone of voice to capture interest of audience |

# Assessment in reading

In assessing children's reading, it is important to remember that reading is a complex process that varies in different contexts. Ultimately it is about gaining meaning from written texts and assessment should help provide insights into children's ability to read for meaning. Assessments should be conducted within motivating contexts as children's interests in the subject matter will affect the way they engage with a text. A number of ways of assessing reading are outlined below.

## Listening to children read

Listening to children reading and talking with them about what they have read is possibly the most common way of gaining insights into how children read and what they understand. This may occur during independent or guided sessions. Sharing a book with young children also provides an opportunity to assess aspects of children's knowledge about print, such as their awareness of directionality and expectation that the text will carry meaning.

## Reading diaries

Some schools maintain a record of a child's individual reading that lists the titles of books read. These may be in home/school reading diaries in which both teachers and parents make comments about a child's progress. Some schools also encourage children to comment on what they have read, perhaps writing notes or simply placing a smiley face next to the titles of books they enjoyed. Importantly, such records should not become a chore – knowing that a lengthy review must be written after finishing each book can be a disincentive to reading.

## Written/oral responses

Aspects of comprehension can be assessed by analysing children's responses to texts. These may be expressed in different ways, for example orally or through writing, drawing or drama. Some teachers make extensive use of comprehension exercises, which generally involve providing children with a passage to read and questions to answer. As explored in Chapter 4, such exercises can be demotivating and unchallenging. If they are used, they should include a range of questions that invite children to infer and deduce as well as simply retrieve information.

## Miscue analysis and running records

When working with developing readers, it is important to monitor the reading strategies they use. *Miscue analysis* (Goodman *et al.*, 1972) or *running records* can be useful here. These techniques involve viewing children's errors in reading as 'miscues' that are not random but prompted by the reading strategies a child is using. By analysing children's miscues, we can therefore gain insights into the way they are tackling the reading process. 'Miscue analysis' and running records both provide approaches for doing this but miscue analysis is more rigorous. Most teachers find that running records are adequate for their needs. Completing a running record involves marking a photocopy of a passage from the text the child is reading. The teacher listens to the child read and notes any miscues on the passage. Afterwards the teacher discusses the book with the child or asks him/her to retell the story. One way of recording miscues is provided below.

| Miscue | Strategy | Example |
|---|---|---|
| Omission | Put letter 'o' above the word omitted | **O**<br>Up the chair |
| Child is given word (told) | Put the letter 't' above the word told to the child | **T**<br>she laughed |
| Substitution | Cross out the correct word and write in the substituted word | wide<br>the ~~wild~~ sea |
| Self-correct | Write Sc over the word the child self-corrected and add miscue | **SC** – this<br>he put <u>it</u> in the box |
| Insertion | Write in the added word | on<br>Come ^ to my house |
| Hesitation | Insert a stroke where the child makes a long pause | She saw the/fridge |

The running record can then be analysed to reveal the kinds of miscues the child is making. Two short extracts from running records are included below. A far longer sample is necessary (100–150 words) to gain a real impression of the cueing systems a child is using.

The child whose reading is recorded in the first extract is clearly reading for meaning as her substitutions, insertions and omissions do not alter the sense of the text. She also goes back and self-corrects, re-reading the final phrase, 'expecting to hear Sam shout her back', when she realizes 'that' does not fit.

                                               s/c

         quickly                 O        T    that

She went ~~quietly~~ out of the small room, expecting ^ to hear Sam shout her back.

In contrast, the child whose reading is recorded in the next extract seems to be relying on initial phonemes to decode unfamiliar words and is not reading for meaning. Her miscues do not make sense within the context of the text.

         quite   T          smell           T       have       shut

She went ~~quietly~~ out of the ~~small~~ room, expecting to ~~hear~~ Sam ~~shout~~ her back.

Incidentally, the fact that the teacher has to supply so many words and that the child makes so many miscues suggests that this book is too hard for this child.

(She might use a wider range of cueing strategies with a simpler text. A teacher would need to check this.)

The results of conducting a running record can be used to inform future planning for children: for example, the teacher could develop a programme to encourage the second child to use a wider range of cueing strategies. She might encourage her to widen her knowledge of high-frequency words, make analogies between known and unknown words using graphic cues and extend her use of semantic and syntactic cues.

### Standardized reading tests

Many schools use commercially produced standardized reading tests (available from educational publishers and organizations) to measure children's progress in reading. These tests often focus on limited aspects of reading, for example word recognition or graphophonic skills, and rarely assess reading in a range of contexts. Extensive trials are carried out by the publishers to identify how 'average' children of different ages score on these tests and children's scores are often used to determine a 'reading age', which can then be compared with the child's chronological age. Importantly, the results should be treated with caution and teachers need to be absolutely clear about what a given test actually measures; indeed children frequently obtain markedly different 'reading ages' from different tests. These tests may prove useful to schools in monitoring cohorts of children, but they provide limited information to guide teaching and need to be used alongside a range of more informative assessments.

There are also several computer-based programs available to support assessment in literacy. Again, these should be evaluated carefully to identify the aspects of language and literacy they actually test.

## Assessment in writing

In assessing writing, it is particularly important to make assessments within a range of contexts. Teachers need insights into how children approach writing, what they find difficult and their ability to make effective choices about their language use in different situations.

### Analysis of writing/mark-making samples

As we saw at the beginning of this chapter, analysis of children's writing/mark-making can be highly informative, as long as a number of samples are examined within a varied programme of assessment that acknowledges range, attitudes and process. In setting an assessment task for writing, it is important not to expect a child to focus on all aspects of the writing process at once. Assessments should recognize what the child was trying to do and also any targets or objectives that have been identified. Note that plans and drafts can provide insights into how the child approached a piece of writing.

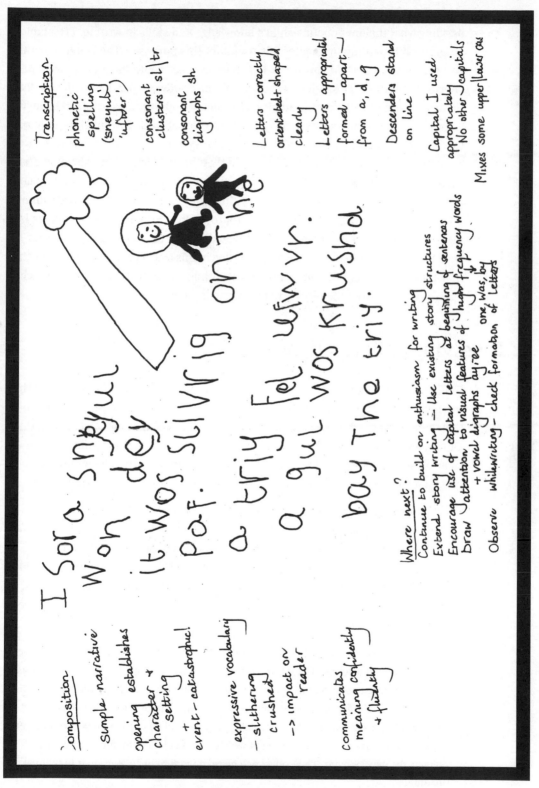

Figure 9.2. Writing sample – the snail

The process of analysis involves looking at a piece of writing/mark-making and deciding what it shows about a child's knowledge and skills in writing. (The table of progression in writing in Chapter 5 is useful for this purpose.) The emphasis at this point is on what a child *can do* rather than on what could have been done more effectively. Figure 9.2 provides an example of a piece of work that has been annotated for assessment. Clearly, other samples/assessment opportunities would help answer some of the questions raised by analysis of this piece of work. It would be appropriate to see, for example, whether this child would have included capital letters at the beginning of sentences if she had been told that this was important; she might have been concentrating so hard on composing her story that she left them out. Similarly, it would be useful to see how effectively this child writes in other contexts and for other purposes. If analysis is being used for formative purposes, the next stage is to identify the kinds of experiences that it would be useful to provide in order for the child to progress (as in the 'where next?' section of this teacher's notes). It is interesting that the teacher has not commented on the child's use of illustrations. The child appears to have used the picture to complement the written text.

## Involving children in assessment

In Chapter 5, we explored the importance of encouraging children to reflect on their learning. If children themselves are involved in their own assessment, this raises their awareness of what they are good at and how they can develop (McCallum, 2000). During any assessment activity, it is important that both teachers and children are clear about the assessment criteria. Involving children in discussing and agreeing criteria for a piece of work is a particularly effective way of achieving this.

> The **nursery** teacher often uses digital photographs to record children's activities and outcomes (for example, browsing through books in the book corner, using mark-making in the structured play area). These photographs are compiled in a book for each child. The teacher uses these photographs as a stimulus for talking to the children about what they did, how they did it and what they learned. The teacher records what the child says in captions that are stuck in the book alongside the photographs. The book is taken home at regular periods for children to show to their parents.

> The **year 2** teacher uses a guided session to conduct a group writing conference. The children look at a series of pieces of writing they have completed during the previous term – a zigzag book containing a quest story, an anthology of jokes and humorous poetry and a printout of an email they sent. They talk through how they approached each writing task, discuss what they enjoyed doing and what they think they did well. Next they discuss aspects of writing at which they would like to improve and set targets for development. They select one piece of work to include in their individual portfolio.

The **year 4** children have been encouraged to complete 'talk logs' over a week long period. These include a space for children to record the kinds of talk they use during this time and comment on their effectiveness. At the end of the week, the children are encouraged to reflect on their overall strengths and weaknesses.

The **year 6** children have looked at the level descriptors for levels 3, 4 and 5 in writing. They have discussed what these involve and re-written them using more accessible language. They are now using these descriptors to assess pieces of their own writing and identify what they do well and what they need to improve.

Various studies have highlighted the importance of feedback in helping children reflect on their learning and become aware of what they are trying to achieve (Weedon *et al.*, 1999; McCallum, 2000). Interestingly it seems that it is frequently the least able children who benefit most from such feedback as they are often unclear about what constitutes a 'good' piece of work (Weedon *et al.*, 1999). It seems that the feedback most welcomed by children is oral and given as they are working on a task or just after they have completed it. Many children cannot read or understand teachers' written comments. Guidelines for giving feedback and sample feedback comments are provided below.

### Guidelines on giving feedback to children:

Schools will have their own policies on giving feedback and some will use an agreed mark scheme. The following guidelines, however, offer some general principles for oral or written feedback.

- always respond to the content of children's reading, writing and speaking;
- do not overwhelm children with feedback but try and make sure it relates to the objective or target the child was trying to meet, for example don't comment on spelling if the emphasis has been on writing an exciting opening that will grab a reader's attention;
- respond to children's writing as a reader or to their speaking as a listener, telling them about how you were affected by what they said or wrote and speculating on the impact of proposed changes on future readers;
- try giving feedback that relates to the process rather than the product. This enables you to value what children have tried to do and help them understand *how* they can improve;
- whilst it can be much easier to identify strengths and weaknesses in sentence and word level features than those at text level, make sure you address a balance of elements over time;
- avoid vague judgements such as 'good', 'super work' or 'messy'. Be clear about why a piece of work is successful or what could be done to improve it. Telling children what they are doing well encourages them to do it again next time;
- remember that feedback should relate to the task rather than the child. It is unhelpful for children to become stereotyped as 'lazy', 'messy' or even 'neat';
- note that feedback can be given to a group or whole class if they share the same needs.

**Table 9.4. Setting learning targets**

| Question | Option | Advantages | Disadvantages |
|---|---|---|---|
| What kind of targets will be set? | Class | • Whole-class teaching towards target possible<br>• Peer support for meeting target | • May not be suited to child's individual needs |
| | Group | • Group teaching and learning possible<br>• Peer support for meeting target<br>• Easy to manage | • May not be most appropriate target for individuals |
| | Individual | • Tailored to child's needs | • Difficult to manage individual targets for a whole class<br>• Time consuming to set/monitor targets |
| Who will set the targets? | Teacher | • Based on teacher assessment | • Child does not have ownership<br>• Child may not understand or be clear about need for target |
| | Child | • Child has ownership | • May not be most important target for development<br>• Time consuming |
| | Teacher and child/group/class | • Child and teacher share ownership | |
| How will you ensure that children do not forget about their target? | Wall chart/display of targets met | • Targets have high profile<br>• Peer support/affirmation for meeting targets | • Children may be uncomfortable with others knowing their targets |
| | Individual target cards | • Low-profile reminder | • Without constant reminders, these may become lost/ignored |
| | Oral reminders and discussions about targets | • Ensures that children understand target | • Time consuming |

# Setting learning targets

Having identified areas for development with children, teachers can then help them set targets for their own learning. Target setting is intended to establish a clear link between assessment and learning through clarifying what children need to do next and enabling them to monitor and take control of their own development. Learning targets can be set for an individual, a group or a class. They should be appropriate to the child and specify exactly which skill, area of knowledge or concept the child needs to develop. Targets should also be manageable – too many targets or too broad a target can be overwhelming. Targets need to be regularly reviewed to avoid them becoming forgotten or outdated.

In organizing target setting a number of key decisions will be taken. These are outlined in Table 9.4, which outlines advantages and drawbacks of different approaches.

# National requirements and documentation

## Foundation Stage Profile

The Foundation Stage Profile provides an overview of a child's development in relation to the 'stepping stones' and Early Learning Goals (ELGs) and must be completed by the end of reception. Importantly the ELGs are not assessment criteria. Children are assessed against scales that relate either to individual goals, parts of or combinations of goals. Details of the scales and exemplification materials can be found in *The Foundation Stage Profile Handbook* (QCA, 2003).

Assessments are made following observations during which practitioners note down what each child knows, understands and can do. The profile can be built up throughout the reception year and assessments take place within the context of normal activities. Observations are supplemented by information gained from records from previous settings and parents. This includes building up a profile of how a child uses any languages used in addition to English.

## Monitoring progress using National Curriculum levels

The National Curriculum Programmes of Study are supplemented by a series of levels of attainment that mark children's progress for the purposes of summative assessment. Most children are expected to reach the second level by the end of Key Stage 1 and the fourth by the end of Key Stage 2. Teachers use *level descriptors* to decide which level each child is at. These broad statements specify the knowledge, skills and understanding that are representative of each level and are intended to help teachers arrive at 'best-fit' judgements of a child's attainment based on a range of evidence. The level descriptors have been subdivided in various ways to facilitate more precise judgements about children's progress, for example Level 2 is divided into three sub-levels to support assessment at Key Stage 1. Teachers also have access to the P-Scales, which support the assessment of children with special educational needs who are working pre-level 1 (DfEE/QCA, 1998).

Given that interpretation of these levels can be very subjective, schools often conduct moderation exercises during which staff work together to ascribe levels to pieces of assessment evidence. This helps them arrive at an agreed interpretation of the level descriptors.

## Standard Attainment Tests (SATs)

Summative assessments referenced to the National Curriculum levels of attainment are statutory at the end of Key Stages 1 and 2 when teacher assessments are supplemented by results from SATs. Current guidelines are sent annually to schools by the Qualifications and Curriculum Authority (QCA) and most schools will keep samples of tests, mark schemes and guidance for teachers. The SATs are intended to facilitate comparisons between schools, enabling them and external agencies to monitor the school's progress. More detail on this process and its implications is contained in Chapter 13.

Many schools also opt to conduct formal summative assessments at the end of each year or even each term, often using the optional tests produced by QCA for years 3, 4 and 5. SATs and optional tests consist of a series of tasks designed to assess children's reading and writing. The SATs may be seen as limited measures of children's ability; aspects such as speaking and listening are ignored and formal timed tests do not provide an environment in which children can demonstrate the full range of their capability. Teacher assessment, which draws from a wider range of evidence, is intended to give an overview of a child's attainment within a broader range of experiences. This assessment is intended to be of equal status to SATs.

# Assessing children with English as an Additional Language (EAL)

Many LEAs have developed scales to describe children's progress in learning EAL but the detail of these differs and it has been difficult to ensure continuity in assessments for children and teachers moving between schools. Consequently, QCA produced *A Language in Common* (QCA, 2000), to provide a common scale linked to National Curriculum level descriptors and ensure greater continuity in assessment. These scales are intended to support teachers with both identifying what children can do and planning future development. Teachers can use them to monitor achievement and build up a profile of children's achievements to share with other professionals and parents. Importantly, children are not expected to progress evenly through each step of these scales. Some children, for example, may read and write more effectively than they communicate orally. As will be explored in Chapter 12, language development in English and other languages is mutually supportive. It is therefore important to find out as much as possible about:

- other languages with which the child is familiar;
- language(s) used by other members of the family;
- contexts in which different languages are used;
- the child's experience of formal teaching in another language;
- whether the child has experience of reading or writing in another language or whether they are likely to learn to read and write in that language;
- the kind of experiences the child has had in different languages, for example being familiar with rhymes or stories in another language.

# Summary

Effective assessment in English involves:

- using summative, formative and diagnostic assessment in appropriate contexts;
- collecting information relating to skills, knowledge, understanding, range, process and attitudes;
- drawing from a range of assessment evidence;
- selecting an assessment focus that is appropriate to the child's stage of development;
- selecting methods of assessment that are appropriate to the assessment focus;
- involving children themselves in assessment and target setting;
- giving focused feedback to children;
- devising manageable recording procedures.

# Reflective questions

1. Consider a series of assessment activities you have used or observed being used. Look back at the principles for English assessment identified at the beginning of this chapter. Evaluate the methods of assessment you used in the light of these principles.

2. Look at the levels of attainment in the National Curriculum and the Foundation Stage assessment scales. Which aspects of English do they reflect? Are there any aspects that are neglected?

3. Assessment has a number of purposes and audiences. Which methods of assessment would you use to enable you to:
   - report to parents about their child's progress;
   - inform a specialist support teacher about a child's strengths and weaknesses in reading;
   - provide information to the head teacher who is collecting information to inform the school governors about pupil progress?

4. Evaluate your own feedback/marking. Does it address a balance of compositional and transcriptional elements? Would it be helpful to the child? How could it be improved?

5. Consider a specific class of children that you have observed/taught. How could you involve them in their own assessment? How could you ensure that your processes for setting targets are manageable and meaningful to the children?

## FURTHER READING

Arnold, H. (1992) *Diagnostic Reading Record*. London: Hodder & Stoughton.
  Provides a detailed description of miscue analysis and examples.

*National Curriculum In Action*: http://www.ncaction.gov.uk
  Contains samples of children's work, some of which are annotated with National Curriculum levels.

Qualifications and Curriculum Authority (QCA) (1998) *Talk about Reading: Gathering Evidence Of Children's Reading through Talk*. London: QCA.
  Booklet and accompanying videos providing guidance and examples of ways to learn about children's comprehension and response through discussion.

Qualifications and Curriculum Authority (QCA) (2000) *A Language in Common: Assessing English as an Additional Language*. London: QCA.
  Provides scales of progression for children with EAL along with exemplification material.

Qualifications and Curriculum Authority (QCA) (2003) *The Foundation Stage Profile Handbook*. London: QCA.
  Provides detailed guidance on completing a Foundation Stage Profile along with plenty of exemplification material.

## REFERENCES

Assessment Reform Group (1999) *Assessment for Learning: Beyond the Black Box*. Cambridge: University of Cambridge School of Education.

Department for Education and Employment/Qualifications and Curriculum Authority (DfEE/QCA) (1998) *Supporting the Target-Setting Process*. London: HMSO.

Goodman, Y. and Burke, C. (1972) *Reading Miscue Inventory*. New York: Macmillan.

McCallum, B. (2000) *Formative Assessment: Implications for Classroom Practice*: http:www.qca/ca/5–14/afl/resources.asp.

Qualifications and Curriculum Authority (QCA) (2000) *A Language in Common: Assessing English as an Additional Language*. London: QCA.

Qualifications and Curriculum Authority (QCA) (2003) *The Foundation Stage Profile Handbook*. London: QCA.

Siraj-Blatchford, I., Sylva, K., Muttock, S., Gilden, R. and Bell, D. (2002) *Researching Effective Pedagogy in the Early Years*. London: DfES.

Weedon, P., Winter, J. C., Broadfoot, P. M., Hinnett, K. V., McNess, E. M., Tidmarsh, C. R. and Triggs, P. (1999) *Learners' Expectations of Assessment Requirements Nationally: How Students Perceive and Respond to Feedback*. Bristol: University of Bristol Graduate School of Education.

# The Learning Environment and Resources for English

In earlier chapters we have established key principles relating to the importance of providing a range of purposes and audiences for language use and the value of authentic texts and motivating activities in teaching speaking and listening, reading and writing. In this chapter, we look at the crucial role of the learning environment in making such opportunities readily available to children at all levels. We aim to show how careful organization and planning of the learning environment and resources can enable all children to see and engage with language used for varied purposes and become active, independent language users.

## The role of the environment in teaching and learning

In every educational setting, children, support staff and teachers need a physical space and the necessary furniture and resources. For staff and children, this provides far more than simply a space for learning. It influences how they feel about themselves, their learning, their relationships with others, the activities that take place, and their role in that environment. It has the potential to be a warm, welcoming, stimulating place in which all involved feel comfortable, secure and motivated, sharing a sense of ownership and pride in its care and development.

Values and attitudes in relation to language and literacy are also conveyed by the classroom environment. The use of space, the selection and presentation of educational materials and children's work, the arrangement of furniture and resources all carry messages. These features reflect values and attitudes in relation to language and literacy and the nature of learning in this area of the curriculum. The environment will convey whether talk is seen as valuable and who is expected to speak and who will listen. The choice of texts, their presentation and use will carry important messages about the nature of literacy and the purposes for which it is used, as well as who can be involved in the production of texts. The environment will reflect assumptions about the status of different languages and those who use them. The organization and presentation will also show who is welcome within that setting and whether language and literacy are considered to be enjoyable, meaningful and relevant to life beyond the classroom.

Consider what messages children in the following reception setting receive about literacy and language and about themselves as learners.

## Reception I

A large sheet on the door presents the word 'Welcome!' in various languages and displays the photographs of all the staff and children in the class. All the children have written their own names next to their photographs.

Inside, the classroom walls are full of pictures, posters, written texts and a wide range of materials. Some of these have been produced by the children, others have been collected by them and others are educational materials. On one wall, there is an alphabet frieze, with familiar packaging, for example supermarket bags, chocolate bar wrappers and crisp bags attached below each appropriate letter with spaces for the children to add more.

By the door there is a class noticeboard. This contains reminders from the teacher to the children and parents and messages from the children to the teacher and parents. A whiteboard is used by the teacher to write reminder notes to herself. Sometimes the children do this for her. On the wall, there is a list of classroom jobs that the children tick when they have completed their tasks. A list of class rules produced by the children is also displayed.

In one corner of the classroom there is a reading corner, with a rug, settee and several large cushions. A wide range of children's texts are displayed on a low set of shelves and in boxes on the floor. The collection includes fiction and non-fiction books, comics, brochures, catalogues and texts in various languages. There are also several books that have been produced by the children in the class and some that have been written for them by older children in the school. The children's possessions are kept in trays, which they have labelled themselves with their name and a small picture.

The role-play area is a home corner, containing a small settee, table, chairs, a cooker and toy food and cooking equipment. There is also a telephone, a note pad, a pencil, a message board, a computer monitor and keyboard, a recipe book, a telephone directory and a variety of magazines and newspapers.

At the side of the room, there is a writing area containing a range of writing implements, forms, cards, note books and various pieces of paper and card. On a low noticeboard, children have put up bits of writing and pictures they have produced. There is also a small post-box, which contains messages to other members of the class.

In this environment, children are clearly invited to use their language skills and see themselves as readers and writers. Their own writing is valued even if it is not formally accurate. They see that writing is used for communication and they make use of it.

They regard themselves as authors and are encouraged to be independent in their writing. Reading is an activity involving choice, pleasure and a wide variety of texts and is presented as a pursuit with relevance beyond the classroom. In their play in the 'home corner', the children share magazines, check the *TV Times* to find out what to watch, they choose recipes, make shopping lists and leave notes for others. In doing so, they demonstrate their understanding of the wider purposes for literacy and their confidence in themselves as literacy users.

This example relates to an early years setting, but it raises issues that are equally relevant to children in the primary years. In order to create a positive learning environment for the development of language and literacy for children of any age, the setting needs to convey the following messages:

- language is alive, interesting and changing;
- literacy involves a diverse range of texts used for a variety of purposes;
- classroom use of literacy has a relevance to the world outside literacy;
- language is a source of interest, entertainment and pleasure;
- languages other than English are important;
- learning is challenging, rewarding and achievable;
- individuals are valued, respected and expected to be independent;
- children are encouraged to take responsibility for their learning;
- all members of the learning community are encouraged to contribute to the successful use and development of the learning environment.

The rest of this chapter examines ways in which such an environment can be created through the organization and use of:

- the reading area and resources for reading;
- the writing area and resources for writing;
- the role-play area;
- the use of display;
- the involvement of parents.

# The reading area and resources for reading

A reading area is an important feature of any early years or primary setting. An attractive, comfortable area invites children to regard reading as a pleasurable activity. By providing a range of texts it can offer children the opportunity to explore and develop their own interests and gain independence as readers. Even if it is not feasible to provide space for children to sit and read in comfort, the area where books and other texts are housed needs to be inviting, stimulating and attractive. Books need to be displayed so that covers are visible; racks, bookstands, low bookcases and boxes are useful for this purpose. Although it is important that the reading area is organized and tidy, it is also essential that children feel able to pick up books and look at them before making their selection. Posters produced by the children or by publishers to advertise particular books or authors provide an attractive support for children in selecting titles that interest them. Such displays need to be changed frequently to ensure that they continue to have an impact. An ongoing list of recommendations created by the children is also helpful as are brief reviews attached to book covers.

### *Texts for the classroom:*

- a range of children's literature;
- books written in different languages;
- dual language texts;
- books created by the children in the class and by other children;
- magazines, newspapers, brochures, catalogues, comics, texts related to children's current interests, popular music, television programmes, films, and so on;
- talking books, living books and CD-ROMs;
- non-fiction texts including those supporting current topic work;
- reference books: picture dictionaries, regular dictionaries, glossaries, thesauruses, encyclopaedias, atlases and so on.

Audio tapes and headsets offer all children access to literature. Groups can be encouraged to share the experience of listening and discuss their responses.

## Children's literature

It is important to ensure that, at every level, children have access to a wide range of children's literature including poetry and picture books. As discussed in Chapter 4, picture books have an important role to play throughout and beyond the primary years.

In selecting texts for the classroom, it is essential to provide a wide range of genres and cater for diverse tastes. It is also essential to include up-to-date children's fiction.

### *Range in children's literature:*

- science fiction, fantasy, adventure, historical fiction, autobiography, mystery, everyday realism, comedy, biography, autobiography, letters, diaries, and so on;
- open texts which invite questions;
- familiar texts which have been read aloud or enjoyed in guided reading;
- traditional tales and alternative versions;
- traditional and modern poetry;
- plays;
- dual language texts;
- several copies of texts by popular authors;
- a wide range of picture books using a variety of kinds of illustrations in different ways;
- novels of varied length, serials and series.

It is important that the collection includes texts which:

- are fun, interesting, challenging, thought provoking and entertaining;
- reflect different cultures;
- provide positive images of gender, class, disability and different types of family unit;
- contain interesting and memorable use of language, for example rhyme, rhythm, repetitive structure or refrain.

# Reading schemes

Reading schemes are sets of books carefully organized into different levels according to assumptions about the nature of progression in reading. Most reflect a relatively controlled vocabulary which builds up gradually as the child moves through the scheme. In the past, schemes were criticized for offering a contrived form of language and predictable unimaginative texts that failed to relate to children's interests and experiences. They were also contrasted with 'real books' (Waterland, 1988), children's literature, which is more likely to provide experience of the pleasures and challenges of reading. Reading scheme books were generally presented in a uniform way with uninspiring covers and little indication of authorship or content. Often the most noticeable aspect of the cover was the symbol or figure signifying the level of the text. The main focus of these schemes therefore seemed to be to provide material for children to practise reading, rather than to stimulate or entertain.

Recently published schemes differ widely in their content, presentation and language use but generally reflect greater effort to contain more natural use of language and appealing, relevant content. Some children's authors now write for schemes and many texts are presented as fiction and non-fiction for children. They often include wordless picture books that are useful in encouraging children to use illustrations to explore narrative. These schemes offer a clear system of progression that can be easily monitored and texts that can be selected to suit the ability of individual children. As reading is presented as a process of progression in clearly identified stages, however, reading schemes may still encourage competition and a sense of failure for some children. Even more importantly, as many have pointed out (for example, Browne, 2001; Meek, 1988), reading scheme texts are rarely as rich as children's literature in terms of plot development, characterization, depth of emotion and language use. In offering children a richer and more rewarding experience of reading, children's literature may be more likely to encourage children's interest and progress. Many schools therefore find it useful to incorporate both reading schemes and children's literature within their reading programme. Various guides are available to support teachers in grouping books from current reading schemes and children's literature which share common levels of challenge and are suitable for use in guided reading (such as Hobsbaum, 2002; Buckler *et al.*, 2003).

Whether or not reading schemes are used, all children need to see that reading offers opportunities, challenges and rewards and access to an increasing range of different kinds of texts. It is also important to remember that children's interest and motivation are crucial to success in reading and will enable them to enjoy texts that far exceed their independent reading ability. This underlines the importance of reading aloud to children, making these texts available to them and offering frequent and varied recommendations.

## Resources for developing response to literature

Young children welcome the opportunity to explore and extend their understanding of familiar stories and characters through play. The following resources are useful in this respect.

### Small world play

Puppets, dolls, toy people and animals can be used to recreate scenes or retell a story. Settings can enhance such play, and are particularly useful for stories in which the setting is significant or a journey takes place.

For example, in *We're Going on a Bear Hunt* (Rosen, 1989) a family run into a series of natural obstacles including long grass, a river and mud on the way to find a bear. A refrain is repeated as each obstacle is encountered: 'Uh-uh . . . we can't go over it. We can't go under it. Oh no! We've got to go through it!' with noises made to match the experience, like 'squelch squelch' as they go through the mud. Providing figures to represent the family and a model landscape containing these features, or even better, encouraging the children to create the different settings can reinforce the narrative and encourage repetition of the refrain.

### Socio-dramatic role play

The provision of costumes and props can encourage children to act out sequences from a familiar narrative. Story settings can also be recreated. For example, *Whatever Next!* (Murphy, 1985) presents the story of a teddy who makes a journey to the moon, using a box for a spaceship and a colander as a helmet. Provided with these same items, children who are familiar with this book will happily recreate the teddy's adventure.

In *It's the Bear!* (Alborough, 1992), Eddy and his bear Freddy go with Eddy's mum for a picnic in the woods. Eddy encounters a huge bear clutching his own teddy and hides in the picnic basket. With bears of different sizes and a large box to represent the picnic basket, children can re-enact the story.

*Can't You Sleep, Little Bear?* (Waddell, 1988) tells the story of a small bear who lives with a big bear in a cave and spends one sleepless night repeatedly disturbing Big Bear with his fear of the dark. The cave and its homely environment can be created in the classroom and PowerPoint used to project a starry night sky onto one wall. Role-play areas can also be created from traditional tales, for example Seven Dwarves' Cottage, the bridge from the Billy Goats Gruff, the kitchen from Cinderella. Children can be involved in planning what should be included.

## Storysacks/resource packs

Storysacks are a popular resource pioneered by Neil Griffiths (Bird, 2001) in family literacy groups but now widely used in schools. A storysack is a cloth bag containing a book and puppets, masks, toys or props and sometimes a map or setting relevant to a story. The bag also holds a non-fiction book and a game related to the story. Parents and older children have often been involved in designing and creating such bags and their contents although they are also available commercially. Such bags may be used at home or to support shared text work and independent activities and storytelling in the classroom.

For example, *Where the Wild Things Are* (Sendak, 1963) tells the story of a young boy, Max, sent to bed without any supper as a result of his naughty behaviour. During the night his room changes into a forest and Max embarks on a voyage by boat to an island where he is welcomed by friendly 'wild things' who invite him to join their 'wild rumpus' and make him their king. Max later realizes that he wants to return home, so he sets off in the boat again and arrives back to find that his supper is 'still hot'!

A storysack for this book could contain:

- Max – a model or puppet;
- puppets or models of wild things;
- crown;
- boat;
- a cloth/collage painted or marked to show an island;
- a box to show Max's bedroom;
- a game – for example, 'how many things starting with "B" can you find in the book?';
- a book about boats.

Resource packs are a similar resource, aimed at older children. They also contain a range of artefacts and texts related to a text and often provide opportunities for extending themes raised in literature across other areas of the curriculum.

## Topic boxes/discovery kits

Storysacks have been adapted in various ways. Topic boxes/discovery kits relate to non-fiction. They may contain non-fiction texts on the same subject and then relevant resources which are likely to stimulate interest in this topic. For example, a topic box on the Fire of London might contain:

- a time line;
- pictures of London, fire engines, people and houses at the time;
- a report from a witness;
- a book about the Fire of London;
- a book about modern fire engines and the job of a firefighter.

When such kits are used as part of a home reading programme, a related adult text on the same subject is often included to offer opportunities for extending interests and enjoyment.

Topic boxes could be created for topics in science, geography and religious education or linked to the children's own interests and hobbies. Older children can be involved in the design and preparation of the contents of these boxes.

# The writing area and resources for writing

The purpose of the writing/mark-making area is to encourage children to write independently. Although more frequently found in early years classrooms, it can be valuable at any stage of the primary years because it provides children with the opportunity and resources to develop their personal interests in writing. This area can offer children scope to enjoy the freedom to write as they wish, explore their interests and to experiment. The writing area can also provide a space for children to use on a regular basis to concentrate on specific aspects of the writing process. Prompts, dictionaries, thesauruses and highlighter pens can encourage children to apply themselves to the editing of their work.

In planning a writing area, it is necessary to consider the setting and the materials. Clearly the size of the classroom dictates how much space can be devoted to it. At its most limited, the area could consist of a table and chairs and some form of storage for a range of writing equipment. In the early years, the teacher can make explicit her own use of writing for different purposes by announcing, for example, the need to visit the writing area to note down something to remember or write a message or list. It is important to provide an extensive and varying range of writing equipment, particularly for young children who need the opportunity to experiment with their handwriting and presentation. Older children also gain pleasure and satisfaction from experimenting with the presentation of their writing.

### Resources for the writing area:

- pens, pencils, marker pens, crayons of various thicknesses, highlighter pens;
- a variety of types of paper, card, pre-made books, forms, plain postcards, note pads, letter writing paper, envelopes, calendars and diaries;
- hole punchers, paper clips, folders;
- dictionaries, thesauruses;
- examples of authentic texts, for example shopping lists, formal and informal letters, greeting cards, postcards, invitations and forms;
- computer and printer;
- laptop;
- spellchecker;
- noticeboard;
- post-box for sending messages to others in the class;
- lists of high-frequency words.

## Mini-whiteboards and dry wipe pens

Mini-whiteboards and dry wipe pens are a valuable resource for encouraging interactive learning particularly during whole-class sessions. Children can use whiteboards in many ways, for example:

- to jot down ideas for a class piece of writing;
- to complete a sentence or continue a paragraph started in shared writing;
- to note down adjectives which could be used to describe a character;
- to create a new line of a dialogue;
- to experiment with spelling;
- to practise the formation of a letter;
- to write a specific letter for a given phoneme;
- to list words which include a particular spelling pattern, rhyme or a common root or suffix.

Whiteboards are often shared between pairs of children. At times a teacher may select pairs and decide which partners will scribe in order to provide support for less confident writers.

## A class message board

A class message board is a valuable resource for communicating information to children and, depending on the situation, to parents. Reminders can be posted there by the children or the teacher. Children can also use the board to advertise for lost or desired items, tell jokes or pass on messages. It provides a dynamic and meaningful context for children's reading and writing.

## Journals and jotters

Journals provide a space for reflection through writing. They enable children to express emotions and clarify thoughts. Reflective journals may be used on a regular basis or when children feel the need or desire to write in them. Some teachers regard these journals as the children's personal and private possessions and do not read them. Others engage in a dialogue with each child, by writing regular responses to a child's entries.

Journals can also be used in more specific ways:

- spelling journals and vocabulary books provide a space for children to record words that they need to learn to spell and to collect interesting words and phrases from reading;
- reading journals can be used to keep a record of books read with brief comments on responses to them;
- talk journals are useful for recording reflections on participation in discussions and oral work;
- learning journals can be used to highlight key learning points in any subject, reinforcing understanding and a sense of achievement.

Jotters or rough books are used to make notes and record ideas and drafts. When children are given such books for recording these unformed thoughts, they can see that this kind of writing is valuable. They can also see that at the initial stages of writing they do not need to be concerned with presentation. Such books are useful in keeping notes and drafts together so that there is less chance of rough pieces of work being lost.

# The use of display

Displays are important in every learning environment in providing information and valuing pupils' work. Children can be encouraged to engage actively with the content rather than simply observe passively. Interactive displays invite children to respond to questions, contribute answers, compare and speculate. Sometimes they encourage children to contribute their own questions or add comments, which will invite responses from others. Clearly it is important to consider the height of displays and ensure that children can read them. Post-its can provide a useful means for children to add comments to existing displays.

Children of all ages can also take an active role in planning and producing displays. From the early years, children can discuss what should be included and how it will be presented. As they gain experience and confidence, the activity of planning and producing a display can provide children with a very valuable focus for discussion, research and the presentation of information. Displays produced by children also promote a sense of ownership of the environment and are likely to generate interest amongst other members of the class. Whilst the standard of presentation of the final product may not be professional, the process of creating a display provides a highly motivating activity, encouraging reflection on learning and a meaningful purpose for using a range of skills in language and literacy.

Displays based on children's literature can employ a wide range of materials, props, children's work and pictures to promote interest and also encourage children to consider particular events, characters, motives or techniques used by the author. In the early stages of introducing a topic or text, interest can be stimulated by a display produced by the teacher, which provides an introduction, stimulates interest and raises questions. Teacher-made resources may gradually be replaced or supplemented by material produced by the children.

Another valuable use of display is to encourage an interest in language, the origins and development of words and reinforce recognition of letters and spelling patterns. They can also invite children to be creative, to play with language and reflect on their reading, writing, speaking and listening.

*Sample challenges for use in display:*

- How many words can you find that end in –ful?
- How many words can you find with '–cept' in them (reception, deception, intercept)? What do you think 'cept' might mean?
- How many words can you find that mean . . . small? . . . nice? . . . said?
- Many words in English come from other languages. Here are some examples: anorak, bungalow, spaghetti, mosquito, restaurant . . . Can you find out which language each word comes from? How many others can you find?
- Here's a space to put favourite, memorable, interesting or unusual words/phrases that you find in your reading!
- What's the shortest sentence you can find? What's the longest sentence you can find?
- Here is an opening line to a poem. What might the next line be?
- Match the description to the photo.
- How many heroes and superheroes can you list? How many adjectives can you find to describe them?
- Use these words to make a poem.
- Find as many things as you can that start with 'b'.
- How many words can you add that rhyme with 'two'? Guess how many different spelling patterns there are for this phoneme.

## Alphabet friezes

In the early years, alphabet friezes provide an important support for children in identifying the relevant graphemc. Although these can be purchased, friezes created by the children are likely to be more relevant to them and offer additional advantages in reinforcing understanding through their creation. In the example presented earlier in the chapter, familiar packaging and wrappers have been used. Ketch (1991) describes the use of sweet wrappers as a means to develop children's awareness and recognition of the letters of the alphabet through a class dictionary. This idea can easily be adapted and developed as an alphabet frieze and can include a wide range of wrappers, packaging, familiar logos and cereal packets. Marsh (1999) suggests an alternative presenting popular media characters (such as Barbie, Nemo, Lilo and Stitch).

# Exploring and celebrating linguistic diversity

The classroom environment has an important role to play in the celebration of linguistic diversity. In any classroom, whatever the background of the children, it is important for the following to be visible and available:

- scripts and languages that exist in the wider community and across the world;
- 'welcome' messages, notices and labels, food wrappers, newspapers, magazines and film posters in children's home languages;

- food wrappers, newspapers and magazines;
- comparison of different scripts;
- simple greetings and common phrases in a variety of languages;
- a variety of texts in different languages.

In settings where there are bilingual children it is essential that their home languages are recognized and valued. Whenever possible, texts in home languages should be made available and their use encouraged. In monolingual settings, it is just as important that children are aware of the existence of different languages and scripts and that interest in and respect for such diversity are demonstrated and fostered.

# The role-play area

Over the past 20 years, there has been increasing acknowledgement of the value of the role-play area in providing children with a setting to explore their understanding of literacy. A key influence has been Nigel Hall (1987 and 1999), whose work has shown how role-play areas offer young children meaningful contexts in which they are empowered to use literacy in a wide variety of ways. Children's awareness of print and of the purposes for which adults read and write in familiar settings can be transferred to the role-play area, where they can engage with and explore such use of literacy.

A common use of the role-play area is as a home setting. As discussed in Chapter 1, children will be familiar with language and literacy use in the home. Including a range of resources, such as a telephone, television, newspapers, letters, note pads, catalogues and recipes, encourages children to explore these activities through their role play. Resources such as cooking equipment, items of food, clothing and artefacts of the home are also valuable. These need to be familiar to children in the class and reflect their varied cultures. A valuable source of information and help in providing relevant resources will be the children themselves, their parents and families.

Children are familiar with a wide range of settings, which reflect varied uses of literacy and can also be created in the classroom. For example, the role-play area could represent a shop, doctor's surgery, office, café, library, police station, museum, hairdresser, travel agency or tourist information office. Settings are often linked to work in other curriculum areas – for example, a baby clinic or garden centre may support work in science on growth and change. A health centre, opticians or doctor's surgery may be introduced to reinforce work on the senses. Role-play areas do not need to be confined to imitations of real-world settings but can also be successfully related to popular culture (Marsh *et al.*, 2000). A Batman and Batwoman HQ successfully engaged the interest of children who had previously shown limited interest in the role-play area (Marsh *et al.*, 1997).

Having selected an area, it is then necessary to consider the following:

- roles involved in this setting;
- equipment needed to simulate this setting;

- relevant literacy events;
- resources needed to encourage use of literacy.

The following example shows how these relate to the development of a role-play area as a hairdressers' shop.

Roles: customers, receptionist, hairdressers, assistants.
Equipment: chair, towels, mirror, combs, overalls, posters, till . . .
Literacy events: looking at magazines, selecting hairstyles from books, taking phone messages, booking appointments . . .
Resources: appointment book, pen, pencil, telephone, message book, magazines, posters, till, receipts, and so on.

The preparation of the role-play area can also provide an exciting focus for discussion and a variety of literacy-related events for younger children. A visit with the children to the relevant setting is extremely useful in enabling them to understand the kind of roles, activities and interactions that take place there. It also offers the opportunity to draw children's attention to texts found in the setting. They may then be able to collect examples or produce their own imitations within the classroom. Lists of equipment and plans can be created and letters written to parents asking for useful items. Hall (1999: 115) describes how a teacher successfully and imaginatively incorporated this process within role play. Having decided that the existing area would be changed into a garage, the children wrote letters and filled in forms to request planning permission. They received and responded to letters of complaint from neighbours, drew out plans for a workshop and office area, created a name for the garage, produced health-and safety notices and labels and went on to plan and hold an opening event.

In planning a role-play area, it is also helpful to consider the roles which could be adopted by adults. Consider the following example based on an incident in a nursery class.

Some nursery children have chosen to play in the role-play area, which is a shoe shop. Two children are wearing stickers marked with a picture of a shoe and the words 'shop assistant'. All the children are engaged in playing with the shoes, trying them on and piling up the shoe boxes. The teacher enters the area and says: 'Excuse me, is anyone serving here?' The children turn to look at her. She asks one of the children to be her daughter. She then turns to one of the other children: 'Oh you must be the shop assistant. I wonder if you can help me. I've come to find some new shoes for my daughter . . . Can you help me? Could you measure her feet, I think she's grown a bit.'

The shop assistant child responds by bringing a foot measure and proceeds to measure the other child's feet. A size is given and then the conversation moves on to discuss different types of shoes. The shop assistant goes to find the appropriate boxes . . .

By acting as a customer, this adult not only succeeds in engaging and focusing the children's attention, but also provides a model of appropriate behaviour and language use. By assuming the role of the customer, rather than the shop assistant, she is able to guide the child's responses yet still place him in the position of authority.

In addition to encouraging children to engage in and explore roles and activities within the role-play setting, it is also possible to harness their interest and generate interactions with print within and beyond the role-play area. Work by Hall (1999) has highlighted the value of introducing events and problems into the role-play area. Note how interventions are used in the following example:

> The teacher produces an email from Head Office telling the shoe shop staff that they should appoint two new shop assistants. The children discuss what to do and decide to advertise. The teacher shows them adverts for jobs in the local paper and the children create their own. They produce and complete application forms and hold interviews. Later a letter arrives from a customer, complaining about the service in the shop and the poor quality of the shoes and arguing that the shop should be closed down. The children discuss what they should do in response and a class letter and several individual letters are written.

The above example illustrates that the introduction of events and problems can be effective in generating interest, motivation, challenges and further opportunities for using language and literacy. Such interventions provoke thought, provide challenges and engage children in speaking and listening, reading and writing for a wide variety of meaningful purposes. Through extending children's experience in this way, teachers encourage children to develop confidence in themselves as independent users and producers of language and literacy.

Whilst role-play areas are used mainly in the early years, their value and potential to encourage varied use of language, learning and creativity continue throughout the primary years. In particular, they enable meaningful opportunities for literacy and language use to be integrated with learning from other curriculum areas such as history, science or geography. The example below shows how older children can also be involved in planning, preparing and organizing role play.

> A year 6 class is studying the Victorians. Some resources have been borrowed from the local museum by the teacher. The children are given the task of creating a class museum to inform other children and parents about Victorian life. The children discuss what the museum should contain and how it should be organized. Groups of children research different aspects of Victorian life and prepare information sheets and commentary on artefacts. Publicity material and museum guides for younger children are created during literacy sessions and parents and the chair of the school governors are invited to attend the Grand Opening. Adult visitors and children from other classes in the school are given guided tours by members of the class.

# The outdoor environment

In the Foundation Stage, it is particularly important to capitalize on opportunities for promoting use of language and literacy offered by the outside environment. Activities can be planned to encourage children to:

- develop use of oral language through exploring water play, physical activities, gardening and so on;
- experiment with mark-making using paint and chalks;
- gain interest in research into plants, minibeasts and so on;
- create a street scene, for example, with road signs and shops.

The outdoor environment can also be used to create a role-play area, for example a garden centre, garage, street or building site.

The wider school and local community also contribute valuable resources and opportunities for language and literacy use. Within the school, children can make use of the library to support their research and extend their reading interests. Staff, children and visitors to the school provide a range of audiences and purposes for talk and writing. Assemblies offer opportunities for presentations, drama and public recognition of children's efforts and achievements. Beyond the school the local environment and community offer a further range of meaningful contexts for language use. Visits to local places and school trips can also provide a valuable stimulus for children's language and literacy development.

# Information and Communication Technology (ICT)

Information and Communication Technology includes a wide range of equipment, such as tape recorders, video cameras, dictaphones and computers. Such resources can support and enhance the teaching of language and literacy in a variety of ways, which are discussed in Chapter 8. There are considerable benefits of having such facilities in the classroom. The availability of computers allows for their use to be related directly to other aspects of the English and wider curriculum. This enables word-processing facilities to be readily available as an alternative to pencil and paper for all stages of the writing process. It also provides access to the Internet to support classroom research. However, it does require careful organization to ensure that the use of such facilities is enjoyed by all the children. Pairing and grouping children for work on the computer can be effective but only if those involved understand the need for discussion, co-operation and the sharing of roles.

Many schools now provide computer suites to allow for class teaching. This can lead to ICT sessions that are not connected with other classroom learning. It is important for children to see the value of ICT in supporting their literacy, so it is useful to relate its use to classroom activities and learning. A vast range of computer packages and Internet sites exist to provide support for the teaching of specific aspects of reading and writing. These are often attractive to children in their use of graphics, moving images and sound effects. At times they can provide a very valuable means to reinforce a learning point or motivate an individual child. However, it is important to be selective and discriminating in their use. It is always essential to consider the nature of the experience of literacy offered and its relevance to the individual child.

# Encouragement of independence, ownership and motivation

The classroom environment is also important in encouraging children to be independent, motivated learners and regard themselves as significant members of the classroom community. At all stages of the early and primary years, clear systems of organization in terms of procedures and resources are essential if children are to be independent in the classroom. Children at different stages will need to be clear about:

- what to do when in difficulties or when work has been completed;
- how to be a good talk or response partner;
- how to be a good listener;
- how to go about redrafting a piece of work;
- things to think about at the editing stage;
- how to find a good book.

Involving children in developing procedures and producing poster reminders encourages ownership and a meaningful purpose for discussion and writing. The boxes below and opposite provide examples of guidance produced by children.

Access to necessary resources is also crucial if children are to work independently. Involving children of all ages in the organization, labelling and maintenance of resources encourages them to take responsibility for such equipment and be confident in knowing where to find what they need. Many teachers find it useful to allocate resources that are in regular use – pencils, pens, crayons, sharpeners, rubbers and so on on a group/table basis and appoint monitors to be responsible for their upkeep. Clear labelling of places

---

*How to find a good book!*

Look at the front cover and the blurb on the back.

Read a bit of the first chapter/skim a few pages/look at the pictures.

Ask a friend for a good book.

Read something by an author you already like.

---

*How to redraft your work*

Read it to yourself or to a friend.

What do you like about it? Which are the best bits? Why?

Does it make sense and flow? Are there any bits that don't? Why? How could you make it flow more smoothly?

Is the opening clear? Does it make a reader want to read on? How can you make it better?

Are there any words or phrases you could improve?

---

> *How to be a good listener*
> Look at the person speaking.
> Think about what they are saying.
> Look as if you are interested. Nod and smile.
> Don't interrupt.
> Don't talk to anyone else!
> Ask good questions.
> Keep still!

where resources are kept is helpful not only for organizational purposes, but for younger children reinforces recognition of print in a meaningful way.

Registers and lists of children's names are essential for administrative purposes. However, their use can also be shared with the children. Self-registration is a good example of this. Children write their names on a list to show they are present, which provides a meaningful purpose for such practice. Name cards may be available to support them in this activity. At an earlier stage the focus may be on recognition of individual names. In a nursery setting, for example, as the children arrive with their parents or carers, they find a card showing their own photograph and name and fix this on a board to indicate that they are present. Names and photos provide a valuable resource that may be useful for a variety of activities, as discussed in Chapter 4.

At all stages, children benefit from reminders about common spellings. Posters or laminated mats showing high-frequency words can provide children with valuable support and encourage independence in writing. Posters showing common phoneme digraphs, for example ai – ai/ay/split digraph a-e and examples of associated common words (rain, day, came) can also be useful, particularly if the children are able to contribute to these collections.

# The role of parents and carers in the classroom

Positive relationships with parents and carers are essential in promoting mutual support and understanding. The classroom environment plays an important role in making all visitors feel welcome, respected and appreciated. It also provides a means to increase understanding of the nature of the activities that take place in the classroom and their purpose in supporting children's development. However, the relationship is not one-way; parents and carers offer an invaluable resource in terms of skills, experiences and knowledge of children, which can support and extend opportunities for learning within the classroom. This section therefore offers some examples of ways of promoting each of these aspects.

### Making the classroom a welcoming environment

Warm, friendly greetings show all visitors that they are welcome and provide reassurance to those lacking in confidence. Informal conversations at the beginning and end of the session demonstrate interest and approachability.

***Other ways of encouraging positive relationships:***

- welcome notices in different languages;
- informal messages to parents;
- message boards for parents;
- coffee mornings/open sessions.

### Informing parents about classroom activities and approaches to teaching

Parents and carers can be informed about teaching approaches and activities in the classroom.

***Ways to communicate with parents and carers:***

- encouraging children to show parents and carers what they have been doing;
- informal conversations about activities;
- displays of children's work with commentary and translation if appropriate;
- open sessions where parents and carers are welcome to participate or observe;
- regular sessions in which parents or carers are involved in activities with the children, for example reading/writing together – in many early years settings this takes place at the beginning of every session;
- letters/newsletters sent home about activities in school – which may be written by the children;
- messages/articles on the school Web site.

### Encouraging involvement in the educational setting

Depending on their interests experience, skills and availability, parents and carers may be willing to become involved in various ways.

***Ways to involve parents and carers:***

- storytelling;
- translation;
- scribing;
- writing with children;
- reading aloud;

- telling children (or being interviewed) about their interests, hobbies, jobs, personal histories, culture or religion;
- talking to individual children about their reading;
- hearing children read;
- sharing books with children;
- supporting children choosing books in the reading corner or library;
- creating resources, for example puppets, storysacks and displays.

Adults offering support with teaching activities in the classroom need clear information about the children's task, the nature of the learning objective, the level of support required and any anticipated outcomes.

# Summary

This chapter has demonstrated a wide range of ways in which the classroom environment can be used and developed to encourage children to feel welcome, valued and interested in learning. It has also shown how the setting and the use of resources can contribute to children's development in language and literacy and their attitudes to this area of the curriculum and to learning. In particular, it has emphasized the importance of providing the following:

- a welcoming, stimulating environment for all;
- a wide range of carefully selected texts and resources;
- a setting which reflects and values the diversity of languages, children's use of language and literacy and children's own interests;
- an environment which presents language as interesting and alive;
- opportunities for developing independence.

# Reflective questions

1. Whitehead (2002: 83) suggests that teachers considering their learning environment in relation to the teaching of language and literacy should consider the following question: 'Does the appearance of your room or setting or institution . . . give a message that you are nurturing and extending a community of speakers and listeners, readers and writers?' Consider this question in relation to a setting you know. Try to identify what kinds of messages are conveyed in that situation and how these are reflected in the environment and its organization.

2. Select an appropriate role-play area for a particular setting. Use the role-play planning form below to plan resources you will need and how you will engage and extend the interest of the children. A completed example is presented beneath it.

## Role-play planning form

**Role-play area:**

Roles

General equipment and resources

Literacy events

Relevant texts, resources and implements

Introduction of setting

Adult roles

Events and interventions

## Role-play planning example

**Role-play area: SUPERMARKET**

| | |
|---|---|
| Roles | Check out assistant, shelf stacker, manager, customers |
| General equipment and resources | Packages shelving, till, table, seating, carrier bags, money |
| Literacy events | Making orders, restocking shelves, reading shopping lists, writing cheques or signing slips |
| Relevant texts, resources and implements | Till receipts, note pad, pencils, pens |
| Introduction of setting | Visit supermarket, observe contents and layout and interview member of staff about the setting and who works there |
| Adult roles | Customer, check out assistant, shelf stacker, manager, inspector |
| Events and interventions | Need to advertise for new staff<br>Burglary<br>Company drive to improve service<br>Visit from company director |

### FURTHER READING

Drake, J. (2001) *Planning Children's Play and Learning in the Foundation Stage*. London: David Fulton Publishers.
  Chapter 5 on the value of display in supporting learning.

Hall, N. (1999) 'Young children, play and literacy: engagement in realistic uses of literacy', in Marsh, J. and Hallett, E. (eds) *Desirable Literacies: Approaches to Language and Literacy in the Early Years*. London: Paul Chapman Publishing.
  On the use and development of the role-play area.

Siraj-Blatchford, I. and Clarke, P. (2000) *Supporting Identity, Diversity and Language in the Early Years*. Buckingham: Open University Press.

Chapter 7 on the selection of resources.

## REFERENCES

Bird, V. (2001) 'Once upon a time . . .', in *Literacy Today*, 26 March 2001.

Browne, A. (2001) *Developing Language and Literacy 3–8*. Second Edition. London: Paul Chapman Publishing.

Buckler, S., Baker, S. and Hobsbaum, A. (2003) *Book Bands for Guided Reading: Organising Key Stage One Texts for the Literacy Hour*. London: Institute of Education.

Hall, N. (1987) *The Emergence of Literacy*. London: Hodder & Stoughton.

Hall, N. (1999) 'Young children, play and literacy: engagement in realistic uses of literacy', in Marsh, J. and Hallett, E., (eds) *Desirable Literacies: Approaches to Language and Literacy in the Early Years*. London: Paul Chapman Publishing.

Hobsbaum, A. (2002) *Teaching Guided Reading at Key Stage 2*. London: Institute of Education.

Ketch, A. (1991) 'The delicious alphabet', *English and Education*, 25(1), 1–4.

Marsh, J. (1999) 'Tellytubby tales: popular culture and media education', in Marsh, J. and Hallett, E. (eds) *Desirable Literacies: Approaches to Language and Literacy in the Early Years*. London: Paul Chapman Publishing.

Marsh, J. and Millard, E. (2000) *Literacy and Popular Culture: Using Children's Culture in the Classroom*. London: Paul Chapman Publishing.

Marsh, J., Payne, L. and Anderson, S. (1997) 'Batman and Batwoman in the classroom', *Primary English*, 5(2), 8–11.

Meek, M. (1988) *How Texts Teach What Readers Learn*. Shroud: Thimble.

Waterland, L. (1988) *Read With Me: An Apprenticeship Approach to Reading*. Second Edition. Stroud: Thimble.

Whitehead, M. (2002) *Developing Language and Literacy with Young Children*. Second Edition. London: Paul Chapman Publishing.

## CHILDREN'S BOOKS

Alborough, J. (1992) *It's the Bear!* London: Candlewick Press.

Murphy, J. (1985) *Whatever Next!* London: Macmillan.

Rosen, M. (1989) *We're Going on a Bear Hunt*. London: Walker.

Sendak, M. (1963) *Where the Wild Things Are*. London: Bodley Head.

Waddell, M. (1988) *Can't You Sleep, Little Bear?* London: Walker.

# Meeting Diverse Needs in English

In this chapter we explore ways in which all children can be given opportunities to develop their knowledge, understanding and skills in language and literacy to their full potential. The teaching of language and literacy to children with special needs discussed in this chapter is underpinned by the same principles as those that have been reflected throughout this book. Our aim in this chapter is therefore to demonstrate how the approaches discussed in earlier chapters can be adapted to be appropriate, relevant and accessible to *all* children.

In every classroom, a teacher will find children with a wide range of interests, personal qualities, strengths and needs. In a positive learning environment such individuality is valued and children are encouraged to respect differences and build a supportive community. Given movements towards greater inclusion since Warnock (DES, 1978) and subsequent legislation (DES 1981, 1993; DfES, 2003) the range of needs within the mainstream classroom has broadened considerably and includes children with minor and severe needs in relation to social, emotional, sensory, physical and cognitive factors and those described as gifted and talented. All of these children can be encouraged to develop their knowledge, understanding and skills in language and literacy as far as possible. Given the crucial role of language and literacy in providing access to other subjects and as a means to develop and demonstrate learning, such progress is essential in supporting achievement in all areas of the curriculum.

The nature of the provision required to support and motivate all children in developing confidence and making maximum progress inevitably varies enormously depending on the nature of children's needs, for example:

- temporary and focused intervention;
- more permanent provision in the form of physical resources or the adaptation of tasks or the environment.

This chapter does not aim to provide detailed explanations of the nature of specific needs or specialist knowledge on the support required across the curriculum. This is clearly well beyond the scope of this book and further information can be found from the references provided at the end of the chapter. It is also assumed that consultation within and beyond the school would be sought to gain more specific guidance for individual children. Parents or carers, the school special educational needs co-ordinator (SENCO), other teachers and LEA support services including speech therapists and educational psychologists will be able to provide support in catering for particular needs.

In any discussion of provision for children with special needs, there can be a danger of focusing on needs rather than on the individual child. As a result the need may be regarded as the defining factor and consequently children's individual personalities and strengths can be overlooked. Treating children with special needs as a homogenous group is not only inappropriate in failing to acknowledge the diversity of needs but also disrespectful to the individual. Even when children share a condition or experience similar difficulties, they may well have huge differences in their life experiences, personalities and interests. Whatever the nature of the need, children are individuals first and it is essential to demonstrate that they are valued for their strengths and qualities rather than simply labelled for the ways in which they differ from others.

We therefore begin the chapter by discussing differentiation. We then explore difficulties faced by children with speaking and listening, reading and writing and how they can be encouraged to overcome them. Dyslexia is discussed within this section. The last section of the chapter presents practical ways in which the learning of children with a range of special needs can be supported.

# Differentiation – enabling all children to achieve success

A range of strengths and weaknesses in language and literacy will be apparent in any classroom. It is important to take into account such differences and consider ways of engaging all children in learning. Differentiation offers the means to take account of children's needs, promote learning and a sense of achievement for all. This may be provided in many ways depending on the needs of the children, the activity, topic and the learning objective.

In many classrooms there has been a tendency to group children according to ability on a semi-permanent basis. This can provide the opportunity for teachers to plan carefully targeted activities for children who share similar needs. Children of all ages are usually well aware of the hierarchy of grouping. Consequently such practice not only has implications for the expectations of the teacher but also for children's progress and self-perceptions. Children who perceive themselves to be in the least able group, with consistently lower expectations and less challenging work, may suffer from lack of self-esteem and poor motivation.

It is often possible for children of differing abilities to work on the same learning objective and in such cases, mixed-ability grouping may be more appropriate. Mixed-ability grouping not only encourages the sharing of ideas but also promotes collaboration and the satisfaction of being involved in a shared goal.

Within an activity, differentiated support can be provided in:

- level of structure – perhaps organized as a sequence of clearly focused steps/open ended;
- amount of support from peers and adults/level of independence;
- adaptation of learning objective of common activity;
- level of input – for example additional input prior to a class session;
- type of outcome – children produce work of differing quality, depth and quantity;
- use of resources, including:
  - choice of equipment, for instance dictaphone, speech recognition software; concept keyboards, tape recorders;
  - nature of texts: simplified/enlarged;
  - range of texts: restricted or wide;
  - reminders of key vocabulary;
  - visual aids/pictorial support.

Consider how the different forms of differentiation are used in the following scenarios:

In the class pet shop area in the **nursery**, the children are encouraged to produce labels and notices for the (toy) animals. The teacher focuses the attention of some children on the correct pencil grip; with others she talks about the initial sounds of the words they wish to use and encourages them to use their knowledge of letters.

Children in a **reception** class are working in groups to create a welcome leaflet for newcomers. Each day, with the support of the teaching assistant, a group takes digital photos of areas of their area and uses these as the basis for their leaflet which they produce using a word-processing package. By the time the less able children come to tackle this activity they have already seen three versions of leaflets presented, discussed and reviewed. In writing their leaflets they use concept keyboards which present key vocabulary.

Children in a **year 2** class have been collecting and telling traditional stories from their communities. They then plan to create a class book to record the tales. The teacher encourages some of the children to work in pairs. She matches some of those who have excelled in storytelling but find writing difficult with others who are more confident writers.

In a **year 4** class, all the children are involved in creating board games and are then asked to plan their instructions. One group finds the task particularly difficult, so the teacher devotes time to looking closely at some authentic instructions with these children. This enables them to contribute to a class discussion on the effective writing of instructions. In shared writing, the class creates a framework for writing instructions. Some children use this as the basis for their writing and more confident writers are encouraged to adapt it to create instructions for a particular audience.

A **year 6** class is investigating persuasive language. The children have collected a wide range of texts including visual, written and moving image examples. All the children look at a range of texts, but the questions and complexity of texts provided vary according to the ability of each group.

# Supporting progress in speaking and listening, reading and writing

The following section outlines common difficulties within speaking and listening, reading and writing and considers how progress in each area can be supported. Some of the features identified are indicators of normal development; they become difficulties only when they are out of step with the child's age or progress in other areas.

A number of intervention programmes have been devised to support children who experience difficulties with literacy in the early and primary years. Reading Recovery is an early intervention programme to help children with reading difficulties. It was based on the work of Marie Clay (1979) who emphasized the importance of diagnosing children's difficulties and encouraging their progress through the development of key strategies in reading.

The NLS has introduced a range of intervention programmes directed at children who are achieving below the average for their years, but are not included in the lowest range of ability:

- Early literacy support (ELS) aimed at children at the end of the first term in year 1 identified as needing additional support to enable them to achieve the level of their peers by the end of the year. It includes work on reading, writing and phonics.
- Additional literacy support (ALS) aimed at children in year 3 or sometimes year 4 whose level of attainment at the end of year 2 suggests that they would benefit from support in literacy.
- Further literacy support (FLS) is designed for children needing support in year 5. It focuses on writing and providing strategies to enable children to track and comment on their own progress and also provides independent and 'homework' tasks.

All these structured programmes provide materials and session plans for activities led by a teaching assistant working with a group of children for a regular short session over a limited period of time. Such sessions often take place outside the classroom.

## Speaking and listening

Progress in speaking and listening is highly important as it is generally children's first mode of communication and the root from which reading and writing develop. It is therefore important to identify delays in this area at an early age so that action can be taken to avoid problems in the development of literacy and loss of self-esteem.

### Supporting children with difficulties in listening

A child with problems in listening may display the following:

- inability to concentrate;

- inability to recall content;
- constant interruptions.

It is always important to check for hearing problems with children who have difficulty listening. Ways of supporting hearing-impaired children are discussed later in this chapter.

Activities for encouraging listening are discussed in detail in Chapter 3 and would be appropriate for a child with difficulties in this area. For such a child the following would be particularly useful:

- discussing ways of giving attention – for example, the use of eye contact and the importance of keeping still;
- providing clear, structured explanations and instructions;
- using literal rather than figurative language (Martin *et al.*, 1999);
- using resources and visual aids to gain attention;
- asking children to repeat key points;
- encouraging children to ask questions.

## Supporting children who are unwilling to talk

Confidence in speaking can be promoted through encouraging children to feel safe and relaxed by providing opportunities to talk:

- about subjects of interest or expertise or about personal experiences;
- with a chosen partner or in a small group of friends;
- to a familiar group after prior practice;
- about a shared book, tape or game.

For a range of relevant activities, see Chapter 3.

In supporting children who refuse to speak it is important to be gentle and keep expectations very limited, for example beginning with encouraging the child to give a whispered response of 'yes' or 'no' to a simple question addressed to them when on their own. It may take considerable time to build up from single word responses and extend the range of listeners. Steps need to be planned sensitively and outside support may well be needed.

## Supporting children with difficulties in speaking clearly

Lack of clarity in articulation may suggest difficulties with hearing and this needs to be checked. The support of a speech therapist may be needed for children experiencing serious difficulties in this area. In general, clarity in sounds and words can be encouraged through:

- activities to develop phonemic awareness, such as play with rhyme and alliteration, segmenting and blending (discussed in Chapter 5);

- modelling – showing children the physical movement of mouth and tongue necessary to make specific sounds and encouraging them to use a mirror to observe their own movements.

## Supporting children with difficulties in conveying information

The development of spoken language in terms of using relevant vocabulary and connecting words and phrases appropriately can be encouraged through providing children with a version of what they are trying to say. This does not mean interrupting or finishing sentences for the child, but providing a response which models appropriate vocabulary and structure.

A child may be encouraged to be more successful in conveying information if:

- there is a genuine need to pass on information – it is needed by the audience – for example, by another child to complete an activity;
- the child has a clear understanding of the information;
- a structure for presenting or remembering the information which has been provided.

# Reading

Difficulties in reading can limit children's access to literature and the wider curriculum. They can also lead to frustration and lack of motivation. Enabling children to escape from this cycle of failure is essential. Children therefore need to experience the pleasures of reading and a sense of achievement. Careful planning of tasks, selection of texts and the provision of support enable all children to see that reading is a meaningful activity and make progress. The use of praise and rewards encourage children to appreciate their success.

Common problems with reading include a lack of:

- interest and enthusiasm;
- confidence;
- ability to read for meaning;
- ability to recall letters and recognize high-frequency words;
- phonic skills.

## Supporting children who lack interest, enthusiasm and confidence in reading

Interest, enthusiasm and confidence in reading can be encouraged through:

- the provision of carefully selected texts which relate to children's interests and are readable but not patronizing in presentation;
- writing books for/with the children which are then made available for them to read;
- frequent reading aloud by the teacher of a wide range of texts;

- opportunities to listen to tapes and share books with friends;
- opportunities to read to younger children.

Readability of texts is an important factor affecting not only children's access to literature but also their understanding of information texts, worksheets and instructions. In general, texts are easier to understand if sentences are short, the font is clear and vocabulary is simple or explained. Dense print is particularly difficult to read, so texts need to be broken up into sections and supported by illustrations.

## Supporting children in reading for meaning

Indications of reading without understanding would include:

- inability to answer questions on the content of what has been read;
- inability to predict later part of text;
- lack of intonation in reading aloud;
- lack of self-correction when reading aloud and miscues (words included that are not represented in the text) which do not make sense.

Children can be encouraged to read for meaning through:

- opportunities to share and discuss texts of interest with friends;
- DARTs, cloze procedure and activities to develop response (discussed in Chapter 4), using texts appropriate to the reading ability of the child;
- providing meaningful purposes for reading – for example to gain information required for further activity;
- focused activities such as matching pictures and sentences, writing a telegram to summarize a text, a headline for a report or a blurb for a book.

## Supporting children in recalling letters and recognizing high frequency-words

Children can be encouraged to develop visual discrimination through:

- matching games, creating pairs, snap or bingo;
- discussing the shapes of letters and words;
- finding examples of a particular letter or word in as many places as possible;
- highlighting a letter or high-frequency word in a text;
- cutting out and displaying examples of a high-frequency word from newspapers, magazines and comics;
- locating examples of letters and high-frequency words in shared texts.

## Supporting children in the development of phonic skills

The development of phonic skills is often selected as a focus for work with children with difficulties in reading. When activities are meaningful, interactive, multi-sensory and carefully planned to meet individual needs, they can be effective in developing children's phonic skills. The phonics section in Chapter 4 provides a range of practical ideas for this purpose.

# Writing

Lack of interest in writing and unwillingness to write are common in children in the early and primary years. Lack of confidence and enthusiasm may be the result of early difficulties in physical aspects of pencil control, letter formation, handwriting, spelling or punctuation or problems with putting ideas on paper. It is therefore important to explore the reasons for negative attitudes to writing and to ensure that such children have plenty of support in planning their writing and a range of meaningful purposes and audiences. Relevant activities and ways of supporting the writing process are discussed in Chapter 5.

## Supporting children who lack confidence and interest in writing

Children who lack confidence and interest in writing are likely to benefit from:

- opportunities to talk or draw in preparation for writing;
- support through scribing;
- modelling;
- collaborative pair work;
- the use of word processing and speech recognition word programs;
- praise for effort;
- explicit acknowledgement of specific aspects of progress.

## Supporting children with poor pencil control and letter formation

Problems with pencil control and the formation of letters can be a result of difficulties with fine motor skills, which can be encouraged through activities suggested in the handwriting section of Chapter 5. Providing plenty of opportunities to experiment with a wide variety of writing implements is also useful.

## Supporting children with untidy or illegible handwriting

Children who produce untidy or illegible handwriting may benefit from:

- reinforcement of the correct formation of letters as discussed in Chapter 5;
- using smooth flowing roller ball pens;
- reminders abut the correct movements, appropriate posture and positioning of paper;
- explicit reminders and demonstration of the correct positioning and alignment of letters;
- opportunities to write for an audience they value.

## Supporting children who produce disappointing content

Many teachers have met children who are full of ideas in the planning stage but whose writing fails to reflect the same level of imagination, originality or sophistication. Encouraging better results may be achieved through:

- providing a clear and meaningful purpose for writing which is relevant to the child;
- encouraging collaborative writing;
- providing opportunities for publication or work to be seen by a wider audience;
- encouraging ideas to be recorded on tape or pictorially before writing.

## Supporting children who lack ideas in writing

Some children struggle to form ideas for writing and consequently the content they produce can be disappointing or even meaningless. Such children benefit from the suggestions above and from:

- class discussion of ideas for content:
- shared writing, modelling and the provision of an outline of content;
- planning through pictures, diagrams or talk;
- having a good understanding of the content.

## Supporting children whose writing lacks organization

Difficulties with organization can also inhibit children's success in communication. Their ability to structure their work in a specific genre can be supported through the ideas suggested above and through:

- experience of reading authentic examples of the specific text type;
- identification of the structure used in this text type;
- class/group discussion of an appropriate writing frame for this text type.

## Supporting children with difficulties in spelling

Children with spelling difficulties benefit from:

- identifying a specific word or pattern that needs to be learned;
- reminders of ways of learning spelling (see Chapter 4);
- the use of a spellchecker;
- positive correction – ticking words and parts of words spelled correctly;
- activities focusing on different ways of learning spelling;
- words selected for learning carefully selected as relevant and useful to child;
- spelling and handwriting practice linked;
- word books containing common words that present difficulties;
- words learned being kept for future reference and as evidence of learning and success.

Placing too much emphasis on spelling can discourage children from writing. It can also lead to unimaginative use of language. Success in learning spelling, particularly in including words learned in the context of writing, should be praised and rewarded.

# Dyslexia

Difficulties in spelling can also be part of a more general pattern of difficulties in reading and writing known as dyslexia. Children with this syndrome may present a range of symptoms, for example difficulties with words, problems with memory, sequence and fine motor skills. Reid (1994: 2) highlights 'patterns of difficulties relating to the processing of information' as the key indicator. Children who experience dyslexia are often able, creative and imaginative and good at oral work, but experience a range of difficulties with written language. They frequently find learning to read difficult and produce written work that is disappointing in terms of their level of understanding and the quality of their oral responses. Difficulties with reading include:

- difficulties in understanding text and identifying key points;
- difficulties in blending and segmentation;
- reading aloud is hesitant and lacks expression, words are missed out and added;
- failing to recognize familiar words.

Difficulties with writing include:

- poor handwriting:     badly formed letters;
  letters confused for example pg; bd; pq; nu;
  reversal of letters;
- poor presentation: messy work with many crossings out;
- difficulties with pencil grip;
- spelling the same word in different ways in same piece of writing;
- phonetic, odd spelling and unusual sequence of words and letters;
- letter confusions.

Children who experience dyslexia may also lack concentration in class and appear dreamy and easily distracted. They may find it difficult to follow instructions.

Not all of these characteristics are reflected in all dyslexics. In the early stages it can be difficult to diagnose, as symptoms are also indicators of normal development. Nevertheless, as early support is crucial in avoiding frustrations and lack of progress, it is important to be alert to possible early indications.

Examples of early indications include difficulties in:

- learning nursery rhymes, songs and alphabet;
- listening, paying attention and following content of stories;
- following and repeating rhythms;
- fine motor skills;

* remembering names of people, colours and so on;
* following a sequence of instructions.

## Supporting children with dyslexia in learning across the curriculum

In catering for dyslexic pupils it is important to be particularly sensitive to difficulties with organization, following instructions, writing and reading. The following may be useful:

* providing a partner to do the recording or a copy of the required text rather than expecting children to copy from the whiteboard;
* providing a tape recording of instructions;
* suggesting visual strategies such as mind mapping as a means to plan or record understanding;
* providing ways of recording that do not depend heavily on writing – for example posters, charts, tables, cloze procedure;
* using practical demonstrations or diagrams to present concepts and ideas;
* giving children key texts in advance;
* providing cards showing key subject vocabulary.

When producing worksheets it is useful to provide:

* clear and uncluttered text;
* headings and subheadings;
* numbered paragraphs;
* underlining of key points;
* a taped version of the content.

## Supporting dyslexic children in literacy

Support in literacy for dyslexic children may be provided through:

* adult or peer help in reading and making sense of texts;
* taped recordings of texts;
* work in pairs – encouraging a dyslexic child to work with a partner who is more confident in transcription;
* visual reminders of formation of letters and key spellings;
* mnemonics and visual reminders of letters – like b e d makes a bed shape when the letters are correctly positioned;
* alphabet strips to support the use of a dictionary.

The British Dyslexia Association (BDA) (www.bda-dyslexia.org.uk) recommend that help with literacy focuses on the development of phonic skills through

* a carefully structured programme of simple steps;
* constant reinforcement of what has already been taught;

- multi-sensory work – the use of visual, aural, oral and kinaesthetic senses, as discussed in the section in the writing chapter on spelling;
- an emphasis on learning kinaesthetically, for example using wooden or plastic letters;
- the use of Look Cover Write Check . . . (as discussed in Chapter 5).

Information and Communication Technology has a particular value in supporting children with dyslexia, as highlighted by Keates (2000), through:

- word-processing programs enabling children to focus on compositional aspects of writing;
- concept keyboards or programs such as Clicker Plus (a concept keyboard on screen);
- predictive or voice-operated software;
- hand held spellcheckers, especially those that allow phonetic spelling;
- software packages designed to develop children's phonic skills.

The provision of texts to meet children's level of maturity and interests is essential. It is important not to patronize or insult children by giving them books aimed at younger children. Many picture books are particularly useful in offering open, challenging and sophisticated content without relying on complex text.

# Providing support for children with special needs

The following section explores the nature of the broad range of special needs presented in the classroom. In discussing these needs the main concern is to identify ways in which progress in language, literacy and learning may be affected.

## Supporting children with physical disabilities

The range of physical disabilities experienced by children is extensive and the aim of this section is simply to draw attention to some implications for teaching. It is important to stress that many physical conditions are unlikely to have an impact upon children's learning. However, for some children extended absences from school and hospitalization may lead to difficulties with progress. Specific resources or aids and adaptations to classroom organization and management may be necessary for some children; for example, those with hearing or visual impairment or with difficulties in mobility or confined to wheelchairs. Children with difficulties in fine motor control benefit from support with pencil control and writing using activities discussed earlier in this chapter.

A common problem for children with physical disabilities is tiredness as a result of the effort of dealing with difficulties and medication. As a teacher it is important to avoid misinterpreting such fatigue as indicating lack of interest or motivation. For all children who suffer from physical disabilities there is a danger of self-consciousness and low self-image. In any classroom it is therefore essential that positive attitudes to differences are fostered within a supportive, caring environment.

# Supporting children with hearing impairment

Hearing loss may be conductive and temporary or sensori-neural and permanent. Conductive hearing loss tends to be caused by blockages, for example wax or fluid that prevents or restricts vibrations in the air from reaching the inner ear. Children with colds often experience this but conditions such as glue ear can be more lasting. Such conditions can be treated medically and hearing is generally restored. However, the impact of such hearing loss may be considerable. When such conditions are not diagnosed, the following may occur in the child's language use and behaviour:

- difficulties in understanding spoken language;
- limited use of spoken language;
- limited vocabulary;
- difficulties in discriminating sounds;
- lack of attention;
- lack of concentration.

Conductive hearing loss can clearly result in difficulties in development in language and literacy. Children's lack of response and limited use of oral language are sometimes misinterpreted as evidence of learning difficulties (Wilson, 1998) and it is therefore important to be alert to the possible cause of such behaviour and to discuss any concerns with parents or carers and seek outside advice.

Sensori-neural loss of hearing is permanent. It is caused by faulty nerve connections and often leads to difficulties with particular frequencies of sounds. Hearing aids can help some problems, but may cause distortion and pick up and amplify all sounds, not only the ones that are needed. Children who rely on a hearing aid need to be reminded and encouraged to use it.

In supporting children with hearing impairment it is important to:

- face the child when speaking;
- avoid moving around whilst talking;
- speak clearly but not in an exaggerated or unusually slow way that interferes with the normal rhythm;
- make key vocabulary and instructions simple and clear;
- provide written and visual reinforcement, such as pictures and objects;
- encourage the child to participate in class oral work;
- use the child's name to gain attention or address questions;
- encourage peers to ensure the child can see their faces when they address the class.

Hearing-impaired children may use Sign Supported English (SSE) or British Sign Language (BSL), which rely on systems of precise gestures alongside facial expressions. SSE follows the grammatical system of spoken English whereas BSL has its own grammar and is a distinctive language. Encouraging all children to learn some of the sign language used by a hearing-impaired child is not only important in encouraging communication and tolerance but also provides interesting opportunities for deepening understanding of language diversity.

## Supporting children with visual impairment

Visual impairment may be moderate or severe and may improve or deteriorate. It may result in a range of difficulties including:

- difficulties in reading;
- poor handwriting;
- dizziness and headaches;
- poor co-ordination;
- clumsiness;
- tiredness.

In supporting children with visual impairment it is important to:

- ensure the child is seated near the whiteboard or teacher;
- avoid moving around when talking;
- encourage involvement in the session, using the child's name when addressing a question;
- be aware of information carried through gesture and facial expression and make this explicit;
- provide commentary on any teacher demonstration or writing using another child, supporting adult or the teacher;
- enlarge written texts for whole-class or individual work or record them on tape;
- make use of ICT packages such as TextHELP which will read aloud anything displayed on the computer screen.

## Supporting children with learning difficulties

Learning difficulties range from mild to severe and from specific to complex; they may be cognitive or the result of social and emotional problems. This section will provide a brief overview of learning difficulties in relation to cognition.

Cognitive problems can lead to difficulties in all areas of language and literacy, for example difficulties in:

- understanding or communicating through oral language;
- understanding abstract concepts;
- developing vocabulary;
- generalizing learning from one area to another;
- concentration;
- contributing to group or class sessions;
- engaging in the world around them.

In supporting children with learning difficulties it is essential to:

- use simple clear language and instructions;
- focus on, repeat and reinforce key vocabulary;
- use interactive techniques to hold attention;
- make abstract concepts more concrete and real through the use of visual aids, objects and experiences;
- break down learning into small achievable steps;
- repeat and reinforce learning;
- provide adult support for tasks;
- ensure tasks are clearly structured and achievable;
- provide clear models for completion of task;
- acknowledge and reward achievements.

'Autistic spectrum disorders' provides an umbrella term for a number of disorders including autism and Asperger's syndrome. The spectrum includes those with very severe learning difficulties who make very little social contact, have limited use of speech and engage in repetitive behaviour. It also includes children of average and above average intelligence who are fluent but may simply exhibit some unconventional mannerisms. All disorders within this spectrum have certain common characteristics including difficulties with social relationships, communication and imagination (see www.nas.org.uk).

Depending on the needs of the individual it may be appropriate to consider the suggestions above and also:

- devote energy and time to forming a relationship – don't be deterred by lack of non-verbal communication, for example eye contact or facial expression;
- encourage response – even if no response is forthcoming;
- accept that the child may express extreme dislikes;
- use clear and precise language – avoid or explain metaphorical use of language;
- avoid sudden changes in routine – prepare child in advance for any changes which occur;
- accept solitary play but gradually encourage interaction with others;
- provide clearly structured rather than open-ended tasks;
- be prepared for a lack of interest in toys and imaginative play, but gradually show how these might provide pleasure.

## Supporting children with attention-deficit (hyperactivity) disorder AD(H)D

Attention-deficit (hyperactivity) disorder AD(H)D is a physical condition with biological origins which leads to lack of concentration and organization. A child with ADD may display the following:

- carelessness;
- lack of concentration;
- inability to listen;

- forgetfulness about regular activities;
- problems retaining interest;
- avoidance of tasks requiring extended effort;
- problems with organization of self and property.

Not all children with attention deficit disorder are hyperactive; those who are have difficulty remaining still. Examples of such behaviour include:

- inappropriate movement around the classroom;
- constant fidgeting;
- interfering with others' activities;
- interrupting and blurting out answers;
- difficulties with turn taking.

In supporting children with AD(H)D it is important to:

- make expectations of work and behaviour clear and praise achievement;
- reward strategies for exerting greater control over behaviour;
- ensure tasks are clear, focused and brief rather than long and open ended;
- reinforce instructions for tasks;
- provide variety of tasks;
- engage interest through interactive activities and the use of resources, visual aids and so on;
- organize seating to minimize distractions;
- provide adult support to encourage concentration in class and individual work;
- provide reminders of routines and activities;
- encourage child to produce own reminders;
- discuss and make explicit preparation and organization.

## Supporting children with emotional and behavioural difficulties (EBD)

Emotional and behavioural difficulties may result in a wide range of behaviours ranging from highly disruptive, aggressive, volatile actions to total withdrawal. Such behaviour may be a consequence of a variety of factors relating to experiences within and around the home. Examples include changes affecting family relationships, for example divorce, separation, death, birth of a sibling, abuse, neglect and poverty. It may also be the result of over anxious or demanding parents, negative comparison with sibling(s) and frustrations with difficulties of any kind in school or at home.

Children who have EBD may display any of the following behaviours:

- isolation;
- aggression;
- disruptive;
- immaturity;
- lack of self-esteem;
- attention seeking;

- volatility;
- lack of concentration.

In order to support children with emotional and behavioural difficulties and minimize disruption to others it is important to do the following:

- use praise and show the child that he or she is valued;
- find out about the child's interests and strengths and find ways to relate to these or incorporate them in teaching;
- avoid confrontation – find ways to offer the child choices and ways to save rather than lose face;
- use humour to ease tension but not at the child's expense;
- ensure that any negative comments clearly describe behaviour and not the child;
- provide clear routines, expectations and instructions;
- maintain pace in sessions;
- develop targets for behaviour improvement with the child and monitor and reward progress;
- break up long sessions with bursts of pair discussion;
- discuss causes for anger and anger management strategies as a class;
- use adult support to encourage child to focus on task.

# Challenging gifted and talented pupils

Giftedness generally refers to specific areas in which a child works at a faster pace than peers and pursues learning to a far greater depth. Such giftedness in language and literacy may apply to a child who is particularly able in reading, displaying understanding and appreciation of texts far more challenging than those read by peers. A child may be very articulate, able to use a wide range of vocabulary and speak confidently, effectively and fluently in a variety of situations. A gifted writer is able to produce well-structured, original and effective writing for a range of purposes. Giftedness may apply to more than one area.

Gifted and talented children may become bored or frustrated by a lack of challenge and consequently engage in disruptive behaviour. They may dominate others and behave in an intolerant way or underachieve in order to avoid drawing attention to themselves.

Children who are gifted and talented tend to:

- learn new concepts and skills with ease;
- demonstrate imagination, creativity and originality and a desire for knowledge;
- research, compare and synthesize information collected from a range of different sources;
- create reasoned arguments at an abstract level and justify opinions effectively;
- show persistence, resourcefulness, determination and an ability to work independently;
- use and understand an outstanding range of vocabulary;

- display speed and agility of thought;
- use language effectively to capture and maintain the interest of a range of audiences selecting from and adapting a variety of styles.

(Advisory Services Unit, 1995)

In order to challenge and extend children who are gifted and talented in aspects of English, it is important to provide:

- challenging texts;
- open-ended tasks;
- tasks involving analysis;
- extension work which provides opportunities to take learning further;
- problem solving;
- opportunities for autonomous work;
- opportunities to work at their own pace;
- opportunities to work with others who are gifted and with those who are not;
- opportunities to work with older children;
- praise and recognition for their achievements;
- encouragement to recognize and support the achievements of others.

# Summary

This chapter has outlined a variety of strategies for supporting children with special needs. It is clear that there are many similarities in approaches to catering for different needs. Effective teaching relies upon careful planning, differentiation of tasks, appropriate resources and the provision of support when necessary. Through such provision, barriers to progress should be limited and all children should have the opportunity to develop competence and confidence. Indeed, in order to achieve their potential in language and literacy all children need:

- meaningful differentiated activities;
- opportunities to communicate with others;
- texts that interest them;
- encouragement and praise;
- opportunities to experience success.

# Reflective questions

1. Shared reading and writing sessions pose particular challenges in terms of catering for children with special needs. Consider key strategies that you need to use in order to

engage the interest of all children, maintain their involvement and provide support and challenge for learning.

2. Some primary schools choose to set children in classes according to their ability in literacy. What are the advantages and disadvantages of such an approach?

3. A child in your class has recently begun to behave badly during shared reading and writing sessions. She had previously taken an interest in reading but now refuses to read during class reading time. She has declared loudly on several occasions that she hates reading. What might be the reasons for this change in attitude? What would you do?

## FURTHER READING

Bentley, D. and Reid, D. (1995) *Supporting Struggling Readers*. Widnes: UKRA.
  Practical and constructive strategies based on clearly explained principles.

Dean, G. (1998) *Challenging the More Able Language User*. London: David Fulton Publishers.
  Shows how to promote development in language and literacy in the most able children.

Gross, J. (2002) *Special Educational Needs in the Primary School: A Practical Guide*. Third Edition. Buckingham: Open University Press.
  A comprehensive, readable guide providing clear explanations of theoretical principles and practical guidance including chapters on speaking and listening, reading and writing.

Keates, A. (2000) *Dyslexia and Information and Communications Technology: A Guide for Teachers and Parents*. London: David Fulton Publishers.
  Practical guidance on facilities and resources.

Stakes, R. and Hornby, G. (1996) *Meeting Special Needs in Mainstream Schools. A Practical Guide for Teachers*. London: David Fulton Publishers.
  A very readable, practical and useful guide.

## REFERENCES

Advisory Services Unit (1995) *Report of the Very Able Working Party*. Rotherham: Rotherham Department of Education.

Clay, M. (1979) *The Early Detection of Reading Abilities*. Auckland: Heinemann.

Department for Education and Skills (DfES) (2003) *Disability Discrimination Act*. London: HMSO.

Department of Education and Science (DES) (1978) *Special Educational Needs (The Warnock Report)*. London: HMSO.

Department of Education and Science (DES) (1981) *Education Act*. London: HMSO.

Keates, A. (2000) *Dyslexia and Information and Communications Technology: A Guide for Teachers and Parents*. London: David Fulton Publishers.

Martin, D. and Miller, C. (1999) *Language and the Curriculum. Practitioner Research in Planning Differentiation*. London: David Fulton Publishers.

Office for Standards in Education (OFSTED) (1994) *Exceptionally Able Children October 1993*. Report of Conferences. London: DFE.

Reid, G. (1994) *Specific Learning Difficulties (Dyslexia): A Handbook for Study and Practice*. Edinburgh: Moray House Institute.

Wilson, R. (1998) *Special Education in the Early Years*. London and New York: Routledge.

## USEFUL WEB SITES

| | |
|---|---|
| The Alliance for Inclusive Education | www.allfie.org.uk |
| British Dyslexia Association | www.bda-dyslexia.org.uk |
| Dyslexia Institute | www.dyslexia-inst.org.uk |
| DfES Web site | www.dfes.gov.uk/sen |
| National Association for Special Educational Needs | www.nasen.org.uk |
| QCA Guidance on Teaching the Gifted and Talented | www.nc.uk.net/gt/english/ |
| National Autistic Society | www.nas.org.uk |

# 12 English and Equal Opportunities

For almost 30 years, there has been legislation in place in England and Wales that requires schools to promote equal opportunities and positive relations between staff, pupils and parents. The Race Relations Act (1976) and the Sex Discrimination Act (1975) make discrimination on the grounds of 'race', colour, national origins or gender illegal. This was reinforced by the Race Relations Amendment Act (2003). Discrimination involves behaviour or action based on prejudice which results in unfavourable treatment. This may be direct discrimination involving verbal abuse, violence or limitations on access to opportunities or services. It may also be indirect, when individuals appear to be treated equally but decisions or outcomes are still based on prejudice. Discrimination is often so well embedded in society that it may be accepted as normal (Lane, 1999).

The Education Reform Act (1988) takes this legislation further, giving all children the right to expect that they will have opportunities to achieve their full potential irrespective of their gender, 'race', ability or class. In all subjects, it is important to examine teaching approaches and identify ways of facilitating the success of all children. However, the agenda of equality has particular significance for the teaching of language and literacy. As discussed in Chapter 1, language itself can convey value judgements and prejudice in spoken and written form; such prejudice may be intentional, explicit and used deliberately to create an impact, or unintentional but equally damaging. Within our teaching of language and literacy, we therefore need to find opportunities to develop children's awareness of the central role of language in discrimination. We need to encourage them to become aware of the implications of their choice of language and use it with thought and respect for others. We also need to develop their ability to recognize prejudice and manipulation in the language they encounter.

In the promotion of equal opportunities, this subject has further significance in relation to the status given to languages other than English. Fluency and confidence in spoken and written English are clearly needed for progress and achievement within and beyond the education system in England. However, many children in early years and primary settings have been brought up in households where languages other than English are dominant. Such experience is important, not only in relation to children's fluency and skills in language but also in terms of their identities. As discussed in Chapter 1, language and identity are closely related. In promoting equality of opportunity it is therefore important to consider the value attributed to children's knowledge and skills in languages other than English and provide opportunities for their use.

In this chapter we refer to issues relating to gender, culture and class but are keen to acknowledge that children are individuals first, with their personal strengths, interests and needs. We explore some findings from research, which highlight particular issues relating to certain groups of children. However, this is not to suggest that all members of a group share the same characteristics or to deny that an individual may be a member of more than one group. For example, boys' underachievement in literacy has received considerable attention over recent years. However, this does not apply to all boys. Those most likely to underachieve are white, working class or African-Caribbean. In these cases, class, gender and ethnicity are all influential in the child's construction of identity. Given that these factors can influence academic progress, it is essential that teachers actively encourage and support children in developing their identities as individuals and as successful learners (Siraj-Blatchford, 1998).

Within this chapter we aim to highlight particular areas of concern in the teaching of language and literacy. We begin by examining issues relating to gender and then consider provision for children with English as an Additional Language (EAL). The final section of the chapter discusses ways in which classroom teaching of English can promote equal opportunities and children's awareness of the use of language to reinforce stereotypes.

# Gender and literacy

For some time there has been concern about differences in boys' and girls' interests, attitudes and achievement in literacy. In the 1970s and 1980s there was an emphasis on ensuring that literature did not reflect stereotypical roles. Early research also reflected a growing concern with disadvantages faced by girls in school and drew attention to the tendency for boys to dominate classroom talk. It was noted that this was sometimes unintentionally encouraged by teachers (Swann et al., 1988). This research highlighted the need for teachers to support and encourage girls' contributions to discussions and boys' skills in listening and response. Research also drew attention to differences in children's reading habits, noting the tendency for girls to take more interest in fiction, in particular stories in which relationships and feelings were central. In contrast, boys were found to be more interested in non-fiction.

More recently attention has shifted to the underachievement of boys. Analysis of SATs results highlighted differences in boys' and girls' achievement, which were particularly apparent in writing. The lower level of achievement of boys provoked considerable concern (see, for example, QCA, 1998) and prompted a number of initiatives devoted to raising their achievement (see www.rba.educ.cam.uk).

Research around boys' underachievement in writing (for example Barrs *et al.*, 2002; Graham, 2001; Millard, 1997) has identified key features of classroom practice which tend to increase boys' success. These are listed below.

### Encouraging boys' achievement:

- use talk, drawing, drama and storytelling as preparation for writing;
- intersperse writing and drawing;
- write as experts, in other words about subjects in which they are confident;
- write about things that matter to them and first-hand experiences;
- use ICT;
- write in collaboration with others;
- write with clear time limits, purposes and outcomes;
- experience a genuine response to their writing;
- hear their writing read aloud.

According to Millard (1997) boys tend to perceive accuracy in spelling and handwriting as the factors of greatest importance in successful writing and consequently they may feel daunted by the prospect of making mistakes in transcription. Boys tend to be more successful when they are more confident in taking risks in their writing. It is particularly important to capture boys' interest in literacy at an early age, for example by building on their interests in popular culture. In a small scale study, Marsh *et al.* (1997) found that using popular culture as a focus prompted a high level of participation in literacy related activities from boys who had been regarded by their teacher as lacking interest in this area. Such activities also provided opportunities for discussion about the stereotypes implicit in such media.

Recent work by Moss (2000) has examined boys' preferences for non-fiction in greater depth. She suggests that this tendency may be driven by boys' need to be seen as proficient readers. Moss points out that the grading or level of difficulty of non-fiction is less obvious than that of fiction. In storybooks, the length of the text, use of images and size of print may signal that books are 'easy' to read. Based on research in Key Stage 2, she argues that boys who find reading difficult choose non-fiction because it generally lacks such evidence of grading. By selecting such books, boys retain self-esteem, as they appear to be reading on a level with competent readers. In contrast, Moss found that girls who found reading difficult tended to be quite content with less challenging narrative texts provided by teachers. Importantly, girls' lack of interest in non-fiction has implications for their ability to handle such texts and their development of knowledge.

Bearne (2002) and Millard (1997) also explore the way that boys' and girls' writing tends to reflect the kinds of texts with which they are familiar. Bearne argues that boys draw on their experience of multimodal texts when writing. As a result they often try to represent sound, image and movement in words. For some, this task is impossible and the resulting written text not only fails to reflect the visual, dynamic sound-supported story imagined by the child, but also seems to lack the organization and cohesion typical of written narrative. In contrast, girls tend to read fiction more widely and be less interested

238

in multimedia texts. According to Bearne (2002), their stories tend to reflect these preferences and their written narratives are consequently more straightforward than those of boys. Girls tend to produce more static images (Millard, 2001) and represent sounds and visual effects through writing. Texts produced by girls consequently conform more closely to formal assessment criteria and this may be one of the reasons why they often achieve greater academic success than boys.

However, girls' tendency to be less interested and involved in multimedia, computer games and digital animation also has significant implications for the provision of equal opportunities. As Rowan *et al.* (2002) have pointed out, boys' interest in such ICT enables them to gain important skills for the future. In contrast, the comparative lack of experience of girls may place them at a serious disadvantage in responding to an increasingly technologically driven world in which multimedia dominates communication (Bearne, 2002).

The research discussed above has raised important implications for the teaching of reading.

- An active reading culture needs to be promoted in which reading is enjoyed, shared and not regarded simply as 'a matter of proficiency' (Moss 2000: 102).
- Fiction needs to be available that is not too demanding to read but not babyish in appearance.
- From an early age, all children need to be encouraged to make choices in their reading and to read fiction and non-fiction.

In addition, it is important to ensure that girls are encouraged to:

- develop confidence in their use of ICT;
- enjoy and experiment with a variety of multimedia forms of narrative;
- explore the use of the visual and moving image in the production of narrative;

and that boys are:

- introduced to models of effective writing;
- explicitly encouraged to represent images, sounds and movement through words;
- given opportunities to exploit interests in multimedia.

# Supporting children with English as an Additional Language (EAL)

Levels of confidence, fluency and skills in English vary considerably amongst children with English as an Additional Language (EAL). Given the impact of the dominant culture and in particular the media, most children arrive in early years settings with some awareness of English; many have already gained considerable understanding and fluency. However, throughout the primary years there are also children who arrive in classrooms with very little understanding of English. In promoting equal opportunities it is essential to consider how the progress of all children with EAL can be facilitated, not only in terms of their understanding and use of English but also in their use of language as a means to access the wider curriculum.

The backgrounds and origins of children with English as an Additional Language vary widely, including those who:

- have been born in Britain and speak varying amounts of English in the home depending on family members, culture and religion;
- have come from countries outside Britain to join extended families;
- are on an extended visit as a result of parents' work or study;
- are refugees or asylum seekers.

(Mills *et al.*, 1993)

Children with EAL are often described as bilingual. The term 'bilingual' is sometimes assumed to mean that the child is equally fluent in two languages, but this is problematic. Bilingual children are often multilingual, able to operate in more than two languages. Each of their parents may speak a different language or the language of their religion may be different from that which is spoken in the home. Ideas of equivalence in fluency or use are also problematic, because different languages may be used in different contexts and for different purposes. Children may or may not be literate in their home language; they may be able to read but not write, or decode but not read with understanding.

Children's understanding of other languages is invaluable in learning English. Their experience enables them to recognize ways in which language varies according to audience and purpose. They may also bring awareness of the existence of individual words and have some understanding of sentence structure. Research has shown that valuing and maintaining children's skills in other languages helps them to be successful in acquiring new ones. Where home languages are not valued, less progress is made (ILEA, 1990; Edwards, 1998).

### Valuing home languages:

It is important to ensure that children's home languages are used and included in the classroom environment. This can be encouraged through:

- use of home languages in displays, labels and notices;
- provision of texts written in home languages and bilingual texts;
- storytelling in home languages;
- support from same language speaking adults;
- encouragement to work with other children who speak the same language;
- attempts by the teacher and the class to learn and use greetings in home languages;
- translation into home languages by adults and children.

# Supporting children with very limited knowledge of English

Some children who have recently arrived in the country or have been exposed to little English enter early years and primary settings with very limited understanding of English. Such children need considerable support, encouragement and understanding for what can be a very intimidating and isolating experience, particularly if there are no other speakers of the child's own language. It is essential that teachers show warmth and encourage involvement in practical classroom activities, dealing sensitively with any reluctance to join with others in the earliest days.

On arrival such children generally go through a silent period. Although they may say little or nothing in English, they are active in listening and absorbing the use of language around them. Gradually, with encouragement, children will use non-verbal communication. They will then begin to use single words such as 'me', 'lunch' and 'play'. At this time, children may easily become frustrated by difficulties in communicating. It is therefore important to be patient and supportive, allowing time for them to convey what they want to say. Increasingly children will begin to put words together to make meaning, for example saying: 'here stay!', 'where go you?' These utterances will grow longer and the child will begin to show greater understanding of word order in English.

As children begin to communicate in English, they may use the grammatical structures of the first language to help them to make use of the second. However, differences in grammar between languages can result in sentences that are organized unconventionally, for example in Panjabi and Urdu the word order is subject-object-verb ('she book brings') unlike English in which the order is usually subject-verb-object ('She brings the book').

Throughout this period children benefit from the same kind of activities that support monolingual children's development. They need opportunities to:

- interact with others in meaningful contexts, for example through play, games, collaborative and investigative activities;
- hear familiar objects labelled;
- learn from good models of language use through being sometimes grouped with fluent English speakers;
- participate in group/class activities and storytelling where language is supported through visual aids (gesture/images/props);
- join in repetitive rhymes, refrains, songs or circle time activities – where they use phrases rather than isolated words;
- hear their home language alongside English where possible;
- use their home language (for example, with bilingual teacher or teaching assistant or by sometimes being grouped with other children who speak the same language);
- receive plenty of praise for their attempts at using English;
- enjoy texts with interesting storylines, bold illustrations, repeating sequences and predictable structures, for example *Dear Zoo* (Campbell, 1984), *'Pardon?' Said the Giraffe* (West, 1986) and *Inky Pinky Ponky* (Rosen, 1989);

- enjoy songs and books, poems and rhymes that include repetition or patterned use of language, for example 'Not now!' from *Not Now, Bernard* (McKee, 1980);
- introduce texts that are also engaging and challenging, for example *Sam's Duck* (Morpurgo, 1996) and *My Grandfather is a Magician* (Onyefulu, 1998);
- learn essential pieces of vocabulary that they will need in school, such as 'toilet', 'lunch';
- participate in activities to reinforce a specific aspect of grammar, for instance a circle game in which each child in turn completes the sentence 'I like . . .' This reinforces the word order and use of the personal pronoun 'I' (often substituted with 'me' by bilingual children) (Browne, 2001);
- develop their use of tenses within meaningful contexts, for example practising formation of the past tense through relating experiences or storytelling.

In the early stages, as with children learning a first language, it is not appropriate to correct mistakes, as this may result in loss of confidence. Instead it is important to focus on the meaning of the child's utterance and, if appropriate, model the appropriate use of language in response. Children will soon develop their understanding and use of language so that they can interact with others. At these early stages, communication is easier when the context is clear and shared, for example in talking about photos of the child's family, discussing pictures of places the child has visited or commenting on the weather viewed from the window. Visual aids are therefore extremely important. Objects and artefacts used in storytelling support the child in understanding the narrative. In teaching a child to remember the names of the colours, it is helpful to encourage them to collect or identify relevant objects in the environment. As they learn, children will often match the vocabulary they meet with words from their home language. However, they will inevitably encounter new vocabulary in school with which they are not familiar in their home language. It may then be useful to seek help from same language speakers in the classroom or parents or consult a dictionary.

It is important to ensure that children's learning in other areas is not hindered by their lack of understanding of English. It is often helpful to ask children who speak the same language to explain concepts, tasks and content. Where such support is not available, it is essential to communicate content in other ways. Practical tasks, objects and images enable children to tackle more cognitively demanding concepts within a clear context. Cummins (1984) suggests that children take five to seven years to become less reliant on context and more able to deal with abstract concepts and situations. In planning for children's progress it is therefore essential to balance the provision of more abstract subject matter with less cognitively demanding tasks. Work on an abstract concept which is also cognitively demanding may well be too challenging and frustrating for the child.

# Supporting children with English as an Additional Language in reading

Like monolingual children, children with EAL will arrive in school with an understanding of different types of literacy and the purposes of reading and writing. Many bilingual children will bring understanding of another script and its use in their lives. In learning to read English, they are able to draw on this understanding of written language and its uses. They may also build on the understanding of phonology, and grammar from their own languages and apply the skills of making meaning from text.

Previous experiences of reading also have a considerable impact on reading and writing behaviour in school. In a study of literacy practices in the homes of bilingual children, Gregory (1996) highlights the very varied ways in which reading is presented and children's literacy development is encouraged. Such differences illustrate the importance of gaining understanding of children's experience of literacy within the home. Many children attend additional classes in order to develop their ability to read and write languages for religious purposes. In some cases such teaching can be based on developing skills in memorization and decoding and may well influence children's expectations of approaches to learning to read and write in English.

Interestingly, the difficulties encountered by bilingual children learning to read may relate more to lack of knowledge of cultural contexts and the unfamiliarity of vocabulary and idioms than to actual difficulties with reading (Merchant, 1992). Without knowledge of the dominant culture a child may simply not recognize the phrase 'fish and chips' and be confused by idioms such as 'raining cats and dogs'. In oral language such difficulties are less problematic as the context is often clearer and there are opportunities to ask the speaker for clarification. It is therefore important to ensure that unfamiliar vocabulary included in the text is made explicit and idioms are explained.

The effective support for bilingual children learning to read in English relies on those approaches to effective teaching discussed in earlier chapters in this book. Children with EAL, like their monolingual peers, benefit from the following:

- opportunities to see that reading provides pleasure and information;
- a wide range of texts, including patterned, repetitive texts;
- texts in familiar languages;
- the availability of familiar texts for independent reading;
- support through shared and guided reading in developing the use of the cueing systems discussed in Chapter 3;
- the availability of familiar texts for independent reading.

243

## Supporting children with English as an Additional Language in writing

In order to develop skills in writing in English, children with EAL need the same opportunities and encouragement as their monolingual peers. In the early years children's emergent literacy is likely to involve reproduction of print from home languages as well as of English. It is important for the child to experiment with both in order to gain understanding of the differences between them. This can be encouraged in the role-play area but can also benefit greatly from the involvement of parents.

Children with EAL therefore need opportunities to:

- write for real audiences and purposes;
- experiment with mark making;
- represent home scripts and write in their home languages;
- use writing in role play;
- collaborate with a peer or an adult when writing;
- have a clear structure to imitate – such as a story based on a simple narrative, instructions based on an example and a frame prepared by the class;
- talk about and rehearse what they intend to write.

## Promoting equal opportunities and challenging prejudice through the teaching of English

Having discussed specific equal opportunities issues in relation to the development of language and literacy, it is now important to broaden the focus. In this section we consider ways in which the teaching of English can encourage all children to make progress, irrespective of differences in culture, gender or class. This subject area offers possibilities for teachers to tackle prejudice and discrimination, promote tolerance and raise children's awareness of the role of language in reinforcing stereotypes.

As teachers it is our responsibility to try to ensure that our behaviour is not influenced by assumptions about individuals based on generalization, stereotypes and prejudice. Expectations about children in relation to their intellectual, emotional, social and physical attributes are particularly dangerous because they are likely to be reflected in our behaviour. This may have an influence on children's self-esteem, aspirations and achievement. Examples of such behaviour include:

- expectations of girls' neatness in writing, which may limit their ability and willingness to draft and edit their work;
- assumptions about lack of motivation of boys from particular ethnic or social backgrounds, which may result in the provision of unchallenging work and consequent underachievement;

- reinforcement of lack of participation from girls from particular ethnic backgrounds through lack of encouragement to join in class discussion;
- assumptions about literacy practices in children's homes, which ignore the vast range of experiences and skills they have developed beyond the classroom.

It is clearly important to reflect upon our beliefs, attitudes and expectations and aim to facilitate the progress of all children, removing barriers to achievement wherever possible. All children need encouragement to make progress, uninhibited by expectations of their limitations or strengths. It is therefore essential to treat children as individuals and demonstrate that differences are respected and valued.

The appropriate use of children's names is crucial in affirming respect for individuals and their culture. For many teachers, some names of children may be unfamiliar. However, it is essential to devote time and effort to learning to pronounce the name correctly, checking with the child to ensure success. Such attention affirms a fundamentally important aspect of identity. A teacher's willingness to learn phrases of a child's language is also valuable in recognizing the child's language and culture and promoting interest in language diversity.

# Classroom organization

Classroom organization to promote equal opportunities demands flexibility. At times it may be appropriate to group children according to common needs, for example:

- children with EAL who speak the same language for a specific task;
- girls who lack confidence in ICT for an activity using the computer;
- a group of boys, who share a reluctance and lack of confidence in writing, who will be working with the teacher.

In these examples the grouping of the children is dictated by common need and learning objective.

# Resources

In any school, the use of resources needs to reflect the multicultural society in which we live. A variety of cultures needs to be represented, not only in the context of learning about a specific religion or group, but as the norm. Resources need to show men and women, girls and boys from different cultures and religions in a variety of roles. Literature has a particular importance in actively challenging children to reflect on their assumptions and beliefs. If resources are selected carefully, then children can be presented with images that underline the breadth of possibilities open to them and to others. Collections of resources should present:

- adults and children in a variety of roles;
- men and boys, women and girls as active and passive, quiet and aggressive, neat and practical;

- everyday life in a variety of cultures;
- family life in varied forms.

The following list contains some examples of authors who produce texts that present positive images, some of which directly tackle issues of prejudice, racism and sexism. Further suggestions can be found in Stones (1999).

**Early years/Key Stage 1**    Molly Bang, Christopher Hope, Caroline Binch, Rita Philips Mitchell, Eileen Browne, Peter Bonnici, Trish Coole, Mamta Bhatia, June Counsel, Miriam Smith, Tony Brennan, Errol Lloyd, Penny Dale, Khadijah Frischauer, Mary Hoffman, Niki Daly

**Key Stage 1/2**    Floella Benjamin, Valerie Flournoy, Marjorie Blackman, Jamila Gavin, Judy Blume, Rumer Goden, Ann Cameron, Chris Powling, Vivian French, John Steptoe

**Key Stage 2 +**    Bernard Ashley, Gene Kemp, Anita Desai, Robert Leeson, Peter Dickenson, Beverley Naidoo, Anita Desai, Mildred D. Taylor, Farukh Dhondy, Benjamin Zephaniah, Rosa Guy

## Challenging prejudice in language use

As mentioned earlier, prejudice is often conveyed by language in the written or spoken form. The spoken language used by children in the primary and early years can be particularly insensitive in drawing attention to differences in a negative way. Prejudice, direct and indirect discrimination always need to be tackled irrespective of the age of the children, but in different ways according to the situation, incident and individuals involved. Circle time can be an effective way to raise issues. As discussed earlier, stories and picture books also provide a way of opening up a topic and exploring feelings and attitudes.

# Challenging stereotypes

Children can be involved in looking at ways in which language reinforces stereotypes through class activities.

### *Activities which help challenge stereotypes:*

- collecting and comparing images and words used to describe boys and girls on birthday or birth arrival cards;
- discussing the representation of different ethnic groups in the media;
- analysing the range of roles represented in classroom texts in relation to gender and ethnicity;
- collecting words used to describe men and women and their behaviour from newspaper accounts;
- comparing comics or toy catalogues aimed at boys with those aimed at girls.

# Summary

This chapter has drawn attention to ways in which equality of opportunity can be promoted within and through the teaching of language and literacy. In particular it has raised the importance of teachers' willingness to:

- reflect on their own attitudes and behaviour;
- select resources with care;
- use children's literature to promote positive images, challenging stereotypes and raising issues;
- find ways to engage the interest and expand the language and literacy skills of boys and girls;
- value children's home languages and provide practical support and encouragement for the development of skills in English;
- challenge prejudice in the classroom;
- encourage children to recognize the use of language to reinforce stereotypes.

# Reflective questions

1. A child brings a comic from home that seems to reinforce stereotypes. How do you respond?

2. Review the resources in a familiar classroom. Consider the range of roles represented.

3. A child with very limited English has recently arrived in your classroom. Consider how you would make him/her feel welcome and promote development in understanding of English.

## FURTHER READING

Barrs, M. and Pidgeon, S. (eds) (2002) *Boys and Writing*. London: Centre for Literacy in Primary Education.
A collection of articles exploring ways of raising boys' achievement in literacy and raising interesting issues.

Mills, R. and Mills, J. (eds) (1993) *Bilingualism in the Primary School*. London: Routledge.
A readable and useful collection of readings on understanding the experience of bilingual children and issues relating to their support.

Siraj-Blatchford, I. and Clarke, P. (2000) *Supporting Identity, Diversity and Language in the Early Years*. Buckingham: Open University Press.
Provides a detailed overview of the development of English as an Additional Language and practical suggestions for effective support of bilingual children in the early years.

# REFERENCES

Barrs, M. and Pidgeon, S. (eds) (1993) *Reading the Difference. Gender and Reading in the Primary School.* London: Centre for Literacy in Primary Education.

Barrs, M. and Pidgeon, S. (eds) (2002) *Boys and Writing.* London: Centre for Literacy in Primary Education.

Bearne, E. (2002) 'Multimodal narratives', in Barrs, M. and Pidgeon, S. (eds) *Boys and Writing.* London: Centre for Literacy in Primary Education.

Browne, A. (2001) *Developing Language and Literacy 3–8.* Second Edition. London: Paul Chapman Publishing.

Cummins, J. (1984) *Bilingualism and Special Education: Issues in Assessment and Pedagogy.* Clevedon: Multilingual Matters.

Edwards, V. (1998) *The Power of Babel: Teaching and Learning in Multilingual Classrooms.* Stoke-on-Trent: Trentham.

Graham, L. (2001) 'From Tyrannosaurus to Pokémon: autonomy in the teaching of writing', *Reading Literacy and Language,* 35(1), 18–26.

Gregory, E. (1996) *Making Sense of a New World: Learning to Read in a Second Language.* London: Paul Chapman Publishing.

Inner London Education Authority (ILEA) (1990) *Language and Power.* London: Harcourt Brace Javanovich.

Lane, J. (1999) *Action for Racial Equality in the Early Years.* London: The Early Years Network.

Marsh, J., Payne, L. and Anderson, S. (1997) 'Batman and Batwoman in the classroom', *Primary English,* 5(2), 8–11.

Merchant, G. (1992) 'Supporting children for whom English is a second language', in Harrison, C. and Coles, M. (eds) *The Reading for Real Handbook.* London: Routledge.

Millard, E. (1997) *Differently Literate. Boys, Girls and Schooling of Literacy.* London: Falmer.

Millard, E. (2001) 'Aspects of gender: how boys' and girls' experiences of reading shape their writing', in Evans, J. (ed.) *The Writing Classroom: Aspects of Writing and the Primary Child 3–11.* London: David Fulton Publishers.

Mills, J. and Mills, R. V. (1993) 'Language activities in a multilingual school', in Mills, J. and Mills, R. (eds) *Bilingualism in the Primary School.* London: Routledge.

Moss, G. (2000) 'Raising boys' achievement in reading: some principles for intervention', *Reading,* 34(3), 101–6.

Qualifications and Curriculum Authority (QCA) (1998) *Can Do Better: Raising Boys' Achievement in English.* London: QCA Publications.

Rowan, L., Knobel, M., Bigum, C. and Lankshear, C. (2002) *Boys, Literacies and Schooling: The Dangerous Territories of Gender-based Literacy Reform.* Buckingham: Open University Press.

Siraj-Blatchford, I. (1998) 'Criteria for determining quality in early learning for 3–6 year olds', in Siraj-Blatchford, I. (ed.) *A Curriculum Development Handbook for Early Childhood Educators.* Stoke-on-Trent: Trentham.

Siraj-Blatchford, I. and Clarke, P. (2000) *Supporting Identity, Diversity and Language in the Early Years.* Buckingham: Open University Press.

Stones, R. (ed.) (1999) *A Multicultural Guide to Children's Books 0–12.* Reading: Books for Keeps with Reading Language and Information Centre.

Swann, J. and Graddol, D. (1988) 'Gender inequalities in classroom talk', *English in Education,* 22(1), 48–65.

www.standards.dfes.gov.uk/genderandachievement

*Sex Discrimination Act.* (1975) London: HMSO

*Race Relations Act*. (1976) London: HMSO.

*Education Reform Act*. (1988) London: HMSO.

*Race Relations Amendment Act*. (2003) London: HMSO.


### CHILDREN'S LITERATURE

Campbell, R. (1984) *Dear Zoo*. London: Puffin.

McKee, D. (1980) *Not Now, Bernard*. London: Red Fox.

Morpurgo, M. (1996) *Sam's Duck*. London: Walker.

Onyefulu, I. (1998) *My Grandfather is a Magician*. London: Lions.

Rosen, M. (1989) *Inky Pinky Ponky*. London: Lions.

West, C. (1986) *'Pardon?', Said the Giraffe*. New York: HarperCollins.

# 13 Co-ordinating English

This chapter focuses on the roles and responsibilities of the English co-ordinator. Guidance is given for addressing key aspects of the role with a particular emphasis on managing curriculum development. Whilst the Teacher Training Agency and some schools refer to 'subject leaders' rather than 'co-ordinators' (TTA, 1998), the title 'co-ordinator' is used in this chapter as it seems to capture most effectively the way that teachers with responsibility for English work alongside colleagues to promote effective practice.

## The role of the co-ordinator

Through working with and inspiring their colleagues, English co-ordinators can make a real difference to children's language and literacy development. Indeed reports on those schools that are most successful in supporting pupils' progress in literacy have highlighted that effective leadership is essential (NFER, 1998; OFSTED, 2002). In such schools, head teachers take a strong lead in the development of the subject and co-ordinators are proactive in supporting colleagues, evaluating teaching and learning and addressing areas that need development.

Interestingly the title given to the teacher who co-ordinates this area of the curriculum has changed over the past few years, reflecting altered curriculum priorities. 'Language co-ordinators' became 'English co-ordinators' when the introduction of the National Curriculum emphasized English as a separate subject. Many of the same teachers became 'literacy' co-ordinators when the NLS prompted schools to focus on reading and writing and have now become English co-ordinators again given the move to re-emphasize a broad and balanced curriculum. These different job titles are clearly not synonymous and new co-ordinators need to be absolutely clear about their responsibilities. Some schools have both an English co-ordinator and a literacy co-ordinator: one concentrates on literacy development whereas the other oversees areas such as speaking, listening and language across the curriculum. In other schools, one co-ordinator works with Key Stage 1 and the Foundation Stage and a second is responsible for Key Stage 2. A clear job description should clarify the role of the co-ordinator in any particular school. If this is not available it should be negotiated with the head teacher on appointment.

The responsibilities of an English co-ordinator relate to four main areas:

- making policy;
- supporting policy;
- promoting continued development in English;
- providing subject expertise and supporting colleagues' professional development.

# Making policy

There are national expectations for the teaching of English, but each school is different: the size and nature of the school population, the catchment area and staff experience all vary. This individual school context will inevitably influence the way English is taught. In order to ensure that approaches are consistent, each school needs a policy that sets out its beliefs and intentions regarding English teaching.

A policy is usually devised by the co-ordinator in consultation with the rest of the teaching staff, although other members of the school community, such as teaching assistants and the literacy governor, may also be involved. This consultation process is important, as staff need to understand and be committed to the implications of the policy. Indeed policy discussions often provide rich opportunities for teachers to share and refine their views on effective English teaching. Once policies have been drafted, these are agreed by the school governors and communicated to all those with an interest in the children's language and literacy development. These may include:

| | | |
|---|---|---|
| teachers | teaching assistants | nursery nurses |
| parents/carers | lunchtime supervisors | new staff members |
| governors | ICT co-ordinator | SEN co-ordinator |
| parent/volunteer helpers | EAL teachers | bilingual assistants |
| peripatetic support teachers | students on work placements and in teacher training | |
| language support teachers | | |

Clearly policies will evolve and it is the responsibility of the co-ordinator to monitor and review them in the light of local and national developments. Any revisions should be discussed and agreed by staff and governors.

Policies are often written using a standard school format that may be based on a local education authority model. There may be separate sections for speaking and listening, reading and writing and possibly further policies for areas such as drama, handwriting or the library. Policies should be succinct but are usually supported by detailed guidelines or references to other school policies, such as those relating to equal opportunities or assessment. A possible framework for writing an English policy is outlined in Table 13.1.

**Table 13.1. Policy framework**

| Section | Focus |
| --- | --- |
| **Policy statement** | What are we doing and why?<br>Which values and principles underpin the teaching of English in this school?<br>What is the role of English in this school?<br>What do we believe about the use of standard English and other languages (if applicable)? |
| **Aim** | What do we want children to achieve in this subject by the end of their time in the school or early years setting?<br>What attitudes and values do we want children to develop in relation to language and literacy? |
| **Time allocation** | How much time should be allocated to English?<br>Is the literacy hour used? Are there opportunities for drama, specific times for speaking and listening, extended writing, independent reading, library time, handwriting, etc? |
| **Planning** | Which long-term plans are in place? Are the Foundation Stage Curriculum and National Literacy Strategy Framework used?<br>How is English planned? What are the school's expectations for medium- and short-term planning?<br>Which principles should inform teachers' interpretation of these curriculum documents (for example recognition of children's experiences and interests)?<br>How are links made with the rest of the curriculum?<br>How is continuity and progression ensured?<br>How are the children's needs met at different stages of learning, i.e. Foundation Stage, Key Stage 1, Key Stage 2?<br>How is planning for children in mixed-aged classes addressed? |
| **Teaching and learning**<br>(This section may be cross-referenced to a generic school teaching and learning policy.) | How is the subject taught in this school?<br>Which range of strategies is employed?<br>(For example play, collaborative work)<br>How is independence promoted?<br>How does the learning environment support language and literacy?<br>How are children grouped for learning?<br>(For example mixed-ability grouping or setting) |
| **Assessment, recording and reporting**<br>(This section may be cross-referenced to a generic school assessment policy.) | What expectations are there for formative, summative and diagnostic assessment in English?<br>How and when are assessments conducted?<br>What needs to be assessed?<br>(For example range, skills, attitudes, process)<br>What are the expectations for giving oral and written feedback to children?<br>How are children involved in their own assessment?<br>How are results of assessments reported?<br>Who is given this information? |

| Assessment, recording and reporting (continued) | How is communication facilitated between teachers and parents/carers about children's progress? |
|---|---|
| **Target setting** | How are learning targets set and used within the school? How do class and group targets relate to school curriculum targets? Who is involved in this process (for example parents, children)? |
| **Links with home** | How are children's home languages and literacy experiences valued? How are carers'/parents' views about their child's language and literacy sought? How are parents/carers involved in literacy and language in school? How often is homework provided? What form does it take? How are parents/carers consulted and informed about school policy and practice? |
| **Resources** | Which resources are available? How are these stored/accessed? How is the library organized/used/operated? What is the system for ordering new resources? How are LEA library loan services used? |
| **Children with English as an Additional Language** | How are children with EAL supported? How are their other language(s) recognized and valued? |
| **Equal opportunities** (This section may be cross-referenced to a generic equal opportunities policy.) | How does the school ensure that children are not disadvantaged as a result of class, ethnicity, disability, language or gender? How are children's varied experiences recognized and valued? How do resources reflect the school's commitment to equal opportunities? How are the achievements of all groups of children monitored? |
| **Meeting varied needs** (This section may be cross-referenced to generic school policies relating to children with special educational needs or who are gifted and talented.) | How are children's special educational needs identified? How are gifted and talented pupils identified? What is the school's approach to meeting the needs of these children? |
| **Roles and responsibilities** | Who is involved in policy implementation? What is each person's responsibility in relation to the policy? Who is available to provide support? How is support accessed? |
| **Monitoring, review and evaluation** | How is implementation of the policy monitored? Who is involved? When and how will this policy be evaluated and reviewed? |

# Supporting policy

As signalled by OFSTED (1999), a detailed policy does not necessarily imply that the school has a consistent approach to teaching and learning. The co-ordinator therefore has a key role in ensuring policy implementation. Aspects of this are described below.

## Demonstrating and supporting the development of effective practice

Co-ordinators can work with teaching and non-teaching colleagues in a variety of ways to support the implementation of policy. Deciding on a strategy relies on an understanding of the different skills and abilities possessed by different members of staff. Much can be gained from finding ways for colleagues to share examples of good practice and talk to one another about difficulties they may be having. This may be done through staff meetings, peer observations or providing opportunities for feedback from courses attended. The co-ordinator clearly needs to ensure that policy is implemented in her own classroom and to ensure that this is visible to colleagues, for example in the way that the classroom environment is organized or the type of work on display. Importantly though, the co-ordinator should not be afraid of talking through and asking advice on any problems she is having. Indeed this helps to establish the kind of reflective, problem-solving ethos that encourages staff to work with each other and share practice and ideas.

Whilst English will be a key area for many schools, co-ordinators may find that other priorities mean that there is little development time devoted to the subject. Alternatively, schools may become so focused on meeting school targets that the excitement and creativity surrounding English as a subject are lost. Co-ordinators can, however, do a great deal to promote the subject. This may involve working with parents and governors, involving external agencies or publicizing the school's successes within the local press. If co-ordinators are imaginative and proactive in ensuring that English retains a high profile, they can help generate a school community where the children are enthused by language and literacy. Suggestions for promoting English are listed below.

## Maintaining a high profile for English

### Raising the profile of English for children

themed displays, for example celebrating linguistic diversity

book weeks and competitions

special events, for example visits from authors, poets, theatre companies

book of the week displayed in the library

sponsored reads and ongoing stories (each class adds a paragraph)

school magazine or Web site (run by children)

extra curricular activities, for example writers' workshop, drama or story club

regular bookstalls

themed weeks during which the whole school focuses on a shared theme, for example poetry, or product, such as a school brochure

### Raising the profile of English for other members of staff

focus weeks – all staff experiment with a new resource, such as the electronic whiteboard, and then share successes, ideas and problems

sharing tips and good work in staff meetings

using good work and class assemblies to showcase the results of successful English work

### Raising the profile of English for other members of the school community

talks to governors

open days for parents or governors

inviting parents to read or tell stories

publishing work on school Web sites and in school newspapers (edited by children)

devising parents' leaflets, for example on approaches to spelling

inviting parents/governors to school assemblies/performances

contacting the local press to publicize events/successes

### Involving external agencies

inviting theatre and puppet companies or writers to give performances or run workshops

providing children with opportunities to talk to writers, such as authors, journalists

registering for local and national initiatives

# Establishing a scheme of work

A scheme of work (the school's long-term planning) specifies what children will learn in each year, ensuring continuity and progression, and should reflect school policy. In most primary schools, schemes of work are structured around the guidance in *National Literacy Strategy Framework of Objectives* (DfEE, 1998) and sometimes *Speaking, Listening, Learning* (QCA, 2003). Many schools use these as the basis for more detailed schemes that specify resources to be used and suggest activities and assessment opportunities for each term and year. These are often developed by compiling medium-term plans produced by different year groups.

As explored earlier, in the Foundation Stage much planning builds on the children's interests, experiences and enthusiasms. A scheme of work in this phase is likely to be far more flexible and less detailed. Practitioners may use a rolling programme of different topic areas that suggests possible activities or learning contexts. This will specify units of work and links with the curriculum guidance for the Foundation Stage.

# Developing and maintaining a school portfolio

Many schools compile portfolios of samples of children's work which are usually assessed against National Curriculum levels of attainment. A portfolio may be paper based or digital and contain a variety of evidence, such as written work, photographs, notes, observation sheets. It may also include a range of work by one child (to demonstrate how 'best fit' judgements are made). School portfolios serve a number of purposes:

- The assessment of work samples is usually moderated by the whole staff and this process helps staff arrive at a shared understanding and interpretation of different levels of attainment.
- They are helpful when making judgements about children's work.
- Examination of work at different levels can inform teachers, parents and teaching assistants about how children develop as literacy and language users.
- They provide examples of the types of assessment evidence that can be collected.
- They supply the co-ordinator with evidence about the kinds of activities children are engaged in and the quality of children's work.
- They provide evidence of progression for external bodies, for example OFSTED, LEA advisers, parents.

# Organizing and managing resources

English co-ordinators need to ensure that colleagues have the resources necessary to implement school policy. Some co-ordinators are given a budget and autonomy over what is bought whereas others must discuss all purchases with the head teacher. In planning purchases, it is helpful to carry out an inventory of all stock in order to identify what needs to be bought, replaced and even thrown out. Inventories should address the following questions:

- Do staff have what they need to teach language and literacy?
- Are current resources being used effectively?
- What is the quality of current resources?
- Are resources up to date?
- Are there appropriate quantities of each resource?
- Is there an appropriate range of texts?
- What is needed to support new initiatives?
- Do resources reflect a commitment to equal opportunities?
- Are resources organized effectively?

The English co-ordinator usually has responsibility for maintaining the school library. This should be an inviting and stimulating place that contains a range of well-organized, high-quality books alongside varied sources of information including digital texts. It is important that the book stock is renewed in just the same way as it is in the classroom: care should be taken over organization; old and tatty books should be discarded and the range should reflect the school's commitment to equal opportunities. Many schools involve children in running the library, electing librarians who ensure that the library remains a stimulating and orderly environment. School library services may offer support and advice for categorizing books and establishing loan systems.

## Participating in local and national initiatives

The English co-ordinator may be invited to involve the school in a variety of local and national initiatives. The impact of these should be carefully considered and decisions to be involved taken in consultation with the rest of the staff. Particularly valuable initiatives include family learning projects that involve children working alongside their parents. These schemes acknowledge the key role that parents play in children's early and continued language and literacy development.

# Supporting ongoing development: the action planning cycle

Over recent years there has been a significant drive for schools to work towards ongoing improvements in pupil attainment, most notably in regard to literacy and numeracy. Each year, schools are expected to set numerical targets for children's attainment in English and mathematics by the end of each key stage. It is expected that these targets are *challenging*, reflecting not just the numbers of children that are expected to reach these levels but those that *could* achieve them with some support. In many schools, children's progress is monitored throughout the school and the teachers are asked to set targets for their classes. Some schools identify those children who are borderline and provide extra resources (such as teaching assistant support, intervention programmes or booster classes) to help them achieve at a higher level.

The English co-ordinator plays a significant role in supporting improvements in the school's provision for language and literacy learning. Such improvements generally occur as a result of an action planning cycle which includes: review, target setting, action planning, monitoring and evaluation (see Figure 13.1).

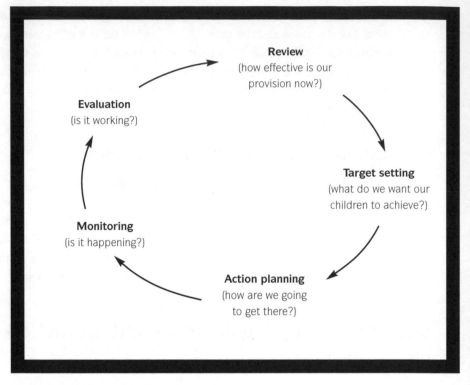

Figure 13.1. The action planning cycle

## Evaluating and reviewing practice

Plans for future development need to be informed by a thorough review of what is happening throughout the school in relation to English teaching and children's language and literacy development: if children are achieving well, why is this the case? If not, why not? This means drawing on various sources of evidence to evaluate the school's current provision.

## Analysis of quantitative data

Schools have access to a range of statistical data that are intended to support them in identifying priorities for development:

- The DfES sends schools statistical information about how their SATs results compare to those of similar schools (for example those with a similar number of children who take free school meals, or proportion of children with special educational needs). They also provide an analysis of rates of progress between Key Stages 1 and 2 and show how their achievements in SATs compare with those in previous years.
- Many schools use the optional tests devised by QCA to track the progress of children through Key Stage 2.

- The local education authority may distribute a statistical profile, facilitating comparisons with other schools in the local area.
- Schools frequently supplement data supplied by external agencies with detailed analysis of their own SATs results, for example comparing children's achievements in reading and writing, responses to different types of questions on test papers or between children of different gender or ethnic group.

Such statistical data can be useful, but they may also be misleading for the following reasons:

- The tests themselves vary from year to year.
- Analysis relies on percentages of children who achieved certain levels in SATs and consequently unexpected success or failure by just a few children can result in a huge percentage swing.
- Some schools have a highly mobile school population and many children will not be at the school from the Foundation Stage through to year 6.
- The data are taken from children's performance in SATs, which involve a limited number of tasks completed in test conditions. Large parts of the English curriculum are not tested at all, such as speaking and listening, or drama, and the results may not reflect a more balanced picture of children's achievements.

Concerns about the use of test results are compounded by scepticism about the accuracy of marking and appropriateness of the mark schemes themselves. Clearly analysis of numerical SATs data is fairly crude. It may be possible to hypothesize that a cohort of children is generally better at reading than at writing, and even that they are better at spelling than composition, but it does not provide any insight into the particular difficulties that children experience. Nevertheless, SATs results play a key role in accountability and OFSTED use them as a significant indicator of a school's success. Consequently, many schools use these figures as a starting point for identifying possible areas of strength and weakness. Once these have been highlighted, these are investigated further by looking at children's achievements in other contexts.

## Analysis of children's work

By examining children's reading, writing, speaking and listening in the classroom, co-ordinators can be more precise about what children at the school are good at and which areas they need to develop. Ideally, any analysis of work should involve the whole staff. If staff themselves are involved in diagnosing areas for development, they are more likely to be committed to helping to address them. This process can also raise staff awareness of the aspects of children's reading, writing, speaking and listening they need to develop.

An English co-ordinator in one school was keen to investigate the quality of talk taking place during collaborative activities. She spent time in each classroom videoing children engaged in classroom activities. Short excerpts were then reviewed with the rest of the staff.

The quality of talk was evaluated and it emerged that some of the most productive exploratory talk was taking place in the nursery and reception. This prompted informal discussion about the best ways to promote talk and helped staff articulate a shared understanding of what effective talk involves.

Having identified that very few children were achieving Level 4 in writing at Key Stage 2 SATs, teachers collected samples of children's writing from throughout the school. They worked in year groups to analyse these samples, identifying what the children could do effectively and what they needed to do next. The teachers found that whilst the work was technically good (accuracy in spelling and punctuation), much of it was unadventurous and formulaic.

The most informative analyses of children's progress rely on a range of evidence. Areas to investigate and sources of possible information are summarized in Table 13.2.

**Table 13.2. Analysing children's achievements to identify trends of strength and areas for development**

| Area to investigate | Sources of evidence |
| --- | --- |
| What progress do children make during their time in school? | Analysis of optional SATs results or work samples from different year groups; school portfolio; observation of children in classrooms; discussions with staff about children's progress |
| How does this compare with children in similar schools? Are there any trends of particular strength or weakness? | Use of statistical data to make local and national comparisons Analysis of SATs and QCA results and papers; analysis of children's work; comparisons with national trends; observing children in classrooms; discussion with SEN co-ordinator; staff questionnaire |
| Are certain groups of children achieving less than others? If so, why? (For example boys, children from minority ethnic groups, children with EAL, certain classes, summer born children, year groups or key stages.) | Analysis of SATs and QCA results; analysis of children's work; observation of children in classrooms; discussions with teachers; discussions with children |
| How does children's achievement in English compare with their achievement in mathematics and science? | Comparisons between teacher assessments, SATs and QCA results in the three core subjects |

Before any plan can be devised to address an aspect of children's achievement, further investigation needs to explore the reasons for the particular area of concern. This could relate to:

- the type of activities children engage in;
- classroom organization;
- teacher interactions with children;
- use of or access to resources (including teaching assistants);
- the specific characteristics of the school population (for example numbers of children with EAL).

Table 13.3 identifies the kind of information that might be useful to co-ordinators in investigating these various aspects of a school's provision.

Table 13.3. Exploring reasons for strengths and weaknesses

| Area to investigate | Sources of evidence |
| --- | --- |
| How does practice match policy? Is policy effective? | Lesson observations; analysis of planning and work; discussions with teachers and children |
| How is the English planned and taught? | Lesson observations; analysis of planning; analysis of work; questionnaire/discussions with teachers; OFSTED reports |
| How confident are teachers in assessing English? | Analysis of marked work; moderation meetings; questionnaire/discussion with teachers; OFSTED reports |
| Which strengths and experiences do children bring to school? | Consultation with parents; information on languages spoken; questionnaire/discussion with teachers; discussions with children |
| How are home/school links fostered? | Consultation with parents; questionnaire/discussion with teachers |
| What motivates the children? | Discussions with teachers, children, parents; lesson observations |
| Which resources support the teaching of this subject? | Inventory of resources (including library); analysis of deployment of teaching assistants; staff questionnaire |

# Target setting

Once an area for development has been identified, the co-ordinator works with the rest of staff and head teacher to set a target for improvement. Such *curriculum targets* relate to achievement in a specific aspect of the English (such as ability to write a range of non-fiction genres, or use different spelling strategies) and may relate directly to National Literacy Strategy objectives. Curriculum targets may be *layered*, translated into specific targets for different classes or groups of children.

In one primary school, monitoring of children's reading by the co-ordinator revealed that most children were able to decode text effectively but inferential comprehension was poor.

The staff decided that there needed to be a greater emphasis on developing response in the early stages of reading. The head teacher, co-ordinator and Key Stage 1 teachers set a curriculum target: ninety-two per cent (all but 2) of the children in year 2 will be able to express their own views on a story referring to words and phrases from a text.

The year 2 teacher identified those children who needed particular support in this area and made it a particular focus in shared and guided reading. Various activities were used to develop response across the school. Teachers in other years also set targets relating to reading comprehension for their classes in order to build towards continued improvement in future years.

There has been much debate over the role of targets in education. Some believe that the process of setting targets involves useful discussion that helps schools to be precise about exactly what they are trying to develop (OFSTED, 2003). Others have expressed concerns about evaluating success using only quantifiable indicators (OISE, 2003). They believe that such a focused approach leads to a narrowing of the curriculum as schools become increasingly pressurized to meet measurable targets.

## Devising a plan

Once an area for development has been identified, co-ordinators work with the head teacher and other colleagues to devise a plan to address this. If the co-ordinator has been able to find out why this was a problem area in the first place, then he or she will be in a good position to decide what action to take. This may mean introducing new teaching approaches, or spreading good practice throughout a school but could also involve purchasing new resources, deploying teaching assistants differently or developing more effective links with parents.

An action plan will identify:

- aims and objectives;
- what will be done;
- people involved;
- resources required (human and material) and relevant costings;
- timing (when it will happen and when it will be completed);
- details of procedures for monitoring, evaluation and review;
- success criteria.

When devising a plan to introduce a new approach, it is often a good idea to start small and not try to have too big an impact too quickly. Approaches must be manageable or they will not be implemented. It is always helpful for co-ordinators to trial approaches in their own classrooms; being enthusiastic about what is working and letting others see what children have achieved can inspire others to have a go.

### *Strategies for encouraging curriculum development:*

- working with a small group of teachers to pilot an approach;
- giving colleagues opportunities to observe teaching in other classrooms or schools;
- leading or organizing whole-school in-service training (INSET);
- introducing special projects to stimulate or motivate staff, for instance organizing for a writer to work in the school;
- buying new resources to support particular activities;
- working with or alongside colleagues to teach or plan and finding other ways for colleagues to support one another;
- facilitating the sharing of good practice from within the school;
- observing and giving feedback to colleagues;
- drawing on external expertise, for example LEA advisors and consultants;
- working with the whole school community, for instance parents, teaching assistants.

Importantly these strategies will not automatically have an impact. New resources may be left in boxes unless teachers are clear about how to use them. Ideas suggested during INSET days can be quickly forgotten and new teaching strategies may be unsuccessful unless the whole staff has a shared understanding of what they involve. It is important to listen to staff feedback and give colleagues time to adapt and consolidate new approaches.

Table 13.4 (see pages 266–7) provides an example of an action plan aimed at developing children's comprehension and response in relation to fiction. The plan uses many of the strategies listed above to stimulate and support curriculum development.

## Managing change

Taking a lead in curriculum development provides a real opportunity to promote the effective and innovative teaching of English. Moreover, the process of exploring and defining effective practice can involve a rich sharing of ideas and experience. However, it is important to remember that whilst the co-ordinator may be enthusiastic about change, other members of staff could have reservations. Lack of enthusiasm may seem like apathy, but colleagues will probably have valid reasons for any reluctance. They may be anxious about trying a new approach or have deeply felt views about how language and literacy should be taught. They may be unsure of what is expected or concerned about the way that change will impact on the rest of the curriculum. They may see the change as unnecessary or remain unconvinced that it will be successful.

Studies of effective schools (HMI, 1977; Fullan, 1993; Mortimore, 1998) have suggested that those that manage change most successfully involve staff at all stages and communicate effectively. English co-ordinators should ensure that they consult with colleagues, listen to and recognize their viewpoints and maintain open dialogue. Importantly, co-ordinators need to avoid taking responsibility for all aspects of the plan themselves as this can prevent others from taking an active role. Including colleagues validates their experience and expertise and provides opportunities for their professional development. Teachers are far more likely to be committed to a new development if:

- they see the need for it;
- they have been involved in deciding what should be done;
- initiative overload is avoided;
- staff needs are recognized and supported through resources/training;
- all those involved are clear about what is expected.

It is crucial that all new initiatives are supported by the head teacher. Unless he or she is committed to the idea, it is unlikely to be prioritized and the time and resources needed for success may not materialize. New practices will take time to become embedded and co-ordinators must be wary of overloading staff. If there is currently a major school initiative underway, this may not be the best time to start something new. English action plans should, therefore, be fully integrated with the school improvement plan.

## Monitoring, evaluation and review

Once action plans are under way, co-ordinators have a key role in monitoring to ensure that the agreed action is taking place, evaluating what happens and reviewing the success of any change. *Monitoring* involves collecting information about how approaches are being implemented and ensuring that staff are confident and clear about what they have agreed to do. Importantly, all staff must know how and when monitoring will occur. This may be done formally through lesson observation or scrutiny of planning and analysis of children's work. (Guidance on these first two approaches is given below.) However, a great deal of information can also be gained informally through chatting to staff and children and looking at evidence in wall displays and class assemblies. Monitoring needs to be done in close consultation with the head teacher, who is ultimately responsible for teaching and learning in the school. Joint monitoring can be particularly fruitful; the process of discussing teaching and learning helps head teachers and co-ordinators arrive at shared understandings of what constitutes effective practice. In some schools, however, all formal monitoring will be conducted by the head teacher.

*Evaluation* involves judging the effectiveness of the intervention and deciding whether success criteria have been met. It is important to involve the whole staff in this process and provide opportunities to share approaches and discuss concerns. Ultimately the focus is on the impact on children's learning, and evaluative sessions often include joint scrutiny of children's work to see if the intervention has had an effect on children's reading, writing, speaking or listening. Points discussed during the evaluation will prompt a *review* of practice during which decisions will be made about what to do next. Many schools plan a mid-point review to allow staff to consider progress made and refine the plan in response to experience.

# Observing lessons

Observing lessons can provide co-ordinators with valuable information both about teaching in the school and children's attitudes and response. Importantly, observations present an opportunity to identify strengths as well as areas for development. It must be noted, however, that some teachers become extremely anxious when they are observed or many feel uncomfortable when asked to observe their colleagues and give feedback. Needless to say, the lessons observed might not be typical of those taught by the teacher every day: strategies used may not be those usually employed or nerves may prevent the teacher from being as effective as usual. The following guidelines can help to ensure that the process is as supportive as possible:

## Before the observation

- Be clear about why this observation is being conducted and agree the focus (for example promotion of independent writing).
- Clarify who will know about the results of the observation (for example the teacher being observed, head teacher).
- Clarify when and for how long the observation will occur and how it will be recorded (for example share observation form to be used).
- Negotiate a time for feedback.
- Provide an opportunity for the teacher to contextualize the lesson. (For instance how does it fit into medium- and short-term plans? How is the focus of the lesson informed by assessment?)
- Make sure you know what the teacher is trying to do. (What are his or her objectives?)

## During the observation

- Concentrate on the agreed focus.
- Note down both what the teacher does and what the children do.
- Note how classroom resources and environment support learning.
- Make sure that written comments are factual rather than judgemental.
- Be a positive presence – smile and show your support for the teacher.

## After the observation

- Ask the teacher to talk through the lesson and give his or her perception of what went well and what could be improved in relation to the agreed focus.
- Discuss the impact on the children's learning. (What was successful? What could have been improved?)
- Be factual rather than judgemental in your feedback– describe what happened and then focus on significant moments.
- Ensure that strengths are identified.
- Identify no more than two points for development.
- Agree how further support could be provided and good practice shared.
- When observing lessons in a number of classrooms, it may be appropriate to give a summary of what has been observed to the staff as a whole.

**Table 13.4. Action plan**

Focus: developing response to text

| Aim | Objective | Activity (What will we do?) | Personnel (Who will be Involved?) |
|---|---|---|---|
| Develop children's ability to respond critically to fiction and poetry | Ensure that high quality fiction is used | INSET: visit from local bookseller to help staff select new books. Order new texts | All teaching staff, English co-ordinator, head teacher, teaching assistants |
| | Ensure that staff are aware of a range of effective strategies for promoting response/comprehension | INSET: introduce and share effective strategies | All teaching staff, head teacher and teaching assistants |
| | Ensure that staff use a range of effective strategies for promoting response/ comprehension | Targeted co-ordinator support | All staff and teaching assistants |
| | Establish guidelines for effective practice | Peer observations | All teaching staff |
| | | Staff meeting: review effective practice | Teaching staff, head teacher and teaching assistants |
| | Encourage children's critical evaluation of books | Evaluate books nominated for Kate Greenaway awards for children's literature | All teaching staff, teaching assistants, parents, lunchtime supervisors, governors |

266

| Resources (What do we need? How much will it cost?) | Timing (When will we do this?) | Monitoring, evaluation and review | Success criteria (How will we know if we have been successful?) |
|---|---|---|---|
| £2000 (books) | January | Analysis of planning by English co-ordinator | Planning includes high quality fiction |
| | January | Discussions between English co-ordinator and rest of staff | Staff can describe effective strategies |
| £160 supply cover for co-ordinator | February | Observations (head teacher with English co-ordinator) | Staff can use effective strategies Children able to express views with reference to text |
| £320 (supply cover) | March | Analysis of notes from peer observations | Staff guidelines established |
| | June | Classroom observations (co-ordinator and head teacher) Analysis of display | Children demonstrate ability to respond thoughtfully to texts |

Observations are not only useful in monitoring practice but provide a valuable opportunity for staff development: teachers can learn a great deal by observing their colleagues. Moreover, receiving feedback on teaching can help colleagues recognize their strengths and identify areas for their own development.

### Analysis of planning

Analysing medium-term and weekly plans can provide co-ordinators with insights into how colleagues interpret the curriculum. Of course, plans evolve in practice and may not always reflect what is happening in the classroom. Analysis of planning is therefore best done alongside other forms of data collection. It can be helpful to invite teachers to talk through the rationale behind their planning. This provides them with an opportunity to explain how it caters for the needs and experiences of the children in their class.

**Questions to address through the analysis of planning:**

Does planning reflect the focus of any recent initiatives?
Is there continuity and progression within and between years?
Are there links between English and other subjects including ICT?
Are speaking and listening planned for?
Will children encounter a range of texts during their time at this school?
Are text, sentence and word level work effectively integrated?
Are children being encouraged to read and write independently?
Are activities meaningful and motivating?
Has differentiation been planned effectively?
Are a balance of texts and activities being used?
How have the needs of children with English as an Additional Language been addressed?

# Providing subject expertise

English co-ordinators are often asked to give subject specific support to other members of the school community. This can be seen in the examples below.

A group of parents have asked for some advice on how best to support their children's reading at home. The co-ordinator is now working with them to devise a set of answers to a list of common queries. These will be compiled into a leaflet and distributed to other parents and carers.

A year 1 teacher is keen to improve the writing of the children in her class. Together the teacher and co-ordinator discuss samples of the children's writing and identify strengths and weaknesses. They discuss the problems the children may be having and identify ways forward.

A team of year 6 teachers are concerned about teaching about the active and passive voice. The co-ordinator explains the terminology and then suggests ways that this objective can be taught in the context of real texts.

The governors have received a complaint from a parent that there is not enough formal teaching of literacy in the Foundation Stage. The co-ordinator must advise the governor on responding to the parent's concerns and justifying school policy.

As the examples show, co-ordinators need a sound understanding of the curriculum requirements for different age groups but also need to understand the rationale for the curriculum and recognize its relevance to the development of children's language and literacy. Not only do co-ordinators need to be aware of recent research relating to English but they must be able to translate this into practical approaches in the classroom and communicate it in ways that are accessible to the non-specialist. They also need to be able to analyse children's work at various stages of development, identifying strengths and ways forward. In supporting colleagues with subject knowledge, the co-ordinator may give guidance, find ways for the rest of the staff to share expertise or help them access other sources of support.

It is helpful to create a bank of resources to support teachers' subject knowledge in English. This might include the following.

## English support file

A file or series of files can be compiled to provide support materials for other members of staff. These could include a database of books representing different genres, publicity material for local theatre groups and samples of successful activities.

## Practical ideas

Co-ordinators can purchase books of practical teaching ideas and direct colleagues towards useful Web sites. Whilst a wide range of materials is available to support English and literacy planning, these vary in quality and need to be evaluated to ensure that the activities suggested promote worthwhile learning experiences for pupils.

## Reference material to support subject knowledge

Co-ordinators need to ensure that teachers have access to materials that will help them expand their own subject knowledge.

## National Literacy Strategy support materials

The National Literacy Strategy has produced an extensive range of teacher resources. Teachers need to be given guidance on how to interpret these.

Co-ordinators can keep up to date with the latest research and approaches through:

- courses run by LEAs;
- conferences run by associations such as National Association for the Teaching of English (NATE) and United Kingdom Literacy Association (UKLA);
- journals and magazines such as *Nursery World*; *Primary English Magazine*; *Reading: Literacy and Language*; *Journal of Early Childhood Literacy*; *Times Educational Supplement*;

- Web sites run by organizations such as the DfES, QCA, and the National Literacy Trust;
- opportunities to network with other co-ordinators live or online and visit other schools;
- reading recently published children's literature (specialist children's book suppliers, children's literature Web sites, school library services and publications such as *Books for Keeps* can direct you to new titles);
- enrolling for a Masters degree or conducting classroom-based research.

# Summary

The role of the English co-ordinator is challenging and rewarding. Being successful involves using and developing a wide range of skills. These include:

- good interpersonal skills;
- being a positive and enthusiastic role model;
- being able to work in a team;
- listening to others and recognizing their concerns and strengths;
- being sensitive to what motivates different individuals;
- being able to plan, organize and prioritize;
- having very sound subject knowledge in English;
- making decisions and delegating as appropriate;
- being able to analyse evidence of children's achievements;
- being able to solve problems and use initiative;
- communicating effectively with a range of people;
- being able to manage time and professional development.

# Reflective task

Download the most recent OFSTED report for a school you know. How do the findings relate to what you know about the school? What else would you want to find out? Consider how you would address any action points relating to language and literacy. What barriers might prevent the changes you have identified? How could these be overcome? Who would you involve and how would you support their development? How would you monitor, evaluate and review these developments?

## FURTHER READING

Merchant, G. and Marsh, J. (1998) *Co-ordinating Primary Language and Literacy: The Subject Leader's Handbook*. London: Paul Chapman Publishing.
  Detailed practical guidance on the role of the co-ordinator.

National Literacy and Numeracy Strategies (2002) *Literacy Co-ordinator's Handbook*. London: DfES.
  File distributed to all schools in 2002/3 to support training for literacy co-ordinators. Provides detailed guidance on use of statistical evidence, monitoring and evaluation.

Tyrell, J. and Gill, N. (2000) *Coordinating English at Key Stage 1*. London: Routledge Falmer.
  Explores effective practice in English at Key Stage 1 and strategies for developing this throughout a school.

Waters, M. and Martin, T. (1999) *Coordinating English at Key Stage 2*. London: Routledge Falmer.
  Explores effective practice in English at Key Stage 2 and strategies for developing this throughout a school.

## REFERENCES

Department for Education and Employment (DfEE) (1998) *The National Literacy Strategy Framework for Teaching*. London: HMSO.

Fullan, M. G. (1993) *The New Meaning of Educational Change*. London: Cassell.

Her Majesty's Inspectorate (HMI) (1977) *Ten Good Schools*. London: HMSO.

Mortimore, P. (1998) *The Road to Improvement: Reflections on School Effectiveness*. Lisse: Swets and Zeitlinger, pp. 49–68.

National Foundation for Educational Research (NFER) (1998) *Evaluation of the National Literacy Project: Summary Report*. London: HMSO.

Office for Standards in Education (OFSTED) (1999) *Handbook for Inspecting Primary and Nursery Schools*. London: HMSO.

Office for Standards in Education (OFSTED) (2002) *National Literacy and Numeracy Strategies: The First Four Years 1998–2002*. London: HMSO.

OFSTED (2003) *Strategies in Action: National Literacy and Numeracy Strategies in Action: Case Studies of Improving Declining Schools*. London: HMSO.

Ontario Institute for Studies in Education (OISE) (2003) *Watching and Learning: Final Report of the External Evaluation of England's National Literacy and Numeracy Strategies*. London: DfES.

Qualifications and Curriculum Authority (QCA) (2003) *Speaking, Listening, Learning*. London: QCA.

Teacher Training Agency (TTA) (1998) *National Standards for Subject Leaders*. London: HMSO.

# Index